ICEBOUND·EMPIRE

ICEBOUND EMPIRE

Industry and Politics on the Last Frontier
1898–1938

Elizabeth A. Tower

Elizabeth A. Tower
5/27/01

Library of Congress Catalog
Tower, Elizabeth, A.
Icebound Empire
Industry and Politics on the Last Frontier 1898–1938
Includes index
ISBN: 1-888125-05-5

Printed in USA
Cover and Book Design by
Hal Gage, Gage Photo Graphics and Shannon Weiss, Illusions Too

But the others, the men of my mettle, the men who would 'stablish my fame
Unto its ultimate issue, winning me honor, not shame;
Searching my uttermost valleys, fighting each step as they go,
Shooting the wrath of my rapids, scaling my ramparts of snow;
Ripping the guts of my mountains, looting the beds of my creeks,
Them will I take to my bosom, and speak as a mother speaks.
I am the land that listens, I am the land that broods;
Steeped in eternal beauty, crystalline waters and woods.
Long have I waited lonely, shunned as a thing accurst,
Monstrous, moody, pathetic, the last of the lands and the first;
Visioning campfires at twilight, sad with a longing forlorn,
Feeling my womb o'er-pregnant with the seed of cities unborn.
Wild and wide are my borders, stern as death is my sway,
And I wait for the men who will win me—and I will not be won in a day;
And I will not be won by weaklings, subtle, suave and mild,
But my men with the hearts of vikings, and the simple faith of a child;
Desperate, strong and resistless, unthrottled by fear or defeat,
Them will I gild with my treasure, them will I glut with my meat.

—Robert Service, *The Law of the Yukon*

Table of Contents

Acknowledgements

The author is deeply indebted to the families of George Cheever Hazelet, David Henry Jarvis and Stephen Birch for their support and assistance in obtaining material for this manuscript.

Hazelet's diaries, letters and pictures were provided by his grandchildren, Harriet Hazelet Flynn, Charlotte Hazelet Turtainen and Calvin Hazelet.
Richard Osborne, a grandson of John Hazelet, provided additional pictures and his grandfather's history of the Chisna mine.

Mary Jarvis Cocke, Capt. Jarvis' granddaughter, provided letters, family photographs and editorial assistance.

William Collins, a great-nephew of Stephen Birch, provided information about the Birch family.

Introduction — Icebound Empire

Gold lured thousands of men and women north in 1898 to Alaska, a vast, underdeveloped subcontinent that the United States had owned for 30 years but made little effort to understand or develop. Most of the gold seekers retreated to their home states or countries after a year or two of adventure and privation but a few stayed, captivated by the challenges that this new land presented.

These new Alaskans assumed naively that Alaska could be developed by the same means that had been successful in developing the western states. They expected the federal government to be generous in granting land for mines and farms, and in subsidizing private railroads. But times had changed. Populist movements in the late nineteenth and early twentieth centuries viewed big business, especially railroad trusts, with suspicion. Furthermore, Easterners, seeing that most of the land in their states was already privately owned, started advocating that more federal land in the West should be reserved for public use. *Icebound Empire* tells the stories of three men whose plans for developing Alaska were thwarted or altered by the trust-busters, muckrakers and conservationists of the early twentieth century.

George Cheever Hazelet came north in 1898, fell in love with the land, and stayed to mold modern Alaska. Hazelet and his partner, A.J. Meals, reached the interior rivers by dragging sleds over Valdez Glacier rather than by climbing the more popular Chilkoot Pass. They never reached the Klondike, but were among the few that found and developed gold mines in the Copper River country. Hazelet's vision for Alaska transcended mining and spurred him on to build cities where families like his could live better lives.

Captain David Henry Jarvis acquired a comprehensive understanding of Alaska's potential while serving as an officer in the United States Revenue Marine from 1887 to 1902 and as customs collector for Alaska from 1902 to 1905. Jarvis' bravery and executive ability earned him nationwide popularity and the respect of

President Theodore Roosevelt, but also marked him as a target for vicious muckraking.

———❦———

Stephen Birch found his fortune in Alaska — in copper rather than gold. With the assistance of wealthy friends he succeeded in developing highly productive copper mines, but took the profits from those mines elsewhere when the federal government blocked further industrial development in Alaska.

———❦———

These three men were associated in the most ambitious of the early Alaska development schemes, the Morgan-Guggenheim Alaska Syndicate, and were implicated in its most dramatic episode — the shootout in Keystone Canyon near Valdez.

This volume also contains brief biographical sketches of other developers and politicians who cooperated with, or opposed, Hazelet, Jarvis and Birch during their efforts to build an industrial empire in Alaska.

Reference Map

Seattle Times   July 16, 1897

FAIRY TALE OF THE FABULOUS WEALTH OF THE CLONDYKE

T.S. Libby's Luck
Former Seattle Man Takes Out $65,000
May Be Fact or Fancy
The Story of the Northern Eldorado

Seattle Times   July 20, 1897

KLONDYKE AROUSES THE EAST

EFFETE CIVILIZATION AND THE DIGNITARIES
OF THE GOVERNMENT AFFECTED BY REPORTS

FIRST IN '49 WANT TO BE FIRST NOW

Seattle Times   July 8, 1897

GOLD MINING CONVENTION MEETS IN DENVER COLO. TODAY

THE OBJECT—GOLD THE
ONLY DEITY—MADE THE WEST

GOLD FEVER IS RAMPANT

THE STEAMER PORTLAND HERE

BOUGHT DOWN A TON OF GOLD

THE PURSER HAS $127,000 AND MEN
HAVE DOUBLED THAT DOLLAR AMOUNT

Seattle Times   July 14, 1897

A GREAT OIL DISCOVERY

Remarkable Flow Found in Southern Alaska

Seattle Times   July 12, 1897

COOK INLET SENSATION

DISSATISFIED MINER SHOOTS
TWO CONTRACTORS

Seattle Times   July 19, 1897

WHERE'S YOUR GRUBSTAKE? – MEN WITH GOLD FEVER HUSTLING TO GO

WORKING MEN WHO GET AWAY LEAVING THEIR WORK. LAWYERS
FORSAKE CLIENTS AND OFFICES, AND MACHINISTS THEIR FORGES.

Seattle Times   July 12, 1897

BULLET IN DESPERATION

J.W. Mathes, Bound for Yukon
Shot with Rifle

Was Probably a Suicide

Lost All His Outfit While
Shooting Rapids in a Raft

WE ARE HEADQUARTERS FOR KLONDYKE UNDERWEAR

For Ladies and Men at Prices Not to Be Duplicated in the City

North to Alaska

I

February 17, 1898 — Left home this day for Alaska, 4:35 PM. Have thought
before that I had endured many hard things in this life, but never came across
anything like parting from my family. I walked to school with my boys to say
goodbye out of sight of my wife. ... The only thought that keeps me up is that
I am going for the good of them and their darling mother. ... I left the house with
dire forebodings, but somehow since the train has pulled out, I have gained
confidence, and especially determination. Determination to go forward and make
one great effort to place my family on the plane to which they belong.

George Cheever Hazelet
PHOTO COURTESY OF HAZELET GRANDCHILDREN

With this entry, George Cheever Hazelet of Omaha, Nebraska, opened the journal in which he would chronicle his search for gold in Alaska. At Alliance, in western Nebraska, he was joined on the train by Andrew Jackson Meals, a seasoned frontiersman with 30 years experience hunting buffalo, driving stagecoaches, locating wagon roads, running cattle, and breaking broncos.[1] Meals, who was nine years older than 36-year-old Hazelet, was leaving a wife and six children in hopes of improving his fortunes in the Klondike gold rush. The future did not look as bright as it had ten years before when Hazelet and Meals were Republican officials of Holt County, Nebraska. Those were the prosperous years before drought, financial collapse, scandal and violence had intervened to dim their prospects.

Hazelet and Meals arrived in Seattle on February 20, 1898, in heavy rain, and checked into the New England Hotel where they shared a bed for $1.00 a day each. Men in "full Klondike dress" filled the streets of Seattle, many of them awaiting passage to Skagway. Unwilling to put up with a long delay, Hazelet decided to investigate the Copper River route and succeeded in purchasing tickets on the EXCELSIOR from Canadians who had decided to change their routing.

On February 23 the partners purchased their outfits and prepared to embark for Valdez. The groceries, which Hazelet and Meals expected to last for one year, cost $129.35, and included 800 lbs. of flour, 300 lbs. of bacon, 100 lbs. of cornmeal, 100 lbs. of sugar, 75 lbs. of salt, 75 lbs. of dried apples and peaches, and 40 lbs. of pea meal, in addition to condiments, baking powder, yeast, coffee, tea, tobacco, matches, candles, soap, and citric acid. Hardware, cooking utensils, firearms, and a tent cost another $110. Winter clothing cost $130. Hazelet was pleased that Seattle merchants were "not trying to beat the poor devils that come here to outfit."

The rain continued while they waited for the EXCELSIOR to arrive. Hazelet "caught cold every day" and treated himself by taking quinine, drinking camphor and whiskey, and rubbing snuff. When the boat finally arrived early on the morning of February 27, Hazelet and Meals put their dunnage bags on board, got acquainted with the steward, and made themselves "solid by means not to be mentioned." Hazelet described the first day of the ocean trip in his journal:

> We expect now to get off by 2 PM. The shrill whistle of the boss freight loader and the hum of voices is all that serves to break the monotony at present except that it be the barking of the poor dogs that seem to be taking this method of protesting against going to the frozen north. 2:40 PM and we are just pulling out. There must be at least a thousand people on the wharf, cheering, waving hats, handkerchiefs and anything they may have. The boat's whistle is blowing a shrill blast and we are off for the frozen north, some of us never to return, others to meet some sort of success no doubt, but more doomed to disappointment. Which class do we belong to? This is all new to me. Strange are the sights and sounds,

and stranger still the feelings that surge through my breast. 6 PM and supper is ready and what a sight. 200 men of all nationalities almost, crowded into the hole. Two long tables swinging from the ceiling, will only hold about one-fifth of those that have to eat. We are told by the Steward that there will be five tables and we go on deck to wait till last call. In meantime to sit among the dogs, smoke our pipes and talk about the prospects for the future.

At about a quarter of eight we go down, find the dishes, of course all of tin and as filthy and dirty as if hogs had just been fed from them, but we must eat something. Hence range ourselves along the table, being thankful that we even get a chance to stand along side. The man in charge dishes up some sort of combination which he calls Irish stew, but much more resembles swill. This we eat, then are helped to a cold potato (boiled), some bread that is not so bad and a large tin cup of black tea. We stow away some of this frugal meal and again go on deck to smoke and dream dreams of gold.

Horace Samuel Conger, a 34-year-old pharmacist from Minnesota endured the same meal and then paid an additional ten dollars "for the privilege of eating in the first cabin." [2]

During the next several days Hazelet escaped sea-sickness and "never felt better." He was enthralled by the mountain scenery, commenting that "there is no other water course in the world like this." While waiting for high tide to pass through Wrangell Narrows, the second class passengers got up a protest about the food, which Hazelet and a "gentleman from Boston" presented to the captain. As a result the dishes were cleaner and the meat better.

While docked at Juneau, Hazelet had the opportunity to go ashore to mail letters, look over the new town, and enjoy a meal "consisting of clam chowder, roast beef, mashed potatoes, peas, beans, hash, bread and butter, mince pie and coffee, all for 30 cents. First decent dinner I have eaten since left Seattle." While Hazelet and Meals were in Juneau, a man who had spent several years in the Cook Inlet region of southcentral Alaska gave them valuable information about the country and reassured them that their supplies of food and clothing were adequate. Hazelet was impressed that the town of 2,000 to 3,000 people was "all lighted with electricity," but expressed concern that there was hardly room for the houses, many of which were built on piles over tidewater while others were perched on the sides of two mountains which looked as if they would "tumble down and cover the town."

As the EXCELSIOR pulled away from Juneau, Hazelet expressed satisfaction that their old boat was still intact while other faster ships, like the COTTAGE CITY, had to return for repairs after suffering rock damage. They anticipated rougher water once they were on the open ocean, but were not prepared for the violent storms they encountered during the next several days. Hazelet was so seasick that he could not write in his journal. A week later he described the ordeal crossing the Gulf of Alaska:

> Well it was simply terrible, if one could only take off his nose and keep from smelling, he might be able to get along, but you smell everything, things you have not seen for years, and all of the disagreeable odors on earth. You seem to smell with your eyes, ears, teeth and everything.
>
> We struck awfully rough weather. The wind blew hard Saturday, harder Sunday, and increased to a violent storm on Monday. The wind blew at the rate of 70 miles per hour so the Captain said. I saw but little of it, raised up on my bunk and looked out of the window a few times. Saw waves that seemed to me as high as mountains. The ship pitched and rolled fearfully and at many times it seemed it would be broken to pieces, but we cared nothing for that. If the ship had gone down, I doubt if we would have made much effort to save ourselves. All on board were sick except five or six.

Horace Conger, who was one of the few not prostrated by seasickness, described the storm in a March 8 letter to his wife:

> Last Monday a southwest storm struck us consisting of snow and sleet, which was blinding in the extreme. The sea was lashed into a foaming caldron. Waves 20 and 30 feet high. We were completely at the mercy of the water and elements. We were lost for 19 hours. Once during that time the cry came, "Rocks ahead." And sure enough, there they were, two hundred feet high, not over 300 yards from us. All steam was applied, and one of the steam pipes burst. I thought we were lost, sure enough. I thought of you and the little ones then and gave myself up to God. Would not go through the same thing again for all the wealth in Alaska. [3]

Port Valdez in 1900 showing glacier.
BENJAMIN BOOHER COLLECTION—ALASKA STATE LIBRARY PCA250-2

The EXCELSIOR reached Port Valdes at noon on March 8, and pulled up to a broad sheet of ice 18 inches thick. Each stampeder looked out for his own provisions as they were thrown off onto the ice. Hazelet and Meals spent several days gathering their belongings and joined about 700 prospectors waiting to cross the glacier. On March 13 they were camped on the outflow of the glacier cutting two cords of dry wood and preparing to move supplies five miles to the glacier. Four days later, with supplies cached at the foot of the glacier, they moved camp. In the meantime two ships arrived with more than 500 gold-seekers.

Prospectors who did not have horses or dogs with them were forced to serve as their own pack animals, as described by Hazelet in his journal on March 17:

> Well I have now learned what it is to make an ass of myself in earnest — one way at least, is to harness yourself up to a six foot sled, put 200 pounds on it and strike the trail for the foot of the glacier, which is five miles away. Repeat this twice a day for a week and you soon have long ears. ... We will in the next two weeks have to reach the summit, and in order to do this we have to cross at least 12 miles of rough glacier, now covered with snow. From the foot to the summit it rises at least 2,000 feet. The trail crosses wide cracks and crevasses which are perhaps hundreds of feet deep; scattered all over it are large boulders weighing thousands of tons waiting for the sun to melt the ice and snow and allow them to tumble down to the sea.

For the next two weeks the men were preoccupied with moving their supplies. Hazelet had no time to write in the journal until March 29 when he gave the following progress report:

> Since writing last we have moved camp and now live on 3rd bench of glacier. Have gotten all of our stuff up to top of 3rd bench by means of the windlass and have pulled two loads 10½ miles up and landed it on top of 4th bench, talk about hard pulls, or labor of the most violent kind. I care not what one might choose but I will put this up as a stand off. Think of a man hitching himself up to a sled, putting on 150 lbs. and pulling that load from 7:00 AM till 2:00 PM, eating frozen bread and beans and drinking snow water for his lunch, then walking back the distance of 10½ miles. If this is not turning yourself into a horse what is it? If men followed this a few generations they would have hooves instead of feet.

Hazelet commented on the death of two men on the trail, one from overexertion and the other from an accidental gunshot wound. While passing the funeral procession Hazelet reflected: "It was a sad sight to see the poor fellow pulled down the glacier on the sled he had pulled so many days and so hard, now strapped to it, just as he had strapped his load, four men pulling the sled and toe holding it back. About 50 men followed the body to the grave at foot of glacier, no coffin, nothing but his blanket to protect him from the damp cold earth." After watching the funeral procession, Hazelet and Meals vowed to avoid overexertion and remove all cartridges from their guns.

The young gunshot victim, whom Hazelet refers to as "Murphy," was actually L.R. Murfin, a member of Horace Conger's Minnesota group. Conger provided details of the accident in a letter to his wife on March 24: "It seems that some of the boys were oiling their guns to prevent them from rusting and one of the party went out of one tent and into another to get his gun out of the case. As there were several guns in the pile, he was pulling them out of the case to find out which one was his. Somehow or other, the gun was loaded and went off." The bullet passed through the walls of two tents before hitting Murfin, who was sitting with six other companions. [4]

Third Bench Camp, Valdez Glacier, 1898
HINCHEY ALAGCO COLLECTION—ANCHORAGE MUSEUM OF HISTORY & ART B62.1.1343

Heavy rains and snow slowed their progress and gave Hazelet an opportunity to give a more complete description of the sights along the glacier trail:

At the present writing there are about 2,200 people on the trail. Goods are scattered from one end of it to the other. There are people of most all nationalities but I think the Swedes predominate. There is the long lean man and the short fat one, who puffs and blows like a porpoise as he tugs at his load up the glacier.

There are old men, boys, middle aged men. Men with whiskers and men, a few, without them. ...

There are at least 20 to 30 women in camp along the trail, one especially I have noticed helps her husband pull every load and seems as happy as if she were presiding over a nice little home in some well-to-do place on earth. She has red hair and is tall and slender, dresses like a woman and seems very ladylike. Others wear the garb of men and look like frights, one especially is fat and chunky with legs big as posts and hips like a Norman stallion, freckles all over her face and her only redeeming quality, that has been noticed, is that she keeps close to their tent. Guess she does nothing but cook. As a whole the people are a fair representation of the average middle class Americans.

On April 9 Hazelet reported that they had dragged all of their goods to the fourth bench at an altitude of 3,660 feet, and were moving loads five miles to the foot of the summit. By climbing an additional mile to the top of the mountain, Hazelet and Meals were able to view "the promised land."

Hazelet, eager for letters from home, walked back to Valdez to meet an incoming ship but came away empty handed. He noted that horses were selling for $350 to $400. The horses appeared to be doing well on the glacier, but dogs were all dying because men treated them poorly. The trail, he observed, was a good place to demonstrate character.

... Men trudge along with a big load behind them, looking as if they were pulling their lives out, all the horrors depicted in their countenances, others go along quietly with a "Good morning" or a "How do you do" seemingly happy or pretending to be. Still others will whistle or sing some old familiar air, but there are few of this sort. The sled really seems to develop the worst side of a man, for most all are ready to scrap on the least provocation. It is very annoying to be pulling a heavy load up hill and some careless fellow coming back down hill with an empty sled catch on to you and yank you back several feet. I always stop if I catch on to a poor fellow and beg his pardon. Some times this makes it all right, other times you have to allow the party to cuss and swear and go away mad. The worst of all is to have a coaster run into you and knock you down and drive your sled away back. You are not only mad because you are hurt, but because he is having it so easy while you are pulling your life out. You don't stop to think that the poor fellow must have gone through just what you are doing before he could have earned the right to coast. We all coast when we get the chance except sometimes fellows that are afraid. Glad to say that the heavy pulling at least on this side will soon be over and we will get to prospect ground and have plenty of food and water.

Hazelet had little good to say about the character of two men who had been camping with them and holding up their progress. When they got to the foot of the summit, these men hired other parties to haul their supplies and took all the wood. Hazelet and Meals had to make a quick trip over the top to cut enough wood to last them until they had all their supplies across the mile-high summit of the glacier.

Traveling was much easier once they were on the other side and could take up to 800 pounds in a load on their sleds. Hazelet and Meals were able to move faster without the other two prospectors and on May 1 they camped beside a lake. Fortunately, they were over the summit when a series of avalanches buried several parties on April 30. Hazelet summed up the exertions of the past six weeks in his journal:

> The glacier is a wonderful thing. It begins almost at the edge of the sound at the time of year we reached it, and extends in a general northerly direction for about 15 miles to its summit. Here it reaches a height of 5,140 feet as indicated by our barometer and crosses over the range. It runs down on the north slope of the coast range for a distance of about 10 miles. ... The man that starts in to pull 1,500 lbs. of supplies from Valdez to the top of summit must needs have plenty of grit and a good supply of muscle, for it is no easy task and I firmly believe that many of the parties now put down at Valdez alone to overcome this task would fail. But seeing others going over, with determination set in every line of their faces, they brace up and proceed and finally, to their surprise almost, they have accomplished what under other circumstances would have proven impossible.

Hazelet realized that he and his partner had passed their first big test. They had succeeded in crossing the glacier while others had failed.

Down the Klutina

III

With the heavy pull up the glacier behind him, Hazelet started to enjoy the new country which was so different from the flat land of Nebraska. "Life in Alaska is fine," he wrote on May 1, "and were it not for the anxiety for the welfare of my loved ones at home this would be a grand 'picnic' despite the hard work, danger and exposure I am subject to." He continued to worry about mail, even threatening to walk 150 miles back to Valdez, but finally received reassuring letters from home brought in by another prospector.

Three Mile Camp beyond Valdez Glacier
PHOTO COURTESY OF HAZELET GRANDCHILDREN

Hazelet and Meals now needed to decide whether to stay and prospect near this lake or to build boats to carry their supplies on down the river to Copper Center. They were pleased to discover from local Indians that they were on Klutina rather than Tonsina lake and thus already about half way to the Copper River where they wanted to start prospecting. After their unfortunate experience with previous partners, they had just about decided to undertake the boat building alone when a young man named Arthur McNeer asked to join them. McNeer had crossed the glacier with a group who chose to camp and prospect around the lake rather than proceed on down the river. After a long discussion, Hazelet and Meals decided to let the 19-year-old West Virginian join them in return for help in building the boats.

During the next week Hazelet and McNeer sawed wood while Meals framed two boats, one 22 feet long and the other 16 feet in length. While waiting for Meals to finishing caulking the boats, Hazelet and McNeer got up one morning at 1:30 AM and hiked to the top of a range of mountains to the north, where they enjoyed the following view:

> Looking east we could plainly see Whitney, Drum, Sanford and Wrangell, all looming up beyond the Copper River, rising to a height of from 12,000 to about 20,000 feet. Wrangell is smoking, we had our first view of a volcano. What a wonderful sight. Here in the far north where perpetual snow covers even the small hills to see a mountain sending forth smoke is a strange sight indeed.
>
> It brings to a man's mind how wonderful is nature and nature's God. Well we didn't get back from the mountains that morning till 9 AM, having been away from 1:30 walking and climbing most of the time and without breakfast, but we felt well repaid for our labor. We may see stranger sights on our journey but we will never see a more beautiful one. One is compelled to exclaim almost every day: "What a wonderful country." For instance we have no night at all, at least we have been unable to find it for the past six weeks. I am writing in our tent without light and it is 10 PM. I wake up almost every night at midnight and can see what time it is by the watch without striking a light and it is still 30 days till the longest day rolls around. We intend to go up on some mountain and watch the sun set some evening, or rather watch it go round us.

On May 23, the three men started down the Klutina River with all their belongings in the larger boat, christened the "Mary Ellen." About two miles down the river they encountered the first rapids and decided to line the boat through them with one man on the boat and the other two walking along the bank with fore and aft lines. After passing through the first series of rapids, Hazelet described the scene that awaited them in the next stretch of rough water:

Here we found a number of camps and lots of wrecks. The river at this point is full of large rocks. Many extend out of the water from two to three feet and some very large ones as close together, so close in fact, that a boat 6 feet on the bottom could hardly get through. The water rushes through here at a terrible rate, making a noise like a waterfall. Rafts and boats were piled high upon each other, goods were spread out to dry, and all looked forlorn enough. We concluded to camp here for the night and determine later what was best to do.

Since they were reluctant to challenge these rapids without help they decided to join forces with a party of nine Swedes from Boston. In spite of having had no previous experience running rivers, they succeeded in guiding their boats through the swift water without mishap. Hazelet commented: "Lucky indeed is the crew that has pulled through safely. The men at the lines must give out and take in slack at just the right time and at the moment the men in the boat command. The men in the boat must be of cool heads, quick eyes and know what to do and how to do it without time for thought. We have been extremely lucky. Have not had a single sack wet and nothing lost." He then described the fate of less fortunate, or less skillful, crews:

This river from here to the lake almost is strewn with wrecks of all kinds. Goods can be seen every few rods along the river put out to dry, broken boats are piled up every little distance and all seems one grand wreck. It takes nerve and plenty of muscles to go through it, besides caution. I believe there is no use of one losing anything if caution is used, but so many are in a hurry to reach the Copper River that they go off half cocked, as it were, and in consequence either lose all their stuff or get it wet which is the next worst thing.

Hazelet was not exaggerating the perils of the Klutina Rapids. Ninety-five percent of the gold seekers who attempted to run the river in the summer of 1898 are said to have wrecked their boats. Captain William Abercrombie, commander of a government party that was sent in 1898 to stake a trail inland from Valdez, estimated conservatively that over $20,000 of supplies were strewn along the river banks. [1] As a result many prospectors who lost food suffered from malnutrition and scurvy the following winter.

Several days later when they reached the Copper River, Hazelet was eager to start prospecting, so he spent several days investigating the streams at the base of Mt. Drum in an attempt to cross overland to the headwaters of the Copper River. Since they were unable to find a passable route, the Hazelet party elected to take their boat further up the Copper River. Four of the Swedes joined them while the rest had to return over the glacier to Valdez for more supplies. Hazelet commented that these were "all young and strong fellows, but with no experience except in a shoe factory."

The Hazelet party nearly capsized when they continued up the Copper River, as described in a diary entry on June 14:

> Came to a high bank of 150 feet, composed of gravel, sand and soft clay. We could see the rocks and gravel start from the top and roll down till they struck the water, but we had come too far to get back and could not cross at this point as the current was very swift and the river full of large rocks, so all we could do was to go ahead and risk dodging the rock. We soon learned that the stones that were falling were from the size of ones fist to that of a half bushel, and some of them just missed us. We pulled for our lives, Jack ahold of the snub rope, McNeer on the pole, and the other five of us tugging at the rope. We waded water up to our waists, crept along the edge of the bank where the water was from 15 to 20 feet deep, and got the boat over half way through when suddenly without any warning the current caught her and shot out into the river like a bucking bronco, getting entirely away from Jack and almost pulling him in. As good luck would have it, the five of us had good fortune and while we were dragged to the waters edge, we succeeded in stopping her. ... A large party just behind us who followed us up to this bank lost two boats and all in them. The last we could see of them they were drifting down the river with the current.

On July 1 the Hazelet party reached the mouth of the Chistochina River where Indians told them they would find coarse gold. The local Indians impressed Hazelet. "Think they are all Catholics," he commented, "as the married women all wear rings. Women much better looking than the average Indian women." He also described a large Indian dwelling near one of their camps:

> A large log house covered with bark and moss has been built here several years ago. I think they use it still in the winter. Gives evidence of a good deal of skill with the axe. No door, but a long coal shute to crawl into. House about 20 x 20 and 8 or 9 feet high, looks as if it had been used by 10 or 12 persons, sort of stalls around the walls which I imagine they sleep in. They build fire in center of room and have a long trough into which they pour the fish or caribou soup and from which they all eat.

Initial prospecting along the Chistochina River confirmed the Indian observations of gold flecks in the river sand, so the Hazelet party decided to move upstream about 20 miles to look for a good site to start mining. By July 27 they had located a promising small bar and were busy sawing lumber for sluice boxes and building a dam.

As soon as these preparations were completed and the placer operation was running, Hazelet and Meals packed 40 miles further up the river into the mountains, hoping to locate a site for a quartz mine. While taking rock samples, they climbed up to the glacier feeding the Chistochina River. Hazelet described the view from high in the Alaska range:

> The whole scene was awe inspiring, not a sound save the mighty rush of waters, not a breath of air stirring, not a human being within miles and miles of us. Truly we were alone with nature and nature's God. Far to the south and east the Chistochina rushed and wound its onward course amid its numerous islands and sand bars to join the Copper, while beyond the Copper rose the mighty Sanford, Drum and Wrangell reaching up toward heaven from 13,000 to 20,000 feet above sea level. We were loathe to leave the spot and could hardly shake off the spell that bound us.

Before returning to camp with the rock specimens, Hazelet had to return three miles to retrieve the pipe that he carelessly set on the rocks while at work. "My advice to anyone going out prospecting is to be very careful of his pipe," he wrote in the journal. "Better make a good strong case out of an old bag and fit it so it can be buckled onto your belt, and under no circumstances lay it down. Always put it in its place when you are through smoking no matter how big a nugget is looking at you from your pan, or how fiercely the mosquitos and gnats are biting."

Food supplies were running short, so when Hazelet and Meals returned from prospecting in the mountains, the seven men prepared to return for more of the provisions that they had cached along the Klutina River. They tore up the sluice box to retrieve the nails, cleaned up the gold and sand, and loaded the "Mary Ellen" for the 85-mile trip down the rivers.

A three-month supply of mail greeted the men when they reached Copper Center and Hazelet spent the next day reading his 44 letters. When they reached the Klutina River they purchased about 1,500 lbs. of supplies from prospectors who were heading back over the glacier to Valdez. Hazelet, Meals and McNeer parted with the Swedes, several of whom were planning to leave, and pulled the "Mary Ellen" 10 miles up the Klutina River to the cache. After loading the remaining 1,700 lbs. of supplies on board, they succeeded in running the rapids back to Copper Center with only minor damage to the boat.

In Copper Center they met other parties making winter plans. Those staying through the winter were either building cabins along the Klutina or heading up the Copper River toward Forty Mile and Dawson. Hazelet considered his decision to spend the winter on the Chistochina as good a plan as any. Capt. Abercrombie had introduced him to a government geologist, named Schrader, who examined some of his rock specimens, declared them promising, and encouraged him to try to reach bedrock. Schrader agreed to take the rocks back to Washington for an assay, but, unfortunately, lost all supplies when his boat overturned while trying to go down the Copper River to Orca.

Some prospectors were not as enthusiastic about the Chistochina country. Horace Conger's party was leaving, disgusted with the area which he described in a September 12 letter to his wife:

> ... I had never seen a country like this before. It all seems to look alike. There is not enough difference in the lakes, streams, and hills to enable one to recognize them the second time. The mountains are a jumbled mass of loose granite and one can feel them move while walking over them. After about five weeks of wading through water, and in moss up to my knees, I started back to Copper Center. [2]

Copper Center, August 1898, prospectors starting on trip
PHOTO COURTESY OF HAZELET GRANDCHILDREN

Although Hazelet and Meals had no previous mountain experience, they were proving capable prospectors, able to live off the land by shooting grouse and squirrels, since big game was scarce.

Hazelet, Meals and McNeer started pulling their boats up the Copper River on September 24 and began encountering ice on October 9. "Weather growing colder each day," Hazelet commented. "Never saw a nicer climate. The mornings and evenings seem like about November 1st in the states." Several days later they had to stop pulling upstream because of ice and camped near the Sanford River to wait until they could pull sleds up the river. In the meantime, they welcomed the opportunity to float down to Copper Center for mail.

While at Copper Center waiting for the mail carrier to arrive, they heard more about problems that prospectors were encountering as they tried to leave Alaska. Some were reported to have gone crazy while going back over Valdez Glacier. "Oh this is a funny old country," Hazelet wrote, "perhaps we are all crazy and don't know it." Then he restated his own determination to continue the quest for gold:

> Since last writing I'm one year older and now have passed my 37th birthday. How old that seems. And that too with a loving wife and two dear boys to provide for, and nothing, nothing, nothing — but I will have it, surely all these hardships and long separations cannot go for nothing. I surely will succeed, I must. Since we have been gone up the river some bad women have come to town and it makes one sick to see how the dogs of men hang round them. Poor fools, men, women and all. And yet it seems to me I am the biggest fool of all, my "fool" should be spelled with a big F, for I need not have been here had I done right. But away with regrets for the past, let me look forward to the future with hope and determination, and I may yet regain what I've lost.
>
> I'm well and strong, the climate is all that could be desired so far, the country is beautiful and if it only holds gold I may yet find it and return to my loved ones, able to take care of them and look after their wants as a husband and father should.

Although enthusiastic about the future, Hazelet was still haunted by past failures.

Nebraska Republican

The prospectors who came north to Alaska and the Yukon in 1898 had various motives for venturing into this unknown and potentially dangerous land. Some came solely for adventure and the promise of wealth, while others, like Hazelet, came in the hope that they could forge new lives for themselves and their families, leaving past failures behind. A review of Hazelet's past ten years in Nebraska will help to explain why he so frequently referred to himself in the diary as a failure.

Hazelet family in Guthrie Center, Iowa.
George Cheever (second from right, back row), John (third from left, back row)

Although Hazelet was born in Ohio, his family moved to Guthrie Center, Iowa, when he was seven. After graduation from Southern Iowa Normal School in 1883 he moved west to Atkinson, Nebraska, where he secured a position as principal of the public schools. [1] "Cheeve" Hazelet was active socially in his new community, politically in the Republican party, and athletically as a member of the Atkinson Reds baseball team. [2] Shortly after his move to O'Neill, Nebraska, and election as clerk of Holt County, he married Harriet Potter on August 11, 1888. *The Frontier*, O'Neill's daily newspaper, complimented the young couple: "He is a gentlemanly young man, intelligent, genial and most popular in the social and political world. He is remarkably fortunate in securing the hand of so estimable a young lady. Miss Potter is the youngest daughter of Mr. and Mrs. A.T. Potter, who have been respected and honored residents of Holt County for a number of years. She is a charming, handsome, young lady, educated and cultured, and remarkably accomplished in music." On June 6, 1889, *The Frontier* noted that Clerk Hazelet was building a house on a two-acre plot in the northeast part of O'Neill, and on August 8 commented that the Hazelets were moving into "one of the finest little homes in the town."

In October 1889, Hazelet was re-elected along with the rest of the Republican ticket. Meals, who had been county treasurer during Hazelet's first term, was succeeded by Barrett Scott who had previously worked for Hazelet in the clerk's office. [3] Republicans had controlled Holt County politically for a number of years and newly elected officials traditionally covered up any shortages passed on from the terms of their predecessors. Meals had inherited a small deficit in the treasury account from David L. Darr, and he passed a somewhat larger shortfall on to Scott, but no note was taken of it at the time. Hazelet continued to collect registration fees in the same manner as his predecessor had done. His accounts were approved without question by the Republican-controlled Board of Supervisors.

Hazelet decided not to run for re-election in 1891 because he was becoming heavily involved in business deals of his own. Under the heading, "New Dirt Deals," *The Frontier* announced that G.C. Hazelet, Barrett Scott and others, had purchased over 90 acres on the outskirts of O'Neill that they planned to plat in blocks and lots and place on the market. [4] Several months later the paper praised Hazelet for the way in which he was developing this property: "Cheeve Hazelet is making some nice improvements on his residence property; laying out sidewalks, driveways, planting trees, etc. The appearance of our city would be vastly improved if others would exert themselves a little in this direction." [5]

Hazelet's development activities extended beyond the subdivision. In January 1891 he was elected secretary of the Nebraska Land and Investment Company, organized for the purpose of handling Holt County lands. A year later he joined G.F. Bazelman in founding the German Chicory Company, an enterprise that he hoped would become a major industry in Holt County. In the February 4, 1892, issue of *The Frontier* Hazelet announced his plan:

> To the farmers of Holt County. As per announcement in these columns last week, an organization has been effected to establish the chicory industry in this county. The factory will have the capacity for working 300 acres this year, and will be ready for operation September 1. All that now remains to be done to give this industry a thorough and practical test is for farmers of this vicinity to raise the required acreage in roots. To this end I have thought proper to give a few facts and figures bearing upon the production of chicory, realizing that it is a subject new to the majority of farmers of this county.
>
> Chicory is a plant resembling in many ways the carrot. ... It is a native of all Europe and has been cultivated for more than a century as a substitute for coffee. When analyzed, it shows no elements detrimental to health, and, in fact, is recommended by physicians as a healthful drink, especially for the young.
>
> It is adapted to a dry climate, needing no rain when once fairly started through the ground. Any soil will produce it well that is not full of gravel or alkali.

The terms of the contract were that the company would supply and plant the seed which the farmers would then cultivate. After the farmers harvested crops in the fall, the company would pay them at least $9 per ton, with $2 deducted to cover the cost of the seed and planting.

While Hazelet was busy persuading Holt County farmers to grow chicory, Barrett Scott continued to serve as county treasurer. He was re-elected in 1891, as were several other Republicans, but for the first time the Holt County Board of Supervisors was controlled by Populists. The agrarian Populist movement was gaining strength in Nebraska and Kansas as destitute farmers started to look to the government for relief. Many families had been lured into the arid regions of central and western Nebraska by the transcontinental railroads on the mistaken assumption that rain would follow the plough. Instead of rain, they were confronted with a decade of drought and dry searing wind.

In the summer of 1892, central Nebraska experienced its worst drought. Arthur Mullen, who grew up in O'Neill, gave the following description in his autobiography *Western Democrat*: "Farmers put in their crops, and never took them out. For six months the wind blew from the south, so flying sand advanced like a moving wall over the fields. Grasshoppers hung in clouds. Day after day, week after week, month after month the people scanned the great high sky of the plains for the sight of rain. Sometimes huge clouds rose from the horizon, but no rain came.

Hope went in August. Despair came in September. By October nearly all the men, women and children in Holt County, as in other parts of the West, knew that they faced dire poverty." [7]

Holt County officials on court house steps.
George Cheever Hazelet (seated second from left), John Hazelet (standing second from left)
PHOTO COURTESY OF RICHARD OSBORNE

The farmers who contracted to grow chicory for Hazelet were among the fortunate few, because chicory grew when nothing else could. The $15,000 factory opened on schedule in the fall of 1892. [8]

The Populist-controlled board of supervisors did what it could to try to help the farmers by spending $3,000 to hire the services of a rain-maker — to no avail. [9] Barrett Scott, the Republican county treasurer, took more direct action — he loaned money from the county treasury to friends who were in financial difficulty resulting from bank failures. [10]

When they became aware of the shortage in the county treasury, the supervisors demanded the treasurer's resignation. Scott, however, refused to relinquish his office. Then the supervisors took direct action to recoup county losses by filing suits, not only against Scott but also against both Meals and Hazelet for shortages during their prior terms.

Frontier Justice – Nebraska Style

IV

In the 1892 elections, Holt County selected Henry Murphy, a Populist, to be its county attorney. With Murphy's assistance, the supervisors started taking legal action. An expert hired by the supervisors determined that A.J. Meals was responsible for a shortage of approximately $10,000 at the end of his two terms as county treasurer. In April 1893 Murphy filed suit against Meals and his bondsmen for recovery of these funds. [1] Meals was fortunate in having a capable attorney, M.F. Harrington, representing him. Meals' bondsmen settled with the county for $3,000 when Harrington demonstrated that Meals had "paid out considerable school money which he had not entered on his books, the aggregate amount of which would cut down the total shortage to quite an extent." [2]

The supervisors also had their expert examine records from the county clerk's office during Hazelet's two terms. The report, published in *The Frontier* on July 20, 1893, indicated that Hazelet had charged fees for "making duplicate tax lists and for making assessors' and road books and also for transcribing numerical index" in addition to receiving a $1,500 yearly salary. The total amount of these additional charges was $3,502.15.

On July 27, 1893, the county attorneys, M.F. Harrington and H.E. Murphy, filed two suits against Hazelet and his bondsmen in the District Court of Holt County, Nebraska, #4022, asking reimbursement of $1,513.11 for charges during his first term, and #4023, for $2,010.40 during the second term.

Harrington, who had defended Meals, prosecuted Hazelet, and continued to represent the county in all subsequent actions against Barrett Scott. Hazelet denied all of the allegations, stating that he had charged fees according to his arrangements with the previous Board of Supervisors and that they had approved his reports without question. These arguments did not sway the jury, which rendered a guilty verdict. Hazelet appealed and asked for a new trial, stating that "damages were excessive, appearing to have been given under the influence of passion and prejudice" and that the verdict was "not sustained by sufficient evidence." [3] After prolonged litigation, judgment in the amount of $3,500 was secured by the county and paid by Hazelet's bondsmen. [4]

The Hazelet trial occurred while Holt County was in a state of financial panic. Several of the Holt County banks were in receivership and only $17,454 in county funds could be accounted for. [5] In July, Barrett Scott refused to pay $9,000 in warrants that were accruing seven percent interest. [6] In August, when the supervisors obtained a mandamus writ and the court ordered payment, Scott abandoned the treasurer's office and left town. [7] After receiving a taunting letter from Scott in Chihuahua, Mexico, the supervisors voted a $2,000 reward for Scott's capture and return to Holt County. [8] On August 19, County Attorneys Harrington and Murphy filed the Scott bond case, #4043 in Holt County District Court, charging Scott and his bondsmen for a $90,000 shortage during his second term as county treasurer. [9] G.C. Hazelet was listed as one of Scott's 21 bondsmen. [10]

Shortly after the supervisors advertised their reward for Scott's capture, they entered into a contract with Sheriff W.P. Cunningham of Santa Fe for the return of Scott. On August 26, Scott was arrested and jailed in Mexico [11], and early in September the Holt County attorneys appealed to President Cleveland for the extradiction of Scott.

Scott arrived back in O'Neill on October 7, 1893, handcuffed between Sheriff Cunningham and another man. They escorted him through town to the jail with guns drawn. [12] At a mass meeting the following week, Harrington accused Scott of plundering the people of $94,000. [13] A grand jury indicted Scott for embezzlement, with trial set for the spring of 1894. [14] In December, Scott was allowed to go free on bond, and a change of venue to neighboring Antelope County was granted.

The criminal trial was convened in Neligh, Nebraska, on April 10, 1894, with Harrington and Murphy representing Holt County. After some legal maneuvering, the defense succeeded in having the trial postponed until September. Scott was again allowed to go free after 26 Holt County citizens traveled to Neligh to put up $70,000 for his bond. [15]

However, before the criminal trial could take place, the civil bond suit was called on August 8 in O'Neill. Scott's bondsmen had met the previous month and offered to settle the case for $50,000 in securities plus $5,000 cash. The supervisors turned down this offer on the advice of Harrington, whom *The Frontier* accused of prolonging the litigation for personal gain. [16] The bondsmen then claimed that the original bond had been invalidated when two additional bondsmen were added during Scott's second term without approval of the original bondsmen. A judge who had been brought in to hear the case agreed with the bondsmen and ordered the jury to release them from liability for Scott's second term shortage, declaring the $76,000 judgment against Scott alone. [17] The bondsmen, therefore, were held responsible only for $5,600 plus interest to cover Scott's first term shortage. [18]

Interpretation of the verdict in the Scott bond case varied with the political alignment of the newspaper. *The Frontier*, which defended Scott throughout presented the following analysis on September 6, 1894:

> Had the board heeded the advice of *The Frontier* two years ago, the county would have been vastly better off today. We told them to let Scott alone, that his bond was good; that at the end of his term, while he might perhaps be a little short, it could be collected from his bond. But they would not do it. For politics they would push him to the wall; they would force him to give additional security, and invalidate the bond; they would declare that the additional security was insufficient, oust him from office and force him to leave the country; they would appropriate thousands of dollars to get him back again; after getting him back they would refuse settlement, and now they have lost the whole amount, together with the almost endless expense that they have gone to in the case.

The *Holt County Independent* gave a different synopsis:

> ... From the start the bondsmen tried to postpone the suit and it took the county a year to force the case to trial, notwithstanding the fact that Harrington and Murphy were demanding and urging a speedy trial. The county did not want Judge Bartow to try the case as it was believed that he stood in with the gang. Judge Kinkaid refused to try the case, so Judge Chapman was brought here to preside at that trial. ...
>
> He was one of the old state house gang. He came here to do the county up and he did the job. [19]

When the criminal trial was finally held at Neligh the following September, Scott was found guilty of embezzlement. He was sentenced to "not less than one nor more than 21 years in the state penitentiary" and fined twice the amount of the embezzlement, which the jury decided to have been $32,000.

Scott was sentenced to five years in the penitentiary and remained in the Antelope County jail through the first week of December. Old friends promptly came to Scott's aid with the necessary bail.

Hazelet may well have been among the friends that greeted Scott upon his return to O'Neill in mid-December; he certainly was one of a group of friends that searched for Scott's body during the first three weeks of January. The former treasurer disappeared after his carriage was hijacked by a band of masked men while returning to O'Neill on New Year's eve after spending a week with friends in nearby Scottsville. [20] On January 24, 1895, *The Frontier* gave the details:

> The long-drawn-out search for the remains of Barrett Scott met with success last Saturday night... He was found 120 feet below Whiting's bridge on the Boyd County side of the Niobrara River... The party which succeeded in locating the body went out to the river last Saturday morning and pitched camp preparatory to remaining until they were satisfied that the body had not been secreted in that locality. Their efforts were rewarded along in the afternoon by finding the quilt which was used by the mob to cover him up when he was captured near Parker. Cheever Hazelet and Charlie Millard, members of the party, left immediately for O'Neill after the finding of this evidence for reinforcements. ...
>
> A *Frontier* reporter, who was a member of the party of reinforcement, viewed the remains by the light of the moon and heard the story of the search and discovery as told by one who was present at the time. The corpse looked very natural. Anyone who had ever seen him in life would have recognized it. His head was bruised as though he had been struck by a blunt instrument. He wore an overcoat and mittens. His arms were tied behind him with a strong rope. About his neck was a rope probably three feet long, showing how he had been killed.

Although Scott's wife, daughter, a friend, and the driver, who were in the carriage with Scott, claimed to have recognized some of the masked men, M.F. Harrington succeeded in defending them. No one was ever convicted of killing Barrett Scott.

The lynching of Barrett Scott demonstrated the vulnerability of public officials, but did not deter Hazelet from continued political involvement — it may even have solidified his commitment to the Republican party in resisting the Populist uprising. In subsequent years, Hazelet served as chairman of the county central committee, [21] and as delegate to the state Republican convention. [22]

Chicory – O'Neill's New Industry

V

Although some of his political aspirations may have been thwarted during the Populist uprising, Hazelet's family life was rewarding. Frequent references in *The Frontier* to parties hosted by the young Hazelets attested to their popularity with a wide circle of friends and family. Harriet's parents and sister lived nearby. Cheeve's brother John, who joined him in Holt County in 1888, also married into the Potter family. [1] Although their first children, twin daughters born in 1889, died shortly after birth, [2] Cheeve and Harriet soon became parents of two sons, Calvin and Craig.

The chicory industry also flourished for several years. Hazelet's factory, which opened in October of 1892, was the first successful chicory business in Nebraska. The factory turned out three products — an all-chicory beverage, a coffee-chicory blend, and a plug to chew. [3] In order to advertise their new products, the company served free chicory beverages to all visitors at the factory and at booths during nearby county fairs. [4] On February 2, 1893, the *Oakdale Beacon Light* commented:

> Friend Hazelet, of the chicory company, O'Neill, Nebraska, presented the *Beacon Light's* family with a supply of that delicate beverage. To mix it one-third with two-thirds coffee, it makes an excellent drink, and is a great saving in expense. Mr. Hazelet says the chicory business is starting out with encouragement to succeed. We wish this old Iowa chum all success possible, and we shall speak at length of his factory soon.

A description of the chicory factory, appearing in the 75th Anniversary history of O'Neill, revealed that "cleanliness was not emphasized and broken windows in the upper stories gave birds free access to the hoppers full of beets. Their droppings and those of mice and rats were processed along with the chicory." [5]

Chicory cultivation received a considerable boost in 1895, when the Nebraska legislature offered a bounty of five-eighths cents per pound on the manufactured product. If the manufacturers built more plants, they could secure an additional three-eights cent per pound bounty. [6] Hazelet opened a second plant in nearby Fremont, Nebraska, and in 1895 his German Chicory Company joined with the American Chicory Company of Omaha. [7]

Hazelet made frequent trips to Chicago, St.Louis, Omaha and Des Moines to market products from the O'Neill plant, and chicory production promised to be a major addition to the area's economy. The editor of *The Frontier* enthusiastically predicted: "When the time comes, O'Neill will be known as the chicory center and lovers of the beverage all over the country will pay tribute to the industry of our people as they do now to the fruit growers of California, and the potato growers of Colorado." [8]

In order to devote his entire attention to the chicory business, Hazelet left O'Neill and established residency in Omaha, where offices for the chicory business were located.

Prosperity was short-lived for the chicory industry. When Populists gained control of the Nebraska legislature in 1897, they cancelled the chicory bounty, which had passed in 1895 over the veto of Populist Governor Silas Holcomb. [9] As a result, the American Chicory Company had to reduce the amount paid for chicory beets, and farmers turned to more profitable crops, such as sugar beets and corn.

Since farmers were no longer raising enough chicory to make operation of the factories profitable, the Fremont factory was converted to storage for dried sugar beets. Hazelet dissolved the German Chicory Company and moved all operations to Omaha. [10] The final blow to the chicory industry came with a sharp drop in the price of coffee. [12]

In retrospect, the author of *Before Today — A History of Holt County, Nebraska* commented: "However, the chicory business had been a life saver to the people of O'Neill. In addition to the cash earned by the farmers in years when corn and hay were worth nothing, the factory had paid $8,000 to $12,000 a year for labor in the plant." [13] At the time, however, Hazelet felt that he had failed in business as well as in politics. Like many other mid-westerners who had suffered during the drought of the 1890s, he decided to join the Klondike gold rush as a possible way to repair his fortunes. He secured a loan from C. Beren Oldfield, a British associate in the chicory business, [14] and headed north with A.J. Meals, a seasoned outdoorsman, as his only companion.

Stephen Birch
Eastern Opportunist

VI

Hazelet and Meals were already prospecting for gold on the Chistochina River in July 1898, when Stephen Birch, from New York City, finally started to cross Valdez Glacier. Although he was only 26 years old, Birch had already acquired assets that most prospectors lacked — a technical education, wealthy friends and remarkable tenacity.

Stephen Birch

Birch's start in life did not promise future wealth. He was the second son of a wounded Union Army sergeant who died when Stephen was 10 years old and his youngest brother, George Howard, not yet born. Three years after her husband's death, Birch's widowed mother moved with her six children from their Brooklyn home to Mahwah, New Jersey, to be near relatives. The young Birches soon became friends and sporting companions of the children of their neighbors, Theodore Havemeyer, the vice-president of American Sugar Refining Company, and his wife, Lillie. Mrs. Havemeyer took a special interest in young Stephen and provided financial assistance for his education at Trinity School, New York University, and Columbia School of Mines.

Unloading horses from SS DORA with a sling at Valdez, Alaska.
ALASKA STATE LIBRARY PCA192-7

At the peak of the Klondike gold rush in 1898, young Stephen announced that he wanted to go to Alaska rather than continue working with an engineering team that was surveying for the New York City subway system. Although most of his friends and relatives failed to take him seriously, Mrs. Havemeyer offered to finance his trip to Valdez.

When H.O. Havemeyer II, Stephen's childhood playmate, realized that his mother and Birch were serious about the Alaska adventure, he enlisted several associates to help pay expenses and arrange for proper connections to assure Birch's safety. [1] As a result of the intervention of these wealthy friends, Birch arrived in Valdez early in the summer of 1898 with a request to Capt. W.R. Abercrombie that he be attached to Abercrombie's Copper River Exploring Expedition in a civilian capacity. Abercrombie, whom President William McKinley had detailed to explore potential all-American routes to the Interior, was not impressed that this New Yorker would be a suitable participant in his wilderness scouting expedition. Birch, displaying the singleness of purpose that would distinguish his later career, took the first steamer back to Seattle and contacted his influential sponsors, who protested to contacts in Washington D.C. When Birch returned to Valdez demanding employment, Abercrombie responded: "Maybe I can't fire you but I can throw you out of my office." [2]

Abercrombie could scarcely afford to be choosy. He initially had planned to use reindeer as pack animals for his military reconnaisance expedition. The deer had been purchased in Lapland the winter before, shipped across the Atlantic, carried by railroad to Seattle, and then by ship to Haines. Reindeer moss ran out in the course of the lengthy journey and many deer died. When Abercrombie reached Haines, he found the surviving deer too debilitated to be used and had to go on to Valdez without pack animals. Realizing that men could not carry all the needed equipment, Abercrombie had to send to Seattle for pack horses, thus delaying the start of a party to establish a route from Valdez to the Yukon River.

As a result of this delay, Birch was back in Valdez in July when the expedition was finally ready to start. Illness had depleted the Army detachment, leaving Abercrombie and Lieutenant P.G. Lowe the only healthy officers. In his official report, Abercrombie described Lowe's part in the expedition:

> ... He (Lowe) was directed to organize a party, consisting of himself and three men, with ten head of stock, and to proceed at once to Forty Mile River via Mentasta Pass, with a view to locating an all-American route from Valdez to the Yukon. On consulting with Lt. Lowe it was decided that the course of duty lay over the glacier, even if all the stock and some of the men were lost in making the attempt. [3]

Birch was one of the civilian guides assigned to Lowe's reconnaissance expedition. After an initial unsuccessful attempt to scale the glacier, the men left Valdez on July 13, 1898, accompanied by Army troops to help get the horses through the crevasse-filled ice field. Lowe told of their hazardous trip over Valdez Glacier in his official report:

By zigzagging, I was enabled to find points along the crevasses narrow enough for the horses to jump over. In many places the snow covered the ice, and the crevasses were not discovered until some of the horses had gotten a leg or two in them. Every horse managed to get one or two legs in a number of times, and they practically hung by their "eyebrows." At times it required the prompt and united efforts of the entire party to rescue them. One horse was saved by his pack striking the edge of the crevasse behind him, when he had both legs in. Had the animal not been sensible and quiet he would have struggled into some other position and gone down for good. This same horse probably saved the life of Private Hilliard, of the Fourteenth Infantry. The latter went down, but held to the horse's shanks, while the animal braced himself and the man climbed out. ...After some pretty stiff floundering, the expedition managed to get through, but we had not an inch too much snow under us. [4]

When the expedition reached the Klutina River, the soldiers returned to Valdez, leaving Lowe and the civilian employees to continue with the horses. Although they were using a prospector's trail, several of the men frequently went ahead to clear brush and find safe places to ford streams. Traveling in this manner, they reached the Copper River at Copper Center on July 31, and Lowe reported:

Copper Center is a sort of interior starting point, the objective appearing to be the headwaters of the Copper and the Tanana. ... Quite a number of cabins were in course of construction; but more than half of the people who had come over the glacier had returned home disheartened, and I met no less than 200 returning prospectors between the glacier and Copper Center. The fabulous wealth of the country had been well advertised, but, the prospectors not finding any gold, the disappointment was too much for them. There may be gold in the Copper River country, but up to the time I passed through it none had been discovered, although several alarms had been sounded. The country was advertised before it was tested.

The men had traveled 100 miles over a known trail to reach Copper Center and had 300 more miles to go through unknown country. Maps that were available proved to be worthless, and the people they talked to told conflicting stories about the terrain ahead.

Lowe described the crossing of their first obstacle, the Copper River:

> Finally I came to the conclusion that, although the animals could in ordinary water be induced to attempt swimming the distance, the swiftness of the current, as well as the extreme coldness of the water, would cause them to turn back. Believing that swimming them behind a skiff would be in every way better, I made a successful test with some of the best water animals. I swam them to an island, and from there they were led behind a boat, two at a time, with a man in the stern attending to each horse.

After crossing the river, they followed an indistinct trail across the big bend of the Copper until they came to the mouth of the Slana River. Here they had to cross the Copper River again, but, since there was no settlement, boats were not readily available to help. Lowe's report contained this report of Birch's participation in the crossing attempt:

> On August 14, I succeeded in finding a ford through an island half a mile below camp... On the following day I moved with my outfit to the island and proceeded to make a raft with which to cross the main channel of the river. My tools were three axes and an auger. The raft was finished and launched the following day and the occupants, lightly clad, started for the opposite bank on the trial trip. The channel was about 30 yards wide, the current very swift, and the raft was immediately at its mercy. To pole was the original intention, but it became evident that oars only could be used, and that a landing must be effected on any shore possible. The raft passed close to the home shore and Birch jumped with the rope; but his feet were instantly swept from under him and he found himself in deep water. He was very cool, however, and held to the rope until hauled on board.

While the group was reassessing their plans, a boat luckily came downstream and they were able to get help again in crossing a major river.

After this crossing, the expedition left the Copper River and followed the Slana up to an Indian settlement on Mentasta Lake, where two English-speaking Natives gave them information about the trail ahead. They crossed Meiklejohn Pass into the Tanana River drainage and reached an Indian settlement where the Tetling River flows into the Tanana. Here they employed the chief's son to act as a guide. Two of the villagers who owned canoes postponed a caribou hunting trip to help the expedition cross the Tanana River. Lowe registered his doubts about the journey ahead:

> ... We had now burned our bridges behind us, as the Indians were off for their annual caribou hunt, and the distance in any event back to Valdez was so much

greater than that to the Yukon that the latter became the preferable objective. Upon leaving the Tanana we entered a country that had not been mapped from actual observation. Information was obtained from the Indians and the country was mapped as well as the imagination could allow. An Indian will tell you it is so many "sleeps" to a certain place, packing so many pounds on your back but he can not tell you the number of miles, and as there is a difference in the endurance of Indians there is a difference in the number of "sleeps."

The men soon found that information obtained from the Indians was more accurate than the Army maps they were attempting to follow. Their objective was a store at the junction of Miller Creek and the Sixtymile River where they hoped to get information about a good trail to the Yukon River. For the next two weeks they continued to travel between branches of the Sixtymile and Fortymile rivers while horses got weaker and the nights colder. When unpacking after a day in the cold rain, Lowe noted that "the hands of my party were so numb that it was hard to handle the ropes and it took three times the ordinary time required to get camp in shape." One of the horses had to be abandoned before they reached Miller Creek, and four more when they encountered a snow storm between Miller Creek and Fortymile River.

As soon as the expedition reached the Fortymile River, they were able to buy a boat in which to cover the remaining 26 miles to the settlement of Forty Mile. The river passed through a tortuous canyon so they left the horses behind with one of the civilian employees who was planning to spend the winter in the area. After lining the boat down one rapid and shooting another, they arrived at the cabin village on the Yukon on September 25.

Although it was too late to catch the last boat down the Yukon River, the group was fortunate to find two American boats that were pushing a barge upriver with supplies for Canadian troops at Fort Selkirk. The expedition landed at Dawson on September 26, and several days later took the W.K. MERWINX, arriving at the White Horse Rapids on October 15. Lowe described the final days of the expedition:

> The steamer NORA was boarded in the afternoon and started for the head of Lake Bennett, but came near having to shoot Miles Canyon and the rapids before getting under way. As the bow left the shore, the wheel got tangled in a raft and could not revolve without tearing off the buckets. For the ship to float down as she was and land would be to tear her bottom off on the rocks. Her nose swung down with the current and was run into the opposite bank the moment she was free. She was tied up, given a chance to breathe, and started on her way again. ...
>
> October 16 the head of Lake Bennett was reached, which is a thriving village with many hotels and an important police station. The day following, the

expedition sent its baggage to White Pass by pack train and walked 8 miles over the Skagway trail to Log Cabin, a large village of cabins and tents. The trail was fair, although wet.

October 18 the expedition walked 20 miles to White Pass, which is quite a town, but will soon disappear, as the railroad is passing around it. ... The trail is rocky, muddy, rough, and about as bad as possible. ... The members of the expedition would occasionally step on dead horses and hogs. ... After 20 miles of stiff walking the expedition entered a canyon that surpassed for beauty and grandeur anything that had been seen. In the afternoon the members of the expedition boarded the narrow-gauge railroad and rode 12 miles into Skagway.

Stephen Birch returned to New York. He had survived his first summer in Alaska and was hardened to the trail.

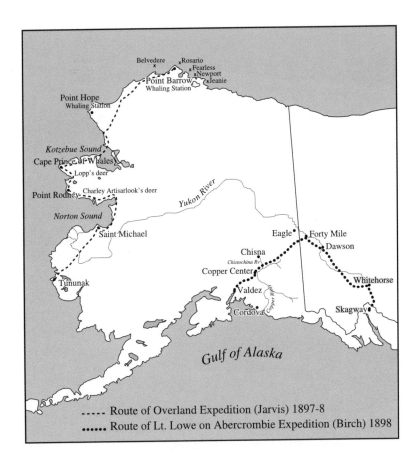

Overland and Copper River Exploring expeditions 1898

Lieutenant David Henry Jarvis
Arctic Hero

VII

Lt. David Henry Jarvis of the United States Revenue Marine was also returning home in October 1898, after spending almost a year in northwestern Alaska on a rescue mission to save icebound members of the American whaling fleet.

Lt. David Henry Jarvis

When news reached Washington, D.C., in October of 1897 that seven whaling ships were trapped in ice north of Point Barrow with insufficient food to last through the winter, President William McKinley convened a cabinet meeting to discuss plans for providing aid. At the suggestion of Rev. Sheldon Jackson, special agent for education in Alaska, Treasury Secretary Lyman Gage ordered Capt. Frances Tuttle of the cutter BEAR to organize an overland reindeer expedition to Point Barrow. Tuttle was instructed to take the BEAR as far north in the Bering Sea as he could sail at that time of year and then land two officers and a surgeon to travel overland to reach the reindeer herds and drive them to the Arctic coast with supplies for the stranded whalers. Reindeer could then be slaughtered to provide fresh meat.

Crew of the Revenue Cutter BEAR.
Lt. Bertholf (front row far left), Lt. Jarvis (front row third from left),
Capt. Tuttle (front row center), Surgeon Call (back row far right)
SAMUEL CALL COLLECTION. ALASKA & POLAR REGIONS DEPT., UAF. A66-10-160

Tuttle chose 1st Lt. Jarvis, a veteran of 10 years service on the Bering Sea, to head the expedition, with 2nd Lt. E.P. Bertholf, Dr. S.J. Call, and one other man to accompany him. Reindeer were new to Alaska. Six years before, Jarvis, under the direction of Capt. Michael Healy and Rev. Jackson, had purchased Alaska's first deer in Siberia. Each succeeding year Jarvis returned to Siberia during the summer voyages of the BEAR and purchased additional deer for the mission schools and the new Government Reindeer Station at Teller. Technically these men were volunteers, but Jarvis was not an eager volunteer. [1] Winter was the only time that officers of the Revenue Marine could spend with their families, and Jarvis was newly married and expecting his first child. However, his participation was considered essential to the expedition because of his experience with reindeer and his friendship with the herdsmen, and also because he had earned a reputation for valor.

Reindeer and sleds on Overland Expedition.
SAMUEL CALL COLLECTION, UAF. B66-10-116

The men, with their supplies and seven sled dogs, landed at Tanunak on December 16, 1897. A trader, Alexis Kalenin, provided additional dogs, drivers, and lightweight sleds. Two days later, they set off for St. Michael with four sleds, 41 dogs, and 1,291 pounds of food and equipment. Jarvis described their mode of travel in his official report:

When the start was made, there were, besides the four members of the expedition, Alexis, who acted as guide, and four Eskimos, who were to help with the sleds and go ahead to break a trail, for where there is no beaten trail or road, it is the custom for one man to go ahead and pick out the road. The team with the best leader comes first, and he faithfully follows the footprints of the man in the lead, and the other teams follow the first one. In traveling over a comparatively level country, with a good road and light loads on the sleds, the dogs will maintain a trot, which is faster than a man can walk, but not as fast as he can run, so the trail maker runs ahead for some distance and then slows down to a walk until the head team comes up with him, when he repeats the operation. By this alternate running and walking, a man can keep ahead of the dogs for a consider-able time without excessive fatigue. Many of the natives who travel a great deal in the winter can keep up this mode of travel all day and show little sign of exhaustion when camp is made at night. When going downhill, the dogs could not keep up with the sleds, so they were turned loose to follow the men as they coasted down on the sleds. [2]

After traveling 20 to 30 miles each day, the group camped at small Eskimo villages, consisting of several small crowded huts grouped around a large "kazheem," which served as dance hall, meeting place and lodging for single men. Although invited to sleep in the huts, Jarvis usually chose to pitch his own tent. The dogs were so ravenous that everything not made of metal or wood had to be taken into the tent for the night. Since they were the first white men to pass through the country in many years, the group created quite a commotion in these small villages.

After three days traveling, two teams, made up of young dogs, could not continue. Since they could find no replacement dogs immediately, Bertholf stayed behind while Jarvis went on to reach the reindeer herds. Jarvis arrived at the Yukon River on December 24 and continued on to St. Michael where he reported to Lt. Col. George M. Randall and refitted the expedition with deerskin clothing, boots, socks and sleeping bags to prepare for colder weather.

> On starting out, I had determined to do as the people who lived in the country did — to dress, travel and live as they did, and, if necessary, to eat the same food. I found the only way to get along was to conform as nearly as possible to the customs of those who already had solved many of the problems of existence in their arctic climate. In this connection, it has seemed to me that the value of deerskin clothing has not always been known or fully appreciated in arctic explorations. The Eskimo of arctic Alaska and northeast Siberia use hardly anything else, and nothing is so warm and light as their dress. [3]

In order to make the expedition self-sufficient, Jarvis arranged for Bertholf to bring provisions across the divide from Norton Bay to Kotzebue Sound and meet him after he had obtained the reindeer. Near Unalaklik [sic], Jarvis met a Mr. Tilton, third mate of the steam whaler BELVEDERE, traveling south. Tilton, who had been sent from the stranded fleet to obtain aid, reported that the ORCA and JESSE H. FREEMAN had been destroyed and the BELVEDERE, ROSARIO, NEWPORT, FEARLESS and JEANIE were icebound. After crossing Norton Bay, Jarvis and Dr. Call met Dr. Kettleson with the government reindeer herd, which was being taken to the aid of stranded Klondike miners. Jarvis reported that Dr. Kettleson accompanied them to the reindeer station at Port Clarence where he provided sleds and deer to pull them. Jarvis explained the difficulties he encountered in driving the deer:

> All our travel heretofore had been by dog teams, and, as we were to have much deer traveling farther on, I was very anxious to try the change and note the

difference, wishing for anything that would hurry us along. There came with Dr.
Kettleson, to manage our train, Mikkel, a Laplander, who was counted a
thoroughly experienced and capable man, and I found him all that. A stolid,
determined character, and possessed of a wonderful patience. He took the lead
with two deer harnessed to his sled, while we had but one. All hands must be
ready at the same time when starting a deer train, for, just as soon as the animals
see the head team start, they are all off with a jump, and for a short time keep up
a very high rate of speed. If one is not quick in jumping and holding on to his
sled, he is likely either to lose his team or be dragged along in the snow. [4]

Jarvis had two accidents the first day on the reindeer sleds and ended up with his
deer breaking loose and stranding him overnight.

A blizzard slowed progress for several days, but they finally reached Charley
Artisarlook's house at Romney Point on January 19. Artisarlook, one of the first
Eskimo herders, had completed a five-year apprenticeship and assumed ownership
of his own herd of 133 deer. Jarvis described his meeting with Artisarlook: "I
explained to him carefully and particularly what the deer were wanted for; that I
had not come with power or force to take his property from him, and that he
must let me have them of his own free will and trust the government, which I
represented, for an ample and suitable reward and return. He and his wife, Mary,
held a long and solemn consultation, and finally explained their position. They
were sorry for the white men at Point Barrow, and they were glad to be able to
help them; they would let me have their deer, which represented their all, on my
promise of return, if I would be directly responsible for them."

When they arrived at the Teller Reindeer Station the sled-deer were too tired to
go on, so Jarvis arranged to continue to Cape Prince of Wales by dog team. After
covering 50 miles, that he called "the most trying and fearful of all I experienced
on the expedition," Jarvis reached the home of Congregational missionary, W.T.
Lopp, on January 21. The sleds were broken, the dogs played out, and he could
scarcely move when he greeted the Lopps, who were amazed to see a Revenue
Marine officer in the winter.

In the interest of humanity, Lopp agreed to provide his entire herd, and join the
expedition with his six Eskimo apprentices. While waiting for Dr. Call to arrive
with Artisarlook's herd, they made careful preparations for the remaining 700 mile
journey to Point Barrow.

They left Cape Prince of Wales with 438 deer and a train of 18 sleds, but Jarvis
soon realized that the sled-deer would give out unless he could reduce the weight
on the train. He divided the load and had Lopp drive him and Dr. Call to a
coastal village to secure dog teams. Eskimos along Kotzebue Sound had never seen
domestic reindeer and Jarvis wanted to tell them that the herd was coming so the

Eskimos would not mistake them for wild caribou and shoot. With the help of Perninyuk, a Native medicine man, they crossed Kotzebue Sound to a Quaker mission at Kikiktaruk, where they met Bertholf with the additional supplies on February 12. They traveled to Point Hope while awaiting Lopp's arrival with the reindeer herd.

Lopp and the herders saved days by driving the herd across the ice of Kotzebue Sound, although they had to retrieve some of the deer that had strayed to find moss while they were camped on the ice. Travel along the flat coastal plain was easier. Jarvis reported that the clear, cold weather, with temperatures between 30 and 42 below zero, was ideal for travel as long as they took the precautions which he described:

> The difference between care and carelessness is slight in arctic travel, and the first let-up is sure to bring its reminder in the shape of a frosted toe or finger or a frozen nose. One must be on guard, and the slightest tinge in the nose or cheek must be heeded, and circulation started again by vigorous rubbing. Though somewhat disagreeable and painful, freezing these parts is not necessarily harmful unless too long neglected. ... But with the hands, and especially the feet, it is different. No part of the body requires more attention than these; socks and boots must be well made and kept thoroughly dry; even the slightest perspiration will, if one stops too long, work disastrously. Both boots and socks should be changed immediately upon going into camp, and dry ones must be put on in the morning before starting. The natives know the importance of this only too well, and if they see one inclined to neglect these precautions, they will insist on his taking care of his foot gear. It is the easiest thing in the world for a man to suffer severely in such a climate, but it is possible, by good care and attention, to avoid what one might call extreme suffering, and live there with only the unavoidable discomforts of the country, to which a man in good health sooner or later grows accustomed. [5]

Jarvis and Dr. Call reached Point Barrow on March 27, after first checking on the status of the men on the ice-bound BELVEDERE. Provisions were low, but Charles D. Brower, manager of the Cape Smythe Whaling and Trading Company, had successfully rationed the available supplies and Eskimo hunters had been able to hunt in the mountains to provide wild caribou meat. Jarvis took charge and arranged housing for the men from the wrecked vessels. He insisted that the men on the intact vessels remain on board to prevent overcrowding in the Point Barrow buildings.

Lopp arrived by dog team on March 30, having left the 382 surviving deer 20 miles away where feed was good. Artisarlook and another herder stayed with the herd while Lopp and the others returned home by dog teams. Dr. Call diagnosed several early cases of scurvy, which were quickly cured with increased rations of fresh meat. Reindeer were slaughtered only as a last resort when adequate wild meat was not available.

Icebound whaling ships, NEWPORT and FEARLESS.
SAMUEL CALL COLLECTION, UAF. A66-10-159A

The whalers were all healthy when the BEAR arrived on July 30, 1898, to remove the 97 shipwrecked men. The BELVEDERE, NEWPORT, FEARLESS and JEANIE had by this time succeeded in freeing themselves from the ice, but the ROSARIO was crushed in the process.

The reindeer were initially left at Point Barrow in the care of Dr. Marsh, the Presbyterian missionary, and four Barrow Eskimo boys trained by Artisarlook. The first fawns were born April 12, and births continued until mid-June, with an increase of 190 deer. Lopp eventually arranged to drive some of the herd back to Cape Prince of Wales, because sufficient replacement deer could not be purchased in Siberia.

Jarvis went back to Romney Point on the BEAR with Artisarlook, whose wife and family had almost starved while the herd was gone. After again promising to reimburse the Eskimo family with reindeer as soon as possible, Jarvis was finally able to return to his own wife and newborn daughter, Anna.

Winter on the Chistochina

George Hazelet wished that he too could be returning to his beloved wife and family in October of 1898, but instead he was at Copper Center preparing to spend a long winter prospecting in Alaska. After reading and re-reading letters from his wife — the last he could expect to receive for months — Hazelet hit the trail with Meals and McNeer to return to the supplies that they had cached 40 miles up the Copper River. Prospectors camping along the river offered them food and shelter as they passed, and they were able to purchase about 30 lbs. of fresh moose meat from one of the groups for $2.

They started the hard work of pulling sleds loaded with supplies up the river on November 7. Overflow of water on the ice forced them to go slowly and they had time to visit with the Indians who joined them at most of their meals. Hazelet was particularly fond of Indian Charlie, who had told him about gold on the Chistochina when they met the previous summer and now helped them pull sleds and set up camp. "He is the most intelligent Indian we have seen," Hazelet wrote. "He can say a few words in English and make one understand much more by signs and illustrations."

This Indian's honesty, theology, and devotion to family impressed Hazelet, as revealed in his November 12, 1898, diary entry:

> It seems he is much more civilized than many of his white brethren in these parts. For he told us in the most earnest way that he had in his cache three cups, three knives and forks, pails, skins, etc., besides some muck-tuck or food, but Oakbine (white man) came along and they were all gone.
>
> We felt so indignant over his loss that we told him and made him understand that if he ever caught a white man taking anything from his cache again he should shoot him on the spot. But he only shook his head sadly, made the sign of the cross, and pointing up said, "No good! Jesus no like, Oakbine take Ingian's [*sic*] cache,

Ingian get more." It was a simple sermon, but uttered with more pathos and feeling than has ever before been my lot to hear. I have sat "for years under the drippings of the sanctuary," I have heard preachers and teachers of almost every denomination expound their doctrine, yet never in my life before have I been moved as I was with the simple utterances of this so called "savage of the north."

The men liked Indian Charlie so much that they invited him to come to their cabin on the Chistochina and use it as a base for trapping.

Weather continued to delay their progress along the river — first, it was too warm and then storms set in. When the weather turned cold, they started pulling the sleds again, but continued to be slowed by overflow. Even when the thermometer registered 30 below zero, they worked so hard that they "perspired like horses." They also ate like horses, although their meals lacked variety. When two prospectors dropped in on them to share their Thanksgiving dinner of bacon, beans, and dehydrated potatoes, Hazelet commented:

> I had begun dinner so we asked them to stay and eat their Thanksgiving with us. Of course they did, for an Alaska man never refuses to eat, be it morning, noon, night or bed time, eat he will and plenty, too. To refuse to eat is to go against all precedent and is considered the sum total of ill manners. During our short stay at Copper Center a few weeks ago, I have gotten up from our table so full I could hardly breath, gone over town and into someone's camp where they were just sitting down to a meal, sat down with them and eaten another hearty repast. So much for appetite in the "Land of the Midnight Sun."

After experiencing an eruption of Mt. Wrangell, which blackened the snow, the Hazelet party reached the mouth of the Chistochina on December 1. All three men adapted well to the sub-zero weather. "Of course it is cold," Hazelet wrote, "in fact we would call it very cold, yet we do not suffer in the least. Work all day with overcoats off and are too warm most of the time."

When they finally reached the site for their cabin on December 11, Hazelet vowed never to pull a sled again. "Life is short enough at best and I feel and know I'm cutting off some of mine each day I pull sled or boat or make a pack horse of myself." Separation from his family was increasingly painful and he dreaded a winter of inactivity — "... it seems at times I cannot stand it, and I know I could not were it not for the fact that I'm so awfully busy that I hardly have time to think. If we make a strike, the winter will pass rapidly, but if we have to lay in cabin two or three months with nothing to do, I can't tell what the result will be."

In spite of two weeks of hard work the cabin was not finished by Christmas and they had to dine on their "bacon, crisp and brown, served with onion and potatoes both of the evaporated kind" in a tent. However, pie made with dried peaches and cherry pudding served to make the meal a special occasion. Hazelet invited a solitary Swede who was camped nearby to join them and had him tell them about Christmas celebrations in the "Old Country." After dinner their guest provided them with a package of tobacco, which was a great treat since they had been out of it for a month. The men celebrated "the death of the old year" by moving from the tent to their new cabin, which Hazelet described as follows:

> Well, now as to our cabin. It stands due north-south as shines Polaris. It is 16x18 in size from the outside. Barring the chimney of logs we erected on top, it resembles a jockey's cap more than anything I can think of, low and squatty with an immense visor in front. Eight logs form each side and ten each end. The roof consists of about 40 logs on each side running in diameter from 4 to 6 inches and covered about 4 inches deep with moss and dirt. This roof extends out in front some 6 feet making a sort of porch and forming what I spoke of as the visor to the cap. A door, high enough so a man can enter without bumping his head occupies the southeast corner. One window in the east and one in the south give us light. Having no glass we had to use flour sacks well oiled with tallow stretched over a frame. This admits a little light and a great deal of cold but is better than nothing. We have chinked between the logs with all kinds of moss, giving the interior a sort of variegated appearance. Two uprights erected about 6 feet from either end in the center of the cabin support the roof, good and strong as well they might be for the roof is heavy. Across the north end we have erected two bunks and along the west side two more. The one with the head in northeast corner is where I lay and dream of my darlings. The next one on the north is Mc's and the one in the northwest Jack's. The extra bunk is for the accommodation of any stray Siwash who may chance to come along. ...
>
> Along the northeast wall hang our clothes, guns, etc., on pegs of wood, while on the west we have a shelf for groceries and cooking vessels. Along the north is also a narrow shelf containing what few books we have and the pictures of our sweethearts, the one best thing of all. That shelf has already gained a place in our hearts. A table built of good, strong lumber and planed to a nicety, stands close to east window, while just above and to the right is a grocery box resting on two large wooden pegs which we call cupboard. The stove that has done such good service for the past ten months stands in the center of the room and throws out plenty of heat as long as we keep its stomach full of good spruce wood. A few boxes used as chairs constitute the remainder of our furniture.

Even before the cabin was finished, Hazelet started digging shafts to reach bedrock, but as soon as they were about six feet deep they invariably filled with water. While waiting for water in the holes to freeze so he could pick out the ice and continue digging, Hazelet started a shaft into the hillside and reached bedrock. Tests on the rock were disappointing and he abandoned this tunnel after uncovering about 125 square feet of bedrock.

On February 17, 1899, Hazelet summerized his first year in Alaska:

> Now for a short resume of the year's work since the day I said the sad goodbye. First, we, A.J. Meals and I, have traveled by rail and water 3,500 miles. Have pulled sleds, loaded with 200 to 800 lbs., 930 miles. Have sawed lumber for two boats and built one. We have gondoliered boat 52 miles. We have shot boat on Klutina, Copper and Chistochina rivers 223 miles. We have towed boat, loaded with from 1,000 to 2,500 lbs., 193 miles. We have packed 50 to 80 lbs. 460 miles, and have not up to date reached a point north of Valdez to exceed 250 miles. We have sawed 800 feet of lumber for sluicing and built 96 feet of sluice box. We have constructed dams on Chistochina 110 feet long, dug a ditch 75 feet long and sluiced 39 ½ yards of river gravel, from which we took $2.24 worth of gold, all of which an Indian stole.
>
> We have panned 300 pans of dirt, in 95% of which we found from one to 30 and 40 colors. Have made at least 50 tests of rock and sent two specimens home for assay. We have built 3 rafts, two of which we wrecked. Built one house on Chistochina 16x18 consisting of 138 logs. ... Started 11 prospect holes, being driven out of 10 of them by water. ...
>
> Have run one tunnel into side hill 25 ft. on top of bedrock, tunnel 7 ft. high and 5 ft. wide, got not to exceed one color to each two sq. ft. of bedrock. We have thus excavated at least 3,675 cu. ft. of dirt. To thaw the same, we cut and burned 50 cords of wood, hauling a part of it ¼ mile. We sawed lumber and made one pump 18 ft. long which we used two days trying to exhaust the water from a prospect hole, but failed. We have sawed lumber and made 7 pair of skis. So much for the work, and now as to results. Must say we have nothing definite. Have found two ledges, or lodes, from which we have not yet got the assay. We still have one dry hole and hope to reach bedrock here and determine whether or not there is any gold on the Chistochina.

After two more weeks working on the last dry hole with no encouraging results, the three men left for Copper Center on hand-hewn skis, 9½ feet long and 6 inches wide. Even though they were not pulling heavy loads this time the traveling was not easy:

> We break trail with our skis and then pull our sleds over it, sometimes breaking in half way up to our shins, then have to get onto skis and double up going ahead for a short distance with one sled and back after the others. The sweat runs off of us in streams, our whiskers freeze stiff — a solid mat over our faces, and our

underclothing is simply as wet as if it had been in a bath tub. The outside garments freeze stiff and we have to camp in this condition on from 3 to 6 ft. of snow with the thermometer any place from 10 to 30 below.

When they reached Copper Center, they realized they were doing much better than many of the prospectors. Hazelet met a Dr. Townsend, who invited him to visit the hospital where he saw "men lying there in all stages of scurvy, some close to death's door, others getting well, most all in bad shape." In contrast, Hazelet and Meals were thriving. "Up to date we weigh more than we ever did in our lives and feel fully as well," Hazelet wrote while summarizing the year's accomplishment.

After receiving reassuring letters from home, Hazelet and Meals made preparations to spend the summer prospecting in the mountains at the head of the Chistochina. They purchased a complete outfit, including "the best horse on the trail," for $150. McNeer had business to attend to in Valdez, so he arranged to escort one of the sick men back over the glacier and return with two more horses.

First Hazelet and Meals cabin on the Chisna, 1898.
George Hazelet (left)

On the way back to the Chistochina, Hazelet and Meals met the Indians again and traded tea for more moose meat. This time Indian Charlie and his family went with them to hunt, trap and show them through the mountains. In mid-April they reached the cabin, where they rested the horse, washed all their clothes, and prepared to start up to higher meadows where the horse could graze. On April 30, while waiting for the snow to melt, Hazelet filled the last notebook that he had with him with the following entry:

> Since we have had to lay off, I'm just about insane, in fact I guess I'm entirely so and always have been, but have just reached a point where I have found it out. However, I've thought the thing all over many times in the last few days and nights, and whether I make a find or not shall go home this summer and lead a different life in some lines. At least I have made some resolves and I propose to carry them out.

Hazelet did go home, but not to "lead a different life." On May 18, Hazelet and Meals found gold on an upper branch of the Chistochina River. [1] Out of 4,000 to 5,000 prospectors who crossed Valdez glacier in 1898 to search for gold, they were among the few who succeeded.

Although Hazelet's diary does not contain details of the gold discovery, additional information provided in a recorded interview by McNeer's friend and mining partner, Henry Watkins, indicates that McNeer was back at Chisna with Hazelet and Meals and, therefore shared in the discovery, as did Melvin Dempsey, a Cherokee Indian who Hazelet and Meals had rescued from the river and befriended. Watkins also revealed that McNeer had found good prospects in a small nearby creek, but had not staked claims or informed his partners, planning to return the following year to stake claims for himself. McNeer's promising prospect was apparently at Miller Gulch on Slate Creek which turned out to be the richest stream in the area. [2]

When Hazelet and Meals left for Alaska, they took with them powers of attorney from friends and relatives so that they could stake claims for them. While back in Nebraska, they planned to organize a company to develop the 25 claims that they had staked. [3] Since no other prospectors were in the area when they made the discovery, they did not anticipate competition for their claims. However, Dempsey, who had agreed to secrecy about the gold strike, couldn't resist telling about his good luck when he returned to Valdez.

Indian Charlie

Although several Indians named "Charlie" lived in the Copper River country in 1898, the man that Addison Powell refers to as "Gakona Charley" in his book *Trailing and Camping in Alaska* is undoubtedly the same Indian Charlie that led Hazelet and Meals to placer gold on the tributaries of the Chistochina River. In *Tatl'ahwt'aenn Nenn, the narrative of Upper Ahtna Athabaskans*, Katie John identifies the Indian who discovered gold on the upper Chistochina River around 1895 as a Mentasta man named Tl'adets, who was "Fred John's uncle Charley."

Charlie impressed both Hazelet and Powell with his intelligence and devotion to his family. Hazelet did not mention Indian Charlie in his diary after 1900, but Addison Powell provided more information about the tragic life of this Copper River Indian:

> That summer (1902) had been an unlucky one for I had arranged to accompany the Indian, Gakona Charley, to a great copper deposit. He had failed to appear the year before, because of sickness in his family, but as they had all died, he was left alone to disclose the secret. He was willing to do so on condition that if it were worth it to me, I should take him out of the Copper River country, so that he would never see it again. We were to meet on August 1, but on the way to our appointed rendezvous, he was drowned in the Tazlina River, on July 28. The secret was lost, and so was an Indian friend whom I had known for four years.
>
> I had often noted his tracks and those of his family as they moved from one hunting-ground to another, and had seen their abandoned camps, where in their all-too-brief period of childish happiness, his little ones had built playhouses (wickiups). Charley had watched his children die, one at a time, and then had seen his wife succumb to consumption. With loving hands he had laid her to rest beside their children, and with tearful eyes had followed the lonely trail leading away from their decorated graves, never to return.

Powell was probably three days off in the date he gave for Charley's death. *The Valdez News* carried the following story on July 26, 1902:

> Tazlina, July 26.
>
> Yesterday the ferry which was operating across the Tazlina river at this place broke away and two Indians were drowned. Mr. Bunday, who operates the ferry was crossing the stream with two Indians as passengers. When about midway between the shores the cable suddenly snapped and the ferry shot down stream at a rapid rate. Mr. Bunday managed to get ashore in some manner but the Indians were both drowned. The ferry was destroyed between Tazlina and Copper Center.

The Valdez News   September 28, 1901

THE PRESIDENT ASSASSINATED
McKinley Shot Twice by Anarchist at the Exposition

The Alaska Prospector, Valdez   June 19, 1902

The New Strike
First Reports Are Fully Confirmed

*The '98ers Missed It—They
Followed the Wrong Trail*

The Valdez News   June 22, 1901

CAPT. HEALY'S BIG SCHEME

*WOULD BUILD RAILROAD TO
SIBERIA—START FROM VALDEZ*

According to reports a company will be
formed early this month, construction
work will begin at once.

The Alaska Prospector   March 6, 1902

BIG $1,100,000 SALE
AGREEMENTS ARE NOW ON RECORD

Alaska Copper Company Buys 45 Copper Claims
From Original Locators for Large Amount

The Seattle Post-Intelligencer   May 31, 1902

From Valdez to Eagle City
M.J. Heney Has Contract for Building Road

Seattle Daily Times   November 13, 1899

DAWSON TO CAPE NOME

Many Miners Preparing to go Down
Over the Ice—No Hardships Now

The Valdez News   Sept. 28, 1901

From Seattle to Interior
New Mail Service Over the
All-American Route

TELEGRAPH LINE
A telegraph line is being contemplated
to run to Slate Creek and Chisna
thence down Delta and Tanana to
Yukon River.

Gold Mine at Chisna

IX

When Hazelet and Meals returned to Nebraska in the fall of 1899, they had a lot to do besides enjoying the long-awaited reunion with their families. On January 4, 1900, *The Frontier* reported that G.C. Hazelet had spent the Christmas season in O'Neill "furthering the plans for the Klondike expedition, which will head for the fields of gold the latter part of the present month." The paper further explained that some 15 or 20 men in the party will be "equipped so as to get out the gold-laden dirt in great quantities."

Chisna Mining & Improvement Co. on the trail.
BENJAMIN WESLEY BOOHER COLLECTION, ALASKA STATE LIBRARY

Later in the month, the paper listed some of the local men going with Hazelet and Meals. They included Hazelet's brother John, father-in-law A.T. Potter, and nephew Ralph Evans. [1] Two more nephews, E.A. and H.G. Tuffin, and cousin, Will Porter, all from Guthrie City, Iowa, also joined the group headed for Alaska.

On February 2, while enroute to Valdez aboard the EXCELSIOR, Hazelet started a journal to record the doings of the Chisna Mining and Improvement Company to "tell somewhat of the success or failure of said company." The Chisna Mining and Improvement Co. had been organized in Omaha in the winter of 1899 and capitalized at $3,000,000. The market for stock was good and enough was sold to outfit the expedition. Each individual for whom claims had been staked agreed to accept $45,000 worth of stock for his interest and donate two years of work in developing it. [2] Some of the men with Hazelet and Meals were stockholders in the company, while others, like young Henry Fleming of Atkinson, Nebraska, were hired to take the place of stockholders who were "too old or tied down" to make the trip. [3]

In Sitka, *The Alaskan* reported that "the Chisna Mining and Improvement Company, of which Mr. Hazelet is the head, have started in with 28 men, 22 head of horses, 4 head of cattle and 100 tons of freight consisting of a hydraulic outfit, saw mill and provisions, expecting to remain two years." [4] Young Arthur McNeer, who had spent the winter of 1898-9 with Hazelet and Meals in their cabin on the Chistochina, his brother George, and Henry Watkins, all from West Virginia, were also passengers on the EXCELSIOR. Although not part of the Chisna Mining and Improvement Company, the McNeer group planned to develop claims in the same area. [5]

After Arthur McNeer left Hazelet and Meals in March 1899, to return to Valdez for more horses, he presumably returned to the Chistochina region long enough to stake claims. The following July, McNeer joined B.F. Millard and a group of prospectors, headed by R.F. McClellan, to prospect for copper in the Chitina River valley. In early August, McNeer, acting as an agent for Millard, Ed Gates from the McClellan group, and James McCarthy located the Nicolai copper vein, which was the first major copper discovery in the area. [6]

During August, while members of the Army Copper River Exploring Expedition were mapping the Chitina and Nizina regions, the cartographer Oscar Rohn wanted to cross the Nizina Glacier into the upper reaches of the Copper River. No one in Rohn's party was willing to accompany him over the glacier, so he engaged McNeer to join him. On August 26, they set out on a harrowing glacier crossing that took a month and was complicated by storms and severe snow blindness.

They crossed by mistake into the White River drainage, but eventually reached the Copper River and returned briefly to the Chisna cabin only to find that all the cached provisions had been stolen. [7]

Since it was already late October when McNeer and Rohn left Copper Center to return on foot to Valdez and catch a boat home, McNeer had only a limited time to prepare for the trip back to Alaska to develop his gold claims. According to a taped interview with Watkins, McNeer approached him and a man named Cameron for grubstakes, offering shares in either the Nicolai copper prospects or gold prospects. Cameron chose the Nicolai holdings and prospered financially as a result. Watkins, who was 19 years old and eager to go to Alaska, borrowed money and chose to share in McNeer's gold prospects. McNeer told of his plan to take a dog team as soon as he landed in Alaska to stake claims on Miller Gulch. Watkins and the McNeer brothers met Hazelet in Omaha while Meals went to Montana to purchase horses. The three West Virginians planned to travel with the Chisna Company and help move the stock and equipment. Aside from Hazelet and Meals, McNeer was the only member of the group with experience in Alaska.

The boat trip was uneventful until they reached Valdez Bay on February 14 and found the weather unseasonably cold and the bay covered with two to three inches

Steer "Jack" with pack.
PHOTO COURTESY OF HAZELET GRANDCHILDREN

of ice. Hazelet and McNeer went ashore to look for a possible place to land the stock, but, finding none, agreed to send some of the men out in small boats to cut through the ice. For the next week they battled ice and high winds while attempting to land the stock and supplies.

As soon as the party was safely on shore, Hazelet hiked up to the third bench on Valdez Glacier, but decided that the animals and heavy equipment would not be able to use that route. The only other possibility was to go by way of the new trail that the government was developing through Keystone Canyon. On March 3, Hazelet reported that they had successfully broken the stock to carry pack and moved all equipment six miles out of Valdez. Hazelet then set out to assess the condition of the trail through the canyon.

Wheel built by Meals with wood pegs.
PHOTO COURTESY HAZELET GRANDCHILDREN

For the next three weeks the group moved slowly because they had to break trail through heavy, wet snow up the switch-backs and over the summit to the Tiekel River. The horses sometimes broke through the crust and had to be loaded on sleds and hauled back to camp.

Hazelet returned to Valdez to see Capt. Abercrombie and received the promise of four men and 10 horses to help in hauling supplies. With the additional help, they were able to prepare about two miles of trail each day, then let the trail harden over night and haul supplies from 4 AM to noon when they would have to stop and prepare trail for the next day. Progress was so slow that Hazelet began to realize that they would not be able to reach the claims while snow was still on the ground, and would have to build boats to complete the last part of the trip on water. [8] His one consolation was that his group was moving faster than the government party of 25 men and eight horses employed to build the road.

By mid-May, rain had melted most of the snow and the group decided to cache some of the supplies and build rafts to move the rest down the Little Tonsina River. With 22 rafts they succeeded in transporting some 20,000 lbs. of goods about 7 miles, only to find that the river below was not safe for rafting. [9] They then tried to corduroy the trail with logs they could pull the sleds over, but found that this hauling was too hard on the horses, which were weak from lack of food. Finally they constructed 20 carts and 20 sets of travois, and succeeded in reaching the bridge across the Tonsina River on June 9.

1900 on trail using Travois and carts.
PHOTO COURTESY OF HAZELET GRANDCHILDREN

While they were at the bridge, Abercrombie came in from Valdez, and Hazelet arranged to have the government party move their supplies to Copper Center on the carts while their horses took a needed rest. Hazelet then went ahead with 15 men and four pack steers to prepare 25 miles of new trail into Copper Center. Hazelet, who was not familiar with this country, made the following comments:

> All I knew was the general direction of the Copper Center from the Tonsina bridge. So I presume I have not the best trail that could be secured, but at least

have one that carts can pass over and much shorter than the way the government horses go.

To make two miles of trail through Alaska timber is big work for the force we have had, and to tell the exact truth have not averaged over one mile a day, but put in at least 10 to 15 corduroys running from 8 feet to 100 feet, built 12 bridges from 6 feet long to 36 feet long and done a good deal of grade work. The boys have stood the work remarkably well, and for men that had never chopped before are becoming quite expert choppers. [10]

Carelessness almost resulted in tragedy on June 24 when one of the men set fire to a tree. With strong winds blowing, the fire was soon out of control. Hazelet's described this near disaster in his diary:

On reaching the fire, I saw that we would not have more than time enough to get our camp to the lake if we could do that much, so I rushed back, called the men in off of the trail and started to cut trail towards the lake. Luckily the timber was not heavy, and the lake not over 40 rods distant. As soon as the trail was through, we ran back for the four carts, the bulls having been long before taken to their pasture, and ran the carts with their loads right into the water and as far out as we could get them. We at once set about to protect the stuff on the carts with wet blankets and to fight the fire by cutting the trees and carrying them off. But so far as fighting the fire was concerned, we might as well have saved our strength for it was down upon us like a fiend, the flames running from 20 ft. to 50 ft. high and the moss and underbrush burning like tinder.

The flames lopped out over the banks as if to quench their thirst, driving us far out into the water and causing us to duck ourselves every moment to keep from catching fire. The smoke and heat was almost intolerable and several of the boys came close to suffocating. ...

Found the fire had burned up several bridges and a lot a corduroy causing us no end of extra work. It took us three days to get out of danger from the fire. These fires will smolder for weeks in the moss and all at once break out with terrible fury. [11]

Fire was not Hazelet's only concern. As the group approached Copper Center, he began getting reports that prospectors without large outfits had already reached the Chistochina and started jumping claims. Hazelet anticipated that his claims would probably be contested, but had already received his recorded location notices back from Sitka and was confident that he could hold his claims. [12]

After a day off to celebrate the Fourth of July, the men resumed trail building with renewed energy. When they reached Copper Center, they picked up five old boats. Since the boats did not have enough clearance to carry heavy loads, Hazelet chose to transport most of the supplies by pack train. The trip up the Copper River required a number of river crossings with the stock swimming and the boats ferrying the packs. Repacking the 23 horses and steers with 175-250 pound packs usually took Hazelet and another man about three hours.

During the pack trip up the Copper River, Hazelet was again helped by his old friend, Indian Charlie, who blazed a trail for them from the Gakona River to the claims on the Chistochina. In his August 5 journal entry, Hazelet described the final day of travel with the Indian family:

> About 3:30 PM of this day we reached Charlie's camp, which was pitched on a small creek of good water and seemed to be an old Indian campground. He met us about 4 miles out from his camp and guided us in. Here we found his Klooch (wife or woman), his little boy and girl, and an old Klooch who was staying with them. I gave him his sack of flour, some corn meal, a cup of sugar and a few other things, and next morning was surprised to find him and his all packing ready to go along. The Kloochman had a heavy pack, the little girl, aged about 12 years I suppose, the same, the dogs with all they could carry, and Charlie a good sized pack on his back ready to show us the trail and cut brush out of the way.
>
> We had traveled about 4 miles when the boy grew too tired to walk and Charlie had to carry him on his back. He however did not allow this to interrupt his trail cutting and that night about 4:30 PM we all camped by a little lake having made about 8 miles. Charlie's family concluded to "sit down" for a day as they call it, and Charlie came on with us. Before I left camp that morning his Klooch came out and gave me a pair of moccasins which I shall take home as a souvenir of the trip.

Upon reaching the claims, Hazelet found claim jumpers already staking and mining some of his claims. Other prospectors were taking out up to 16 ounces of placer gold a day on nearby discoveries. Still hoping to test some of his locations before the end of summer, Hazelet and two other men set out with the pack train to bring in mining equipment from the boats.

Although the pack train, with help from Indian Charlie, had made good progress, the inexperienced men hauling loaded boats up the river were encountering problems. When Hazelet and the pack train reached the place on the Copper River where they expected to meet the boats, they found that the men had cached most of the supplies and gone on up river. Hazelet loaded the horses with all the weight they could carry and returned to the claims where he met Meals, who had accompanied the boat party and had come to get more food for them.

Henry Fleming, who was traveling with the boats, described their problems. They had unwisely camped on an island in the river where they were stranded by rising water. Expecting Meals to return with more food, they soon exhausted their supply and were reduced to chewing shoe leather. Several men who tried to go hunting capsized their raft, lost their guns, and barely escaped with their lives. [13] When the men finally reached the claims on August 25, Hazelet commented:

> Well boys did not get in till Sunday noon. ... Came in with packs on their backs and horses well loaded down. Looked tired and hungry, but few of them know what hardship means. They have simply had a picnic compared with some of us, at least in days gone by. When it comes to four men not being able to pull 2000 lbs. in a boat it looks funny to say the least. Well, as I said, they got here with their camp outfit, and Monday we got strung out for business. Put two to sawing lumber, four to getting out logs, four to making hay, some to help shoeing horses, four to survey out a ditch to run sluices in Discovery claim. [14]

While the men were coming in with the pack train, Hazelet and another man took two of the horses and visited their upper claims, where they found claim jumpers with a crew of seven men taking out up to $25 a day per man. These men paid no attention to Hazelet's warnings. They admitted to having seen the original location notices, but "wanted the claim so took it." Hazelet blamed Melvin Dempsey, the recorder for the mining district, for allowing all the claim jumping. [15] Dempsey, along with Hazelet, Meals and McNeer, was an original locator of claims in the Chisna district. [16]

Capt. Abercrombie was visiting the new mining camp when Hazelet returned from the upper claims. Hazelet reported that Abercrombie was enthusiastic about their prospects. "He thinks our claims better than any, and said we could hold them in spite of anyone." Hazelet, always alert to new real estate prospects, started talking to Abercrombie about acquiring land at Valdez for development of a townsite. They speculated that the time was ripe to "start the boom for this country." [17]

While the men were busy testing several of the claims, building cabins, and moving supplies to the camp site, Hazelet made preparations for the next summer's mining by filing water rights, digging hydraulic ditches, updating information on claim posts, and again informing claim jumpers of his intention to prosecute. He also made provisions for the care and feeding of his party's horses over the winter. Attempts to locate and prepare hay had been disappointing due to the lateness of the season, so he decided to bring the horses back to Valdez after they had finished hauling in supplies.

On September 27 they "pulled the sluice boxes up and quit, having gotten all told one pound of gold." Although Hazelet felt that the man they brought with them as a mining expert had not set up the sluices properly and, thereby, had lost much of the gold, he considered the tests satisfactory and made the following progress assessment:

> The house is well underway, 54 ft. long, 24 ft. wide and about 11 ft. high, having a 7 foot 8 inch ceiling. Built in fort style and very substantial. ...
> Our ground sluice ditch for hydraulic work is well underway and water running over half of it, balance will be well completed by this time next week. [18]

Five of the men were designated to remain in camp over the winter while the rest headed back with the horses to make hay until freeze-up when they could start hauling in the mining supplies that they had cached at the Tonsina River. Hazelet, Arthur McNeer and Henry Watkins left on foot, driving the steers. Hazelet's father-in-law also accompanied them, riding a horse. The older man had found the exertion of the summer difficult and was selling his interest in the mine to one of the younger men. While camped the first night out, Hazelet was at last able to relax and admire the sunset on Mt. Sanford:

> It (Mt. Sanford) stands just opposite the mouth of the Chistochina and from where we are camped we look straight down the river and up to its lofty summit. It is covered with snow from top to bottom and looks for all the world like a big circus tent. Snow as white as can be till the last rays of the setting sun tinge it a beautiful pink. Does man live that can look upon that scene without admiring it? If so, his soul must surely be dead. In his life there must be no hope, in his thoughts nothing pleasant.
> Many times before I have said Alaska could outdo the world for scenery and each time I visit it, I am more and more convinced of that fact. To the north of our camp lies the Alaska range, cold and bleak. Peak after peak reaches away up towards heaven, filled with snow, ice and glaciers, the resting place of the much-looked-for gold. By turning my eyes to the south I see Sanford, Drum and Wrangell, the last puffing away like some huge furnace. While all between is one vast plain covered with moss, grass, bush and timber. The recent frost has left nothing green save the spruce which is gradually taking on its black winter coat.
> So with such scenes around us we will lie down to rest and sleep, protected overhead by millions of stars, having a feeling of safety and security seldom felt in civilized countries. [19]

On the way back to Valdez, Hazelet regretted the passage of another birthday. "This was October 11 and my birthday," he mused, "39 years of my useless life has passed, nothing accomplished." Upon reaching Valdez, however, he was more optimistic and started working on his townsite project. "Well, I took a bath, got a shave, etc., put on a sort of civilized suit and now 'Richard' is himself again.

Tomorrow to business, hard and fast. If the Captain is any good, we will crack Valdez. If not, maybe I'll do it alone."

He spent the next several days lining up support for his case against the claim jumpers, arranging food for his horses, and looking over ground for a townsite. Hazelet had counted on support from Capt. Abercrombie in locating a townsite, but Abercrombie disappointed him. "Can't quite understand the Captain," Hazelet commented on October 17. "He seems to be afraid of something or somebody. If it is I, he should say so. Anyway, I'm going to bring this to a focus within the next three days. Valdez is booming some but wait till we touch her off on the other side." Hazelet was particularly enthusiastic about a potential location across Valdez Bay, near the mouth of Mineral Creek.

After a week passed with no progress, Hazelet was less optimistic. "Nothing in townsite line," he confided. "Captain off. Never in all my life heard of such a thing. He is surely the most uncertain man I ever met. One day everything is all right, next day everything is all wrong. Think I'll quit, don't care much about the thing anyway; will have enough to do to operate our claims." [20]

Hazelet and his father-in-law finally got passage out of Valdez on October 30 on the NEWPORT — a smaller ship than they would have wished. As storms in Dixon Entrance further delayed the trip home, Hazelet again expressed regrets on the course his life had taken:

> Yesterday was Calvin's birthday — 10 years old! How I would like to have been with him, but it seems to be my lot to be away from home and have none of these pleasures. Surely I'm a poor excuse for a man, or I would arrange my matters differently. I'm getting old and have accomplished nothing. My one hope now is to get enough to keep my dear ones fairly well, educate my boys to be upright, honest, industrious men and let it go at that. I have not the stuff in me to do much. I only hope they have. [21]

Time was running short and Hazelet was torn between his two projects — the Chisna mine and development of a Valdez townsite. Real estate development was his first love, and he had demonstated his ability when he promoted his subdivision back in O'Neill, Nebraska. However, he was committed to the mine and felt responsible for involving friends and relatives in the Chisna Mining and Improvement Company.

Hydraulic Mining at Chisna

X

When Hazelet finally arrived back in Nebraska in late November, he was so busy that he did not take time to write in his diary. He resumed his journal entries on February 5, 1901, and explained that the "stay at home was 60 days of hard work mixed with delightful pleasures." In addition to obtaining supplies for the upcoming year at the mine, Hazelet faced foreclosure of the American Chicory Company property. [1] Although he had disclaimed further interest in a Valdez townsite when he left Alaska the previous fall, contacts in Omaha soon reawakened his desire to pursue that project. George W. Holdrege, manager of the Burlington and Missouri Railroad, was developing plans to build a railroad from

Hazelet-Meals cabin, Lower Claim, 1900.
PHOTO COURTESY HAZELET GRANDCHILDREN

Valdez to Alaska's interior and needed ground for an oceanside terminal. Hazelet and Holdrege evidently discussed the advantages of including the railroad port in a townsite proposal. Hazelet referred to these negotiations several days after arriving back in Alaska: "Juneau is full of talk about Valdez. Townsite is talked, and if any knew I had the papers in my grip which told where the town would be, likewise the railroad, they would be excited sure." (2)

Although Hazelet had these papers with him when he sailed from Seattle, his primary efforts were still directed towards the Chisna mine. He was accompanied by A.J. Meals and a Mr. Acton, their hydraulic expert, 10 head of cattle, and $15,000 worth of groceries. (3) While in Seattle, Hazelet had met Melvin Dempsey and bought his interest in the Discovery claim for $500. Hazelet was irritated with Dempsey for having taken undue credit for the Chisna gold discovery. (4) In Juneau, Hazelet learned that the papers for his legal case against the claim jumpers would have to be resubmitted.

After a stormy passage across the Gulf of Alaska, Hazelet reached Valdez on February 18. Arthur McNeer met him with news that the men had succeeded in moving most of the mining supplies up to the Chisna camp. Hazelet helped break the pack bulls and move new supplies through Thompson Pass, and then returned to Valdez to prepare papers for the lawsuit and survey his potential townsite on the west side of Valdez Bay near Mineral Creek. On April 9, he recorded that he had surveyed 720 acres and that Holdrege approved of his plan to obtain it with Soldier's Additional land scrip. (5)

Hazelet admitted that some of the Valdez businessmen and Capt. Abercrombie were "much worked up" over what he was doing. Valdez was growing rapidly in 1901, but there was still contention as to where the permanent town should be located. The prospectors that landed at Valdez in 1898 had camped on the low land between the water and the glacier, which at that time extended almost to the bay. Stores, hotels and cabins quickly sprang up there to serve them. This original Valdez townsite, however, had several problems. Ships had difficulty landing there because of wind and ice, and glacial streams ran down the main streets of the town. Some Valdezians devised schemes for building a wharf and diverting the streams, while others advocated moving the town to a more favorable site. Ships already utilized a port on the east side of the bay, known as Swanport, and speculators, including Abercrombie, were promoting a townsite at the head of the bay, referred to as Bloomerville or New Valdez. (6)

On April 13, *The Valdez News*, a strong supporter of the original Valdez townsite, reported:

> A rumor is going the rounds that the townsite proposition is to be further
> complicated. It is claimed that Mr. George W. Holdrege is about to put scrip on

the tide flats back of the island on the west side of the bay. It is also understood that Mr. George Hazelet has taken up some land over there for the purpose of raising hay for his stock. As this land is valuable chiefly for this purpose, it is no doubt the true one. With a wharf at Valdez assured, the future of this town is certain and any additional paper townsite simply divides the opposition.

After Hazelet finished surveying, he made arrangements for Thomas J. Donohoe, a Juneau lawyer with a practice in Valdez, and his partners "to look after interests of land company for the next six months." He explained further: "If we make a town out of it, am to pay them $100 per thousand. If not, we pay nothing. They are to look after everything in shape of law that may come in securing title." (7) Hazelet then left for Juneau and Sitka to file suit against the claim jumpers and record the townsite.

In Juneau, the *Daily Alaska Dispatch* printed a favorable interpretation of Hazelet's plans:

> The latest to appear in the arena of townsites on Valdez Bay, and one that bids fair to outstrip all its rivals, is what is now known as "Hazelet's Hay Ranch." About three weeks ago G.C. Hazelet, manager of the Chisna Mining and Improvement Co., started a party of surveyors running lines around the base of the mountain from the glacier to the cottonwood flat at the mouth of Mineral creek on the west side of Valdez Bay. This was followed by taking soundings along the western shores of the bay. The results of the preliminary investigations must have been satisfactory to Mr. Hazelet and his associates, for they immediately surveyed and scripted 720 acres of land about two miles west of Valdez, near the mouth of Mineral Creek. The tract surveyed and located includes one of the best wharf sites on the whole bay, being sheltered from the strong winds, free from ice and 36 feet of water at a distance of 200 feet from the line of high tide.
>
> Mr. Hazelet refuses to give out any information regarding the future use of this large tract of land, which has cost over $10,000 in acquiring title. However, it is generally believed that the Burlington and Missouri railroad people are behind Mr. Hazelet in his land scripting scheme, and that this tract is intended for railroad terminals, as it is known beyond all question of doubt that G.W. Holdridge [sic] general manager of the B.& M. railroad, is interested with Mr. Hazelet in this townsite matter to the amount of several thousand dollars. The many natural advantages of the Hazelet location, coupled with the fact that the B.& M. people are investing their money in this land, leaves little room for doubt as to where the future metropolis of Alaska will be situated. (8)

A railroad at Valdez seemed assured on June 24, 1901, when the Akron, Sterling & Northern Railroad Company, with George W. Holdrege as trustee, filed "the map of the railroad company, showing its line of preliminary and actual survey from Valdes Bay through Thompson Pass." [9] The right of way, when definitely located and approved, covered only the 20 miles from Valdez to Dutch Valley, but did include the critical section through Keystone Canyon.

With his initial responsibilities toward the townsite and railroad completed, Hazelet started on foot for the Chisna mine, 250 miles away, carrying 40 pounds of mail for the miners up there. He arrived at the mine on May 25 and promptly served legal papers on the claim jumpers. Two shifts of men were soon running hydraulic nozzles on Discovery claim. Hazelet sent 10 men to the upper claims to set up the equipment only to have them attacked with a gun by one of the claim jumpers. After Hazelet talked to this man, named Fulkerson, he was "convinced that we either had to kill him and while doing so run the chance of having some of our men killed, or take him out of the country by the marshal." [10]

Having chosen the latter course of action, Hazelet started out on foot for Valdez on July 10, covering the 250 miles in 7½ days. At Valdez he found that the marshal was starting for Chisna with a counter injunction to stop Hazelet's group from mining the upper claims. This ended Hazelet's hope for a large return from the summer work. Although *The Valdez News* had estimated in July that Hazelet and Meals might take out about $100,000, [11] they realized only "a little over $2,000" for the year's effort.

Hazelet left four men at the mine for the winter to "saw logs and do other necessary work." The rest left Alaska in October. Some men, like Henry Fleming, who was working for wages, received their pay, but those who had invested in the Chisna Mining and Improvement Company lost out on their hope for a share in the profit. [12]

<hr />

Hazelet arrived back in Omaha on November 15, 1901, with only six weeks in which to raise enough money to operate the mine the following summer and cover expenses of the trial to settle ownership of the claims, which was scheduled for January 15 in Juneau. While contacting potential investors in Chicago, St. Paul and Omaha, he wrote Thomas J. Donohoe, his attorney, about prospects for the townsite and railroad:

> Saw Mr. Holdrege yesterday. Holdrege and associates hold right of way over pass. ... J.J. Hill and Morgan own Northern Pacific and Great Northern and control Burlington and Missouri. Plan to look out for Alaska. ...
>
> If Hill combine don't care to begin the road this year, then Holdrege and associates will do enough work to hold their right of way and act during the summer.

Now, Tom, this is to you on the dead quiet — there is absolutely no question of the road within the next two or three years. Mr. Holdrege speaks a thousand times more confident this fall than last spring. He stands ace high with the Hill and Morgan combine and has complete charge of all lines west of here. There is no question where the road will start from when they start to build it. It starts down on Hazelet's hay ranch. They will, if they do not change their plans, connect that land by survey this spring with the end of the line Gillette ran two years ago. ...

I say without hesitation that it looks well for Valdez this coming year. The proposition is right in line with Hill's plans for development of the Northwest and the trade of the Orient — and Alaska is attracting a lot of attention. [13]

Although Hazelet succeeded in persuading the original investors in the Chisna Mining and Improvement Company to put up more money, he still did not have enough to cover anticipated expenses for the next summer mining. Therefore, he borrowed $5,000 from John McHugh, a Sioux City, Iowa, banker who had financed John Hazelet's participation in the mine development. In return, McHugh took a mortgage on the mine property for one year. [14]

Hazelet left home and loved ones on January 4 and sailed for Juneau on the CITY OF SEATTLE with five horses, 600 ft. of hydraulic pipe, and provisions for 20 men. [15] Five witnesses for the trial joined Hazelet in Juneau bringing news from Valdez that Horace Tuffin, one of Hazelet's nephews, had frozen to death near Mentasta Pass while carrying mail from Chisna to Copper Center. "So ended one of the brighter and energetic lives that I have ever known," Hazelet wrote in his journal. "He was a boy I loved and I'm sure he would have made his mark in this world, but fate decreed otherwise and we must submit. His dear mother has all my sympathy and I feel sorely to blame myself, for I induced him to come to Alaska." [16]

The trial was quickly decided in favor of the Chisna Mining and Improvement Company, giving Hazelet "everything we asked" and assuring the ownership of the property "for all time." [17] Hazelet, Meals, and their witnesses sailed for Valdez on the EXCELSIOR, and, after a smooth three day trip, began moving supplies to the mine. *The Valdez News* provided the following account of their plans in the February 15 paper:

On their property on the lower Chisna will be operated a modern hydraulic giant. A large ditch a mile long will tap the Chisna above the property. This ditch will be 6 feet wide on the bottom, 8 or 9 feet feet on top and from 3 to 4 feet deep. With the end of this ditch will connect 1,500 feet of steel pipe with a six inch giant, and a 120 foot head of water.

On the upper Chisna properties, which have been in litigation for the past year, another hydraulic plant and a "boom" will be operated. Many people who are not familiar with hydraulic mining will perhaps be interested to know what a "boom" is. As explained to *The News*, it is simply a ground sluice on a large scale. A dam is built across the stream with a large flood gate at the bottom, but this flood gate is made to open and shut with a peculiarly ingenious device. On top of the dam is placed a long pole to one end of which is attached a rope which in turn is attached to the flood gate. On the other end of the pole is attached a large bucket. When the flood gate is closed and the reservoir fills, the water overflows into this bucket, and when the bucket is full the weight lifts the gate and the water rushes out with tremendous force. When the water has escaped from the reservoir, it has also leaked out of the bucket through small holes and the gate again drops in place and the reservoir refills. ... The hydraulic giant will be used to loosen the gravel and wash it down into the channel and when the reservoir opens, which it does automatically about every 20 minutes, the water rushes out and carries the gravel out through the sluice boxes which are placed some distance down the stream.

With these appliances the company expects to work out many acres of ground this coming season. ... Mr. Hazelet says the company expects to have the hydraulic plants in operation by the 10th of June, and that a force of at least 20 men will be employed all summer.

While preparing the hydraulic equipment, Hazelet mentioned that the saw mill was operating well and that it had made $1,300 by sawing lumber for other miners in the area. [18] The hydraulic operation, however, was not destined to operate as well as the saw mill. On June 30 Hazelet confided in the journal:

And now June is almost gone. Three and one half months more and I will see my loved ones, whether we do well or ill. My heart is heavy as lead — have not had much hope for a week.

To explain — I came up last Sunday 22nd with 4 men and took night shift at the boom. Well the boom doesn't operate as Acton (the hydraulic expert) claimed it would. We uncovered about ⅓ of all the ground we expected to last week, so far so good, but the boom would not do its work all the way down. The rock is angular and will lodge most any place, hence it will be carried along two or three hundred feet and then stop and gradually spread out all over. So we are unable to boom to exceed say 2 or 3 hundred feet, whereas I was made to believe by Mr. Acton that we would surely boom 500 or 600 feet.

The old man seems confused and I doubt very much whether he makes a success out of it or not. If I could only get wages out and enough to pay the interest, and have something left to operate on next year, I would call it done. ... I would not care for myself, but oh! my wife and boys! I can hardly face them if I fail, for I have failed at everything. Success was never intended for me I guess. Seems to me I work hard enough for it, but don't know how to catch it and hold on to it.

The situation did not improve during the next two months. On August 20, 1902, Hazelet made the final entry in his journal:

All is **failure** — this book is ended — as is also my mining life I guess. There will not be enough taken out of the ground to pay the help let alone expense for next year, so ended it is, I guess. Now if I can only keep it from absolute failure and entire loss! But how? That is the question.

The gold is here but Acton has utterly fallen down on everything he has attempted. Then to cap the climax, water left us early in July and has not yet returned. No rain or snow this year.

Well, it is all off, Old Man. You don't know where you are going or what you are to do. So as you have no more use for this book, sign yourself a failure and quit.

In his report, *Geology of the Central Copper River Region, Alaska,* Walter C. Mendenhall estimated that the "camp produced $25,000 in 1900 and $115,000 in 1901." [19] The yield, however, was not sufficient to cover expenses and Hazelet and Meals were still in debt when they closed the Chisna mine in 1902. They could not pay off the mortgage, so John McHugh foreclosed and took the mine property in his name. McHugh let Meals do some mining there for several years, but eventually arranged for John Hazelet to take charge of the Chisna mines for him. [20]

Hydraulic mining at Chisna, July 19, 1901.
George Hazelet (left)
PHOTO COURTESY OF RICHARD OSBORNE, GRANDSON OF JOHN HAZELET

Little further work was done at the mine until 1907 when *The Valdez News* reported:

> The Chisna Mining and Improvement Co. is taking an outfit into its hydraulic property on the Chisna river. John Hazelet will have charge of the season's operations and now has the outfit on the trail. The company owns a large area of good hydraulic ground on the Chisna and in 1901 took in a small hydraulic plant but owing to the slight elevation of the ground it could not be operated successfully without additional machinery and greater expense. Little has been done since except the assessment work but this year it is intended to open up the ground in many places so it can be thoroughly examined by hydraulic experts who will come in to look at it this summer. It may be found to be a feasible dredging proposition or if it can be worked by modern hydraulic machinery that will be adopted. The ground is rich and some means will be found of extracting the gold. [21]

John Hazelet and his descendants continued to mine profitably in the Chisna area for many years and it is still an active mine. George Cheever Hazelet failed to establish a profitable gold mine because the technology available to him in 1902 was not sufficient to recover the gold. He was haunted by yet another failure — one in which friends and relatives had lost money and a beloved nephew his life.

Hazelet still hoped for success in his townsite and railroad project. Valdez was continuing to grow, with gold discoveries in streams bordering the Chisna and even more promising copper prospects near the Chitina and Nizina tributaries of the Copper River. Hazelet already knew some of the prospectors who had discovered the rich Bonanza copper claims in the summer of 1900. In an April 9, 1901, journal entry, he mentioned seeing Rueben McClellan, the leader of that prospecting group, and the young mining engineer, Stephen Birch, arriving at Valdez on the steamship EXCELSIOR. Another of these prospectors, W.S. Amy, had informed Hazelet that the Bonanza claims were being sold to New York capitalists for $1,100,000. [22] Since the Bonanza claims were 200 miles from tidewater, a railroad to a port city would be an essential part of mine development.

Bonanza Discovery

XI

After returning from Alaska in the fall of 1898, Stephen Birch continued to benefit from having wealthy New York connections with influence in Washington, D.C. Capt. W.R. Abercrombie had no chance to reject him as a member of the Copper River Exploring Expedition when it returned to Alaska in the spring of 1899. The orders from G.D. Meiklejohn, Assistant Secretary of War, stated:

> Capt. W.R. Abercrombie, Second Infantry, commanding Copper River Exploring Expedition, accompanied by Stephen Birch, guide, will proceed at once to Fort Keogh and Livingston, Mont., there inspect, accept, and brand such pack horses, not to exceed 30 head, as come up to the required standard. On completion of this duty, Captain Abercrombie, accompanied by Guide Birch, will proceed to Seattle, Wash. The travel enjoined is necessary for the public service. [1]

Although he is not mentioned again in Abercrombie's official report of the 1899 expedition, Birch presumably spent the summer of 1899 around Valdez and the Copper River country as a horse-packer for the Army during the building of the military road through Keystone Canyon and over Thompson Pass.

Abercrombie found a desperate situation when he arrived at Valdez. Most of the prospectors who had attempted to enter Alaska over Valdez Glacier had not been as fortunate as Hazelet and Meals. Many had perished or returned home disillusioned. Some who remained in Valdez over the winter were ravaged by scurvy, and others in the interior were also suffering from the lack of fresh food. In addition to his other duties, Abercrombie provided antiscorbutics and medical attention to the ailing prospectors.

Some prospectors who were still physically able accompanied the Army expedition into the Chitina River valley in hopes of locating the source of copper bullets that Chief Nicolai of the Native village of Taral, near the confluence of the Copper and Chitina rivers, had shown Lieut. Henry Allen during his 1885 Army expedition. Included in this group were 10 men led by Rueben McClellan, a rugged frontiersman from Minnesota. The McClellan group, which in the coming years would play a crucial role in Birch's career, had agreed to pool their interests in prospecting so that any discovery made by a member would be shared by all. Membership in the group varied from time to time and the arrangement was further complicated because some of the members were also grubstaked with food and equipment from other sources.

When the McClellan group and B.F. Millard, accompanied by Arthur McNeer, succeeded in reaching the village of Taral, they found Chief Nicolai and his people close to starvation. Nicolai agreed to reveal the location of his mine in return for the prospectors' cache of food. [2] This outcropping of ore, located on a small tributary of McCarthy Creek, proved to contain up to 85 percent copper. The Nicolai claims, which were staked in July of 1899 by Ed Gates, James McCarthy and McNeer, were the first copper claims in the area.

When the prospecting season ended, the McClellan group met in Valdez and decided that some of them, including McClellan, would return home for the winter, while others, including Clarence Warner and "Tarantula" Jack Smith, would remain in Alaska to prospect during the winter and return to the vicinity of the Nicolai claims the following spring. At this time they decided to make Abercrombie a shareholder in the McClellan group, presumably for the assistance he had provided that summer. They also started to negotiate consolidation of the Nicolai claims for development, with McClellan representing his group and B.F. Millard, H.G. Allis, and George M. Perine the other interests. [3]

After visiting his home in Minnesota, McClellan met Millard and Perine in San Francisco and transferred the interests of his group in the Nicolai mine to the newly formed Chittyna Exploration Company in return for 150 shares of stock in that company, which would by divided among the original members of the McClellan group and some of the people who had grubstaked them. While in San Francisco, Millard and Perine asked McClellan to be superintendent of the company's affairs in Alaska during the following summer.

McClellan landed in Valdez on April 17, 1900, with a dozen men and an equal number of horses, all purchased with Chittyna Exploration Company funds, to do the assessment and development work on the Nicolai claims. In the meanwhile, Smith and Warner, along with two other members of the McClellan party who had spent the winter in Alaska, left Valdez on March 2 for the Chitina country, pulling hand sleds over Valdez Glacier. These men, who had no knowledge of the formation of the Chittyna Exploration Company, continued prospecting in the Chitina River valley during the summer of 1900 as members of the McClellan group. [4]

In July, Smith and Warner, while prospecting in the vicinity of Mt. Blackburn at the headwaters of the Kennicott River, located the outcropping of copper ore that led to the formation of the Kennecott Copper Company. In a letter to Alaska Territorial Governor Ernest Gruening, written in January 1940, when he was over 65 years old, Stephen Birch gave this description of the Bonanza discovery:

> They (Smith and Warner) made four locations the second day after they had established their camp. These locations were known as the Independence 1 and 2, Excelsior and National. After they had made them, and while sitting eating their lunch, they looked across the gulch and observed a large green spot on the side of the mountain. Jack's companion declared it was a patch of grass. Jack was not certain and said he would like to go over and see it, but his companion wasn't going to climb up the side of that mountain to look at a sheep pasture.
>
> While discussing this they became thirsty and Jack went down to the creek to get some water. While leaning over the bank he saw a piece of float — float is the name given by prospectors to a small piece of rock containing mineral. Jack at first did not know whether it was copper or silver. He took back the piece to his companion, and they agreed to follow up the creek looking for more green rock as they went.
>
> Gradually as they came near the green patch in the mountain the float became thicker, and presently they saw that instead of being a grass plot it was an outcropping of copper ore. When he saw the size of it, Jack exclaimed, "My God, it's a bonanza!" So then and there it was named the "Bonanza."
>
> This was on July 22, 1900. After they had made their location, they returned to their camp and as their provisions were about all gone it was necessary for them to return to Valdez, a distance of 200 miles. This they were obliged to walk, as they had no horses or other means of transportation.
>
> During the fall, the other members of the McClellan party returned to Valdez with reports from various parts of the country, but none of them had been so successful as Jack. The entire party's interest was centered on the great copper discovery, and it was agreed among them to try to interest capital. (5)

Stephen Birch, who was in Valdez in 1900 when the McClellan group returned from their summer of prospecting, was one of the people they approached about financing. Birch had returned to New York the previous winter to continue his studies as a special student at Columbia University. His friends Henry Havemeyer and James Ralph then sent him back to Valdez to look for investment opportunities. Birch's own account of his meeting with the prospectors is contained in the letter to Gruening:

Jack brought his find to my attention. "Mr. Birch," he said, "I've got a mountain of copper up there. There's so much of the stuff sticking out of the ground that it looks like a green sheep-pasture in Ireland when the sun is shining at its best."

But it was too late in the year to go in and examine it, so it was agreed that I should go in the next season, make a proper survey and report to my principals. The latter, on the other hand, agreed if the mine was as represented to put up money for its development.

Birch had so much confidence in the prospectors of the McClellan group that he was willing to start negotiations with them even before he could investigate their claims. The opportunity came in early November 1900, when he received a letter from Dan Kain, one of the McClellan group, offering to sell one half of his one-eleventh interest to Birch.

On December 2, Birch wrote to Havemeyer:

The man who wrote the enclosed letter offered to sell me half of his interest in a number of claims for $2,000 which is dirt cheap. ... I am anxious to get things settled so that I can telegraph him, otherwise he will be apt to sell to some one else.

Now is the time to make a barrel of money. ... After we get hold of these claims we can either sell things to the Lewisohns or some other company or make a deal to go in with them and form a big company. [6]

On December 9, Birch informed Havemeyer that he had closed the deal with Dan Kain, paying him $250 immediately. The final contract provided for Birch to pay $2,500 for a half interest in Kain's property, including his one-eleventh share in the McClellan group claims and all other claims made by Kain for the next three years. In a January letter to Kain, Birch explained: "This I think is a fair work deal to both you and myself. It will give you ready money and me a good speculation and is a better proposition for both of us as you get more money and I get larger interest. I will be on the ground and we can mutually assist each other." [7] The contractual arrangement proved particularly advantageous to Birch because Kain subsequently located rich placer gold claims on a tributary of the Nizina River, named Dan Creek in his honor. Kain promised to use his influence with other members of the McClellan group to help Birch obtain options on their claims as well, but insisted that Birch make no mention of the terms of his contract.

In early February, Kain wrote Birch: "I want you to promise me not to use any information you have received through me unless you have my permission. Do this for me and it will make my work easy with our party and I assure you I will do my best to serve you." [8]

Birch assured Havemeyer that, although the negotiations with Kain had been done in Birch's name, he was only acting as an agent for Havemeyer. On December 31, 1900, he wrote Havemeyer: "I deeply appreciate the interest you take in this matter and feel that you are actuated because of your desire to aid me, and I will not make any arrangements unless they are satisfactory to you." Havemeyer and Ralph formed the Alaska Copper Company, incorporated in West Virginia, and placed Birch on a retainer of $300 monthly plus expenses.

Birch returned to Valdez early the following spring to make a personal inspection of the Bonanza claims. George Hazelet mentioned in his April 9, 1901, diary entry: "EXCELSIOR is laying at anchor and unloading lumber, brought McClellan, Birch and others in." Birch gave the following retrospective account of this trip in the 1940 letter to Gruening:

> In April 1901, I started in with R.F. McClellan. There were no trails in the country and we had to travel on foot a distance of more than 200 miles. It was a hard trip as I think of it now, but mining engineers are prepared for that kind of thing.
>
> The rest of the McClellan party had gone in during the winter months, sledding in the necessary supplies to live on while they did the annual assessment work as required by the Government.
>
> For the first hundred miles we dragged a hand sled packed with blankets and provisions, but when we got to the Copper River the snow had left the valleys and we abandoned the sled and employed Indians to pack the supplies on their backs. That was really an interesting 100 miles.
>
> I remained at the mine during the season, making various examinations and tests of the ore. Then I returned to New York and reported favorably to my principals. They then optioned the property from the McClellan party and agreed to spend money on its development.

This account makes the acquisition of claims from the other members of the McClellan party sound easier than it actually was. Birch spent most of the next winter traveling around the country, contacting members of the McClellan group to obtain options. On March 6, *The Alaska Prospector* in Valdez reported:

> There has been some fear in the minds of many persons that the reported sale of the famous McClellan copper properties in the Chittyna (sic.) river country was merely "talk", started in order to con the country, but such is not the case, as there was filed for record in the U.S. commissioner's office a few days ago a number of optional agreements, deeds and other papers agreeing to sell about ten-elevenths of the entire McClellan property as it is generally known in this place, for the sum of $1,100,000.

These agreements are from R.F. McClellan, E.A. Gates, H.H. Fitch, W.S. Amy, Dan L. Kain, Jno.L. Sweeney, J.H. Smith, C.L. Warner, H.T. Gates and Stephen Birch, and the property agreed to be conveyed consists of 45 copper claims in the Chittyna country.

Birch probably gave this account with the financial details of the options to the Valdez paper himself. A letter to Havemeyer on March 3 tells of his landing at Valdez and making arrangements for patenting the claims. Birch's arrival had been delayed for two weeks because he was a passenger on the steamer BERTHA when it ran aground leaving Seattle on February 9. The *Daily Alaska Dispatch* gives the following account of the mishap:

All went well with the BERTHA until Saturday night, when the weather set in thick, and Sunday morning at 12:30 the vessel struck on Harald Island. All the passengers were in bed, and the shock caused great confusion and a stampede was made for the upper deck. Captain Johnson and the officers of the ship restored order in short time, and on investigation it was found that the vessel was in such close proximity to the shore that the gangplank would reach an elevated rock. The passengers at once walked ashore, and later bedding and baggage were landed, and a camp was made on barren rocks.

On the approach of daylight the work of lightering the vessel was commenced by landing horses and other freight. A kedge anchor was put out, and the vessel hauled into deep water with aid of the donkey engine, but as soon as deep water was struck she began to sink. The vessel was swung on the beach. She has lost her keel, and there is a large hole in her bottom forward engine room and it is believed she will be a total loss.

The first night the passengers camped on the rock they suffered no serious inconvenience, but on the second day a heavy rain set in, with a cold wind, which caused considerable suffering, as the wind swept across the rock with great force. Monday morning the shipwrecked folk were picked up by the COTTAGE CITY and brought to this place (Port Townsend). The loss of freight and baggage, by exposure to the elements, after being landed, is a severe blow to many, as they had their last dollar invested in outfits for the season's prospecting in Alaska.

Dan Kain was one of the prospectors who lost his outfit in the grounding of the BERTHA, but Birch advanced him money for more supplies and was reimbursed by the Alaska Copper Company.

Birch wrote Havemeyer on March 8, thanking him for reassuring his mother of his safety after the shipwreck, and again on the following day, registering concern for the lack of a safe place for keeping records of claims and deeds.

"The way it is now," he wrote, "they are kept on shelves in a wooden building over a saloon. There is always a lot of intoxicated men hanging around both day and night. It is the worst building in town in case of fire. It would play the devil with us if the records should burn up." He went on to urge Havemeyer to have someone contact the attorney general and try to get a safe for the Valdez court. [(9)]

SS BERTHA on the rocks.
ANCHORAGE MUSEUM OF HISTORY & ART. B62.1.381

After registering this concern, Birch left for the mine, writing Havemeyer from Tonsina Bridge on March 24 to tell of his progress. A letter written at the mine site on April 19 tells Havemeyer of his plans to build a cabin and some mountain trails. Birch had lots of work to do during the summer of 1902 in order to prepare for the visit of a group of mining experts, who were coming to assess the potential for both copper and gold mining in the Chitina and Nizina area.

On July 10, *The Alaska Prospector* announced the arrival of the mining experts, including H.A. Keller of Seattle, M.J. Heller of San Francisco, F.H. Blake of New York, and Norris English of San Francisco. The group first toured copper mining sites on Prince William Sound and then met Birch in Valdez for an expedition to the Nicolai and Bonanza claims. On September 4, *The Alaska Prospector* reported the group's return to Valdez, and commented: "Mr. Stephen Birch had charge of the expedition and managed it so well that the trip seemed like a picnic."

The experts apparently were pleased with what they saw. Upon return from the mine in the fall, Birch began actually purchasing the claims, on which he had options, from the prospectors in the McClellan group. A series of letters to

Havemeyer in November indicated that Birch had to travel to Minnesota, California and Arizona in order to complete the purchases. The Alaska Copper Company kept him supplied with ready cash so he was able to buy most of the claims for between $12,000 and $15,000. The largest cash outlay was $25,000 which Birch paid for W.S. Amy's share.

Mining engineers at site of future Kennecott Mine.
Birch (second from left)
VALDEZ MUSEUM ARCHIVES

Although everything went according to Birch's plan for gaining ownership of the Bonanza claims, an unexpected problem soon arose. The September 11, 1902, issue of *The Alaska Prospector* contained the following announcement:

> Notice has been filed in the commissioner's office that suit will be brought by the Chittyna Exploration Co. against R.F. McClellan and others who are interested in the Alaska Copper Co. for an interest in the Bonanza group of claims. The suit has been brought by the Exploration Company on the grounds that the locators of the said claims were in the employ of the company at the time locations were made.
>
> All the parties concerned, who are now here, are very reticent about the matter, and refuse to be interviewed on the subject.

Bonanza Lawsuit

XII

The filing of a lawsuit contesting ownership of the Bonanza claims focused nationwide attention on the potential for copper mining in the Wrangell Mountains. Both sides in the controversy enlisted the support of influential people and additional capital. Birch and Havemeyer, facing a large cash outlay for buying the claims and hiring lawyers, enlisted leather-king Norman Schultz as a major investor and changed the name of their corporation to Alaska Copper and Coal to avoid confusion with another copper corporation with holdings in southeast Alaska. The Chittyna Mining Company, in the meantime, sold interests in its claim to the Bonanza locations to a wealthy syndicate, the Copper River Mining Company, organized specifically to pursue the lawsuit.

Lawyers involved in the Bonanza lawsuit spent the summer of 1903 taking depositions in New York, San Francisco, Manila, and other distant places. Birch commented in a November 9, 1903, letter to Havemeyer that a Senator Heyburn of Idaho, a Congressman Cushman of Washington, and Andrew Burleigh, who were some of the attorneys for the opposition, arrived in Valdez on October 29 accompanied by "a number of professional witnesses and thugs."

"The first thing after their arrival," Birch continued, "they started right in to blow themselves at the various saloons and tried to create a favorable impression on the community." [1] Judge James Wickersham, who was hearing the case, also participated in the socialization. The judge wrote in his diary on October 23 that his wife had invited Birch, McClellan, and some of the lawyers on both sides of the case to a whist party.

Wickersham heard the Bonanza case in November after reading more than 2,000 pages of testimony taken by deposition. On November 28, Wickersham wrote in the diary:

Rendered decision in Copper Co. v McClellan et. al., the celebrated Chitina river copper case. Senator Heyburn of Idaho, Congressman Cushman of Wash., Burleigh of N.Y. etc. were attorneys for plaintiff — decided case for the defendant on grounds that plaintiff's testimony was not sufficient. Great crowd in attendance.

Lawyers for the Bonanza Trial and their wives arrive in Valdez.
ALASKA STATE LIBRARY

The plaintiffs in the case had argued that the locators of the claims were either grubstaked by or employees of the Chittyna Exploration Company when they staked the Bonanza claims. McClellan summarized the case in a Seattle interview for the November 29, 1903, *Post-Intelligencer*:

> The controversy over the Bonanza mine was originally instigated by the Chittyna Exploration Company, but that organization subsequently sold its claim to a title in the property to the Copper River Mining Company, which was organized for the purpose of making a fight for control of the mine.
>
> To understand the situation one must know that the so-called McClellan crowd, which located the Bonanza, was organized and went to Alaska in 1898. We prospected in various parts of the country, and finally made some valuable discoveries in the Chittyna valley. The Chittyna Exploration Company was organized to develop some of these properties, and we retained a one-fourth

interest in the new company. In 1900 I was made superintendent of the Nicolai mine, which the Chittyna Exploration Company decided to develop.

There were at this time 10 members of the "McClellan crowd." When I took the superintendency of the Nicolai mine, two members of the party returned to the states and the other seven went off on prospecting tours. These seven prospectors were working in the interests of the ten members of my party. We furnished our own money to back ourselves and did our own work. J.H. Smith and C.L. Warner located the Bonanza mine in July 1900.

No one ever disputed our title to the Bonanza until 1901, when we endeavored to bond the property. Even then offers were made to me by other claimants to purchase the property outright, as if we owned it beyond any shadow of an adverse claim. But we were anxious to develop the property, and were working at the time to interest the Havemeyers, as we afterwards succeeded in doing. They bonded the property for $1,100,000, or $100,000 less than the parties who afterward organized the Copper River Mining Company offered to give me.

The Chittyna Exploration Company set up a claim for the property. The first contention of the corporation was that they had grubstaked our party and the exploration company was entitled to a half interest. This position was abandoned, and they claimed that our party were in the Chittyna Exploration Company's employ and that organization was entitled to undisputed ownership of the Bonanza. ...

We showed conclusively that I was the only member of our party that was employed by the Chittyna Exploration Company. The men who located Bonanza had never worked for that company. In fact, five of party had never worked for wages while in Alaska. We showed that instead of the Chittyna company grubstaking our party, we had actually given that company provisions to keep the crew at work. This disposed of any shadow of a claim that the Copper River Mining Company had in the Bonanza.

I am told that large blocks of the Copper River Mining Company were sold in Pennsylvania and New York, and that just a short time ago $37,000 was borrowed by the company. In fact, a mortgage given on the Bonanza was sent to Valdez for record. Of course, the court's decree shows that this company has no right to give such a mortgage nor to sell stock.

The parties who we believe put up this fight and who provided the evidence that induced reputable attorneys to make their contest are promoters, headed by F.C. Helm, who is known here. Helm had a railroad and numerous other enterprises projected which he declared would be built in Alaska by his company.

I know the victory of our company means more to the Copper River country than anything that has happened there for years. The Bonanza mine has demonstrated that it will be a valuable freight producer, and the Havemeyers, abundantly able to provide means for the construction of a railroad, will see that one is built. A railroad into the Copper River country is now practically assured.

We have done comparatively little development work, though we have been in undisputed possession of the property. Our company did not care to put out the money necessary for the improvement while the title was in controversy, but we have a tunnel that has struck the vein ninety feet below the surface where the men, at the last time I heard from the mine, had cut through seven feet of copper and had not passed the vein. There are thousands of tons of ore lying on the surface, and it has been estimated that the property shows $17,000,000 of copper in sight. This, of course, is an estimated valuation, but we know that there are millions of dollars' worth of ore to be taken out and I believe the Bonanza will prove to be the richest mine in Alaska.

Now that the title is settled we will push development work as rapidly as possible. Arrangements will be made for the construction of a railroad into the interior and the entire Copper River valley will be benefited.

McClellan was premature in this prediction of prompt development of the mine and railroad. Wickersham's decision in the Bonanza case was appealed to higher courts and the financiers were reluctant to proceed with extensive investment until ownership was assured. Furthermore, reports from Anaconda experts raised doubts about the value of the Bonanza ore deposits in spite of the prior, more optimistic, assessment.

Birch and Wickersham, who were both ambitious men, understood each other and became good friends during the Bonanza hearings. They left Valdez together on December 4 along with other participants in the trial. Wickersham mentioned in his diary that Birch left the SANTA ANA at Ladysmith B.C. on December 16. Four days later they were together again in Washington, D.C., where Wickersham and his wife were attending the graduation of their son, Darrell, from the U.S. Naval Academy.

Wickersham's term as a district judge was about to expire and he stayed in the Washington area in an effort to enlist Congressional support for his reappointment. Birch was one of the friends who helped Wickersham to make valuable contacts, and on January 17, 1904, Wickersham commented in the diary: "Stephen Birch from New York is here today at the Raleigh — working for me." His January 20 diary stated: "Birch is back to the Raleigh — I moved down there today that I might have more time before I go away." Birch also invited Wickersham to New York, where they dined at Delmonico's, attended several

Broadway plays and met Birch's financial backers, James Ralph and Norman Schultz.

On November 17, 1904, Wickersham received word that the President had reappointed him judge of the Third Division in Alaska. The same day he received a telegram from Birch stating: "We all send hearty congratulations on your reappointment." Along with other letters of congratulation, a letter from Senator Knute Nelson of Minnesota, the powerful chairman of the Committee on Territories, prompted Wickersham to comment in his diary: "He is still ugly — but not virulent — He keeps harping upon the idea that Birch supports me — as if a successful litigant ought to be expected to abuse the court."

Senator Nelson continued to be "ugly" where Wickersham was concerned, leading the opposition to Senate confirmation of the reappointment. Wickersham's failure to support Nelson's effort to split Alaska's Third Judicial District had angered the senator. (2) For the next two years Nelson and several other senators used all means in their power, including filibuster, to block Wickersham's confirmation. President Roosevelt, however, continued to keep Wickersham on the bench by giving him interim appointments, largely as the result of the intervention of Birch and two other friends, Capt. David H. Jarvis, Customs Collector for Alaska and a confidential advisor to the President, and Walter E. Clark, the Washington correspondant for the *Seattle Post-Intelligencer*. Wickersham repeatedly gave credit in his diary to these three men for their efforts on his behalf.

Fighting Jim

James Wickersham and his family kept moving west — from Patoka, Illinois, to the Kansas territory after the Civil War, thence to the Washington territory in 1883, and on to Alaska in 1902 when it was still a "district", 10 years before it officially became a territory with an elected legislature.

After graduating from the 8th grade, Wickersham taught in a one-room schoolhouse and then moved to Springfield, Illinois, to study law in the office of ex-Governor Palmer. When the newly married young lawyer moved to Tacoma to seek his fortune, his parents and siblings followed. A dynamic speaker with a swash-buckling manner, he soon became involved in politics — first as a Republican, then as a Populist.

In Tacoma, Wickersham won a probate judgeship, but was indicted as a member of a group organized to fight Oriental immigration, referred to as the "yellow peril", and was convicted of seducing a Sadie Bratner. Wickersham returned to the Republican ranks in time to aid Addison Foster's election to the U.S. Senate, thereby winning a federal appointment through Foster's patronage. He wanted to be counsel to Japan, but instead was offered a federal judgeship in Eagle, Alaska.

Wickersham accepted his appointment as opportunity rather than exile. His first duty was to construct a log courthouse for $5,000, to be paid out of local license fees. An avid outdoorsman, the 40-year-old judge immediately started hunting gold and sheep when not traveling to court sessions by dog team. Always convinced of his own rectitude, Wickersham criticized Alaska courts for lenient verdicts and bribery of witnesses and jurors.

Since the 1,500 residents in his 300,000-square-mile judicial district failed to provide enough crime to keep him busy, Wickersham volunteered to help other districts. He fought sea-sickness on the floating court to Unalaska and then cleaned up corruption in the Nome federal courts. His service at Nome earned many friends, but also made powerful enemies who prevented Senate confirmation of his reappointment for years.

Wickersham succeeded in moving the seat of his Third Judicial District to a new gold-rush town on Chena Slough and persuaded the town's founder, E.T. Barnette, to name it in honor of his friend Senator Charles Warren Fairbanks of Indiana. Shortly after moving to Fairbanks, Wickersham attacked North America's highest mountain with four companions and two mules, named "Mark" and "Hannah" after the senator from Ohio. He published Volume 1, Number 1, of the *Fairbanks Miner* to finance the excursion, which terminated at the 8,100 foot level after encountering an 8,000-foot vertical rock face, recorded for posterity as the "Wickersham's Wall."

Thanks to the intercession of friends like Capt. David Jarvis, Walter E. Clark and Stephen Birch, Theodore Roosevelt continued to keep Wickersham on the bench with interim appointments as long as he was President, but a personal conflict with Alaska Governor Wilfred Hoggatt in 1907 eroded Wickersham's Republican support.

"He has a penchant — almost a mania for stabbing his best friends to the heart the very moment he imagines the idol of popularity demands such sacrifices," wrote the editor of the *Nome Nugget* about Wickersham on August 8, 1908, when he won election as delegate to Congress from Alaska.

Wickersham's dynamic oratory appealed to the populist leanings of an electorate of placer miners fearing the encroachment of capitalists with modern mining technology. He created a "bogey man" and named him "Guggenheim." Wickersham's war on the "Guggs" served him well politically and kept him in office for 10 years. His populist followers, called "Wickites," bested both Republicans and Democrats, even when the two major parties combined against "Fighting Jim."

Wickersham is credited with having Alaska recognized as a territory, with getting a locally elected legislature, and with persuading the federal government to build a railroad from Seward to Fairbanks. His persistent opposition to "big interests" with capital to invest, however, kept industry from coming to Alaska.

Wickersham understood history and contributed to it by writing, collecting, interpreting, and editing accounts of his times, always with an eye to preserving his own image of himself. He also left to posterity a diary in which the thoughts, impressions and motives of an egotistical demogogue are revealed.

BONANZA CASE DECIDED BY JUDGE WICKERSHAM
ALASKA COPPER COMPANY WINS

The Alaska Dispatch, Juneau   April 17, 1903

Collector Jarvis Speaks Good Word for Alaska

CAMPAIGN OF EDUCATION WOULD BRING THOUSANDS OF NEW PEOPLE TO DEVELOPE OUR VAST RESOURCES

The Valdez News   August 6, 1904

To celebrate the birthday of Mr. George C. Hazelet, the Tillicum Club issued elaborate invitations for a reception which was held at the club rooms Tuesday evening. A large number were present, the music struck up at an early hour, and dancing, story telling, eating, and other refreshments were indulged in till another early hour. The headaches of the following day were attributed to excessive laughter. There was a jolly good night, and all are wishing him many returns of the occasion, notwithstanding the fact that restraining orders were issued by the dean of the club, prohibiting George from having any more birthdays. George was born in 1862, and is still able to attend sessions at the Bar, to which he was admitted at an early age.

The Alaska Prospector February 25, 1904

BREWERY OPENED
VALDEZ DRINKS FIRST HOME BREW

Will Supply House Trade with a Better Article Than That Imported From Seattle

---

The Valdez News   April 11, 1903

RAILROAD FROM VALDEZ TO THE INTERIOR

CITIZENS SUBSCRIBE FOR 125,000 SHARES OF STOCK IN COMPANY

ORGANIZED BY A.B. ILES – CONSTRUCTION BY JULY 1

Fairbanks Weekly Times   December 22, 1906

Mammoth Syndicate to Build Railroads All Over Alaska

GUGGENHEIMS AND MORGAN INCORPORATE ALL PROPOSED RAILWAY SCHEMES INTO ONE BIG SYSTEM

Fairbanks Weekly Times   December 22, 1906

ROSENE MAKES DEAL

COLLECTOR OF CUSTOMS FOR ALASKA JOINS N.C. CO.

Old P.P.& N. Co. Cannery Properties Combined as Subsidiary

The Valdez News   Aug. 6, 1904

One of the prettiest social events of the season was the luncheon giving Saturday by Mrs. George Cheever Hazelet, in honor of Mrs. Evans and daughter, Miss Ruth. Coal Black Lady was the game of the afternoon. In the evening the young people enjoyed the hospitality of Mr. and Mrs. Hazelet.

Jarvis And Wickersham

XIII

After returning from Point Barrow in the fall of 1898, Lt. David Jarvis had several months to recover from the Overland Expedition and get acquainted with his newborn daughter, Anna. In the spring of 1899, he assumed command of the cutter BEAR and spent the summer patrolling the Bering Sea, visiting Native schools and missions with Rev. Sheldon Jackson, and transporting reindeer from Siberia to fulfill his commitment to Charlie Artisarlook, the Eskimo herder who had loaned him deer for the expedition. Although still officially a first lieutenant, Jarvis was referred to as "captain" after being placed in charge of the BEAR .

Lt. Jarvis with Siberian Native family.
PHOTO COURTESY OF MARY JARVIS COCKE

Bering coast residents relied on the Revenue Marine officers to maintain law and order and provide relief from sickness and hunger. Jarvis, who had received nationwide recognition during the Overland Expedition, added to his reputation for heroism during the Nome gold rush. Although pox-marked from youth and slight of build, his presence commanded authority, as described in a Valdez newspaper:

> In his adventures in Alaska, whether on relief expeditions or in turning back plague-stricken vessels from northern ports, Captain Jarvis has not gone armed. His mastery over men is due altogether to his wonderful self-command and his moral force. Although beloved by the rough frontiersmen and feared by the outlaw element, Jarvis has none of the rough characteristics which might be supposed to win leadership among these classes. He is modest and reticent, never enters a bar, never makes any sort of burly demonstration, and is not a "mixer." ... In appearance Captain Jarvis gives no hint of his rugged nature. He is boyish in build and almost shy in manner. But those who saw him, single handed, march half a hundred cutthroats of Nome to his launch and embark with them for the BEAR say he was a man transformed. [1]

When a smallpox epidemic hit Nome in 1900, Jarvis took charge of relief efforts and instituted sanitary precautions, which prevented the loss of many lives according to *The Nome Weekly News* on September 1, 1900:

> The smallpox hospital is vacant. The last patient was discharged on Sunday and the hospital and its contents will in all probability be destroyed.
>
> The cost of fighting this dreaded scourge has been heavy, ... but it was wisely incurred. But for the prompt measures taken to isolate the cases that occurred the spread of the disease would have been rapid.
>
> The situation had to be met promptly and it was; there were no funds with which to fight the plague, no organized government to assist in stamping it out, and yet this was done quietly, effectively and without the blare of trumpets. It may not be generally known, but it is a fact, that the money needed to do the work was advanced by the Alaska Commercial Co., without question and without hestitation. This money was expended under the personal direction of Capt. Jarvis, of the treasury department. That it was wisely expended all residents of Nome know.
>
> The death record speaks for itself; of the 23 cases with were domiciled at the pest house all recovered save one, who died June 29th.

As a result of his work in Nome, the special agent of the Treasury in Alaska recommended that Jarvis be appointed customs collector for Alaska, stating that he was one of the brainiest men in the Revenue Service and praising him for geniality and careful business methods. [2]

Jarvis did not seek this position, accepting it only upon the urgent personal request of President Theodore Roosevelt. Jarvis was unwilling to resign from the Revenue Marine, so Roosevelt, in 1902, arranged for Jarvis to be detached for four years and still keep his place in line for advancement on the list of Revenue captains. [3]

David Henry Jarvis.
PHOTO COURTESY OF DAUGHTER, ANNA JARVIS

Judge James Wickersham first met Jarvis in Nome in 1901 while the judge was presiding over the district court. The two men became friends, and Wickersham praised Jarvis in his diary: "I am very fond of Capt. Jarvis: he is a loveable, honest and competent man. I think these three words cover about all that is necessary in a man, — and he is the typical citizen — that he is modest goes without saying — having the other virtues." [4]

Jarvis and Wickersham resumed their friendship the next summer. As custom's collector, Jarvis was responsible for 20 deputies, who were stationed in coastal and river ports throughout Alaska. [5] This required extensive travel each summer. When Jarvis' duties brought him to Nome and St. Michael, Judge Wickersham saw him almost every day. They usually dined together and had long talks about the legal situation in Nome. [6] While stationed in Nome, Jarvis had observed corrupt federal officials attempting to manipulate the law so that they could personally acquire legitimate mining claims of immigrant prospectors. Both Jarvis and Wickersham wanted clean up the corruption, but they were aware that the offending officials were supported by some powerful congressmen and lobbyists.

James Wickersham
ANCHORAGE MUSEUM OF HISTORY & ART

Wickersham continued to correspond with Jarvis and visited him in Sitka in early March when Jarvis was about to leave for Washington, D.C. President Roosevelt, who had been impressed with Jarvis' heroism during the Overland Expedition, had come to rely on him as a personal advisor and had summoned him to discuss conditions in Alaska. Jarvis promised his friend that, while in Washington, he would try to secure the removal of two of Wickersham's adversaries in Nome.

Jarvis spent the next two months in the capital. He recommended that the main custom house be moved from Sitka to Juneau, and he helped promote an agreement with Canada to allow the transport of sealed goods through Canada without paying duty. He also took every opportunity to boost Alaska's potential worth, telling one reporter that "the possibilities of the country are beyond comprehension." [7]

Wickersham and Jarvis met again at St. Michael during their travels in the summer of 1903. They were together for several days, sharing quarters at the Alaska Commercial Company. [8] When Wickersham traveled on the cutter RUSH to hold court sessions in the Aleutians, Jarvis joined him at Unalaska for the remainder of the trip to Kodiak, Bristol Bay, and Valdez. Wickersham stayed in Valdez to hold the long court session during which he rendered his decision in the Bonanza case. Before parting, Wickersham and Jarvis had another long talk about Wickersham's status with President Roosevelt. [9]

In early 1904, the Scripts-McRae news service proclaimed Jarvis and Wickersham, along with Episcopal Bishop Peter Trimble Rowe, to be the three most popular men in Alaska. [10] Later that year, Jarvis received a gold medal which Congress unanimously voted to bestow on him for his heroics in the Arctic in the winter of 1897-98. [11]

Image of hero, Lt. David H. Jarvis, USRM, awarded by act of Congress June 28, 1902.
OFFICIAL US COAST GUARD PHOTO

While Jarvis was receiving these accolades, Wickersham was struggling for political survival. His term as federal judge expired in 1904 and powerful senators and lobbyists, who were angered by his reform of the corrupt Nome courts, were attempting to block his reappointment.

Jarvis was instrumental in obtaining a reappointment for Wickersham. An investigation of Alaskan matters by Assistant Attorney General W.A. Day in the summer of 1904 weighed heavily in determining Wickersham's future. Jarvis accompanied the Day party during the last part of its travels in Alaska. When the group reached Fairbanks, where Wickersham was holding court, Jarvis advised his friend to maintain "a dignified silence." [12] Wickersham followed that advice and noted in his diary that Jarvis "tells Judge Day that, without hesitation, he is making a fair and strong fight for my reappointment and I will always have to thank him for it." Several days later he reiterated: "Jarvis has not hesitated to stand by me from the beginning and will do so to the end."

Judge James Wickersham at work.
ALASKA STATE LIBRARY

Wickersham and Jarvis were together in Juneau in November 1904 when they received the welcome news that Roosevelt had been re-elected. Jarvis talked about his travels with Judge Day and Wickersham recorded that Jarvis "says Judge Day was satisfied with me and my services as judge and will recommend my reappointment." Within the week Wickersham learned that he had, indeed, been reappointed. In his diary he credited the unceasing help of Jarvis.

Wickersham and Jarvis also spoke about Jarvis' political future in their post-election talk. Wickersham wrote in his diary: "Jarvis wants to be Governor of Alaska, but will not say so and even worse won't let anyone else say it." [13] Three days later, the judge took it upon himself to write Vice President-elect Charles W. Fairbanks, urging the new Roosevelt administration to appoint Jarvis governor. [14]

Wickersham's interpretation of Jarvis' political aspirations was not completely accurate. In a press release to the *Post- Intelligencer*, Washington correspondant Walter Clark related that, in early 1905, Roosevelt had offered Jarvis either the Alaska governorship or a position as assistant secretary of the treasury in charge of the customs service. [15] Jarvis declined because he was more interested in taking advantage of a new business opportunity in Alaska.

The Office Seeks the Man

Cartoon that appeared on the front page of Seattle Post-Intelligencer, *February 17, 1906.*

Jarvis was aware of an opportunity to acquire Alaskan salmon canneries. The Pacific Packing and Navigation Company, which owned 23 canneries and several large ocean steamers, had been placed in receivership in 1903, and its assets were to be sold at public auction in Bellingham. Jarvis, who was not a wealthy man, approached John Rosene, a Nome entrepeneur who owned the Northwestern Commercial Company, with a plan to reorganize the Pacific Packing and Navigation Company. Rosene agreed to accompany Jarvis to a meeting with officials of J.P. Morgan and Company, which was a major creditor of the bankrupt firm and anxious to arrange a viable reorganization. Rosene and Jarvis so impressed the Morgan bank executives that they volunteered to underwrite Northwestern Commercial Company's purchase of the fisheries. Rosene immediately sent an associate to the Bellingham auction and succeeded in purchasing most of the assets, which were capitalized at $12,000,000, for $235,000. (16)

On March 11, 1905, the *Daily Alaska Dispatch* in Juneau carried the news that Jarvis had filed his resignation as customs collector and would shortly arrive in Seattle to assume a position as general manager of the Northwestern Pacific Fisheries Company, a subsidiary of Northwestern Commercial Company established to operate the Pacific Packing and Navigation properties.

Jarvis, who had three young children and was tired of the continual travel necessitated by his position as customs collector, welcomed the opportunity to engage in private business and to move from Sitka to Seattle. (17) He immediately took charge of the canneries, announcing that only four of them would open during the next fishing season, but that all would probably operate after that.

The Pacific Packing and Navigation Company had originally been organized in 1901 as a cooperative cannery venture in an attempt to challenge the monopoly of the powerful Alaska Packers. Alaska Packers, however, was able to undersell the competition in the price war that had forced Pacific Packing and Navigation into bankruptcy. A news dispatch on March 30 explained that Jarvis wanted cooperation rather than confrontation with Alaska Packers, and that the two companies had agreed to stop their "old war" and adopt a motto of "live and let live." (18)

Although he was no longer a government employee, Jarvis retained his political influence in Washington, D.C., and used it to assist Wickersham. Wickersham's 1904 reappointment had still not been confirmed by the Senate because Senator Nelson and others continued to oppose him. However, President Roosevelt kept Wickersham as a judge by giving him a series of recess appointments. For two years Jarvis, along with Clark and Birch, continued to promote Wickersham's retention, actions which Wickersham acknowledged repeatedly in his diary.

Jarvis still lacked enthusiasm for a political career. His success in private business also prompted him to sever connections with the Revenue Marine and remove his name from the promotion list, even though he had officially received his commission as a captain in 1905. When Alaska's Governor Brady resigned in 1906,

Roosevelt sent Jarvis a telegram urging him to reconsider accepting the governorship of Alaska. [19] Jarvis conferred with the President in the White House on March 3, but declined the appointment "on business grounds." The President then chose Wilfred Hoggatt on Jarvis' recommendation. Although Wickersham would have preferred Jarvis, he agreed that Hoggatt would make a good governor. [20]

David Jarvis and wife, Ethel.
PHOTO COURTESY OF MARY JARVIS COCKE

Jarvis had other important business in Washington in the spring of 1906. He used his influence to lobby Congress on several matters important to the Northwestern Commercial Company. In the interest of conserving salmon stocks, he supported legislation to exempt canneries that established hatcheries from the license fee imposed on Alaskan businesses by the Nelson Act of 1905. H.M. Kutchin, the United States inspector of fisheries for Alaska, praised this legislation as having the potential to "do more than almost anything else could to perpetuate salmon in Alaska." [21] Yet, it antagonized Senator Knute Nelson, the author of the original taxing legislation, and generated criticism in Alaska for decreasing income for roads and schools which was obtained through the tax on fisheries. [22]

Jarvis further alienated Senator Nelson by lobbying against a bill the senator supported that would have provided government funds to build a railroad to the Yukon River from a site near Cordova, to be named "Nelson." Jarvis argued successfully, in a document known as the Jarvis Memorial, that such legislation was unnecessary and even counterproductive because it would retard private interests that were already building rail lines to interior Alaska. [23]

Although Jarvis did not participate in the 1898 Alaska gold rush or have prior contact with either George Hazelet or Stephen Birch, he had become involved with both Birch and Hazelet in one of the private railroad building ventures in Alaska through his association with John Rosene and the Northwestern Commercial Company.

Railroad Fever in Valdez

XIV

George Hazelet's plans for railroad development in Valdez had suffered a series of ups and downs between 1902 and 1906. Back in 1902, while he and A.J. Meals were still attempting to retrieve gold from their claims at Chisna, Hazelet's friend George W. Holdrege, manager of the Burlington and Missouri Railroad, continued to make arrangements to build a railroad from Valdez through Keystone Canyon to interior Alaska. He acquired a franchise to build along the route surveyed by Edward Gillette as a member of the Abercrombie expedition in 1899. A stipulation of this franchise was that the railroad in question had to be under construction within two years.

Initially Holdrege contacted J.R. DeLamar, a wealthy New York copper magnate, who was considering acquisition of some Alaska copper claims. DeLamar, however, was not prepared to proceed with construction of a railroad until his mining engineers had an opportunity to appraise the Alaska claims. On May 13, 1902, DeLamar wrote Holdrege:

> I am in receipt of a note from Mr. Gillette stating that he is unable to meet me before I sail on the fourteenth. Since that time, I understand that you are negotiating with Mr. Helm for the transfer of your franchise on the railroad from Valdez into Alaska. Of course I would not influence your determination in any manner, but will simply say that I have arranged for three engineers including my general manager, to examine these Alaska mines, which I have under bond, also the coal mines, and as such men as Mr. Charles M. Schwab, President of the United States Steel Corporation, are identified with me in this undertaking, the building of that railroad would be a very small matter to us, provided the franchise was in the hands of parties with whom we cared to do business, or be identified. The question for you to consider is whether a small payment made to you by the London parties is of sufficient inducement to tie up this franchise, or

whether it would pay to wait until about the beginning, or the middle of September, when I shall have all our reports in and be ready to act. [1]

B.F. Millard and family in front of their Valdez home in 1902.
F.C. Helm (seated on steps)
PHOTO COURTESY OF VALDEZ MUSEUM

Holdrege responded from Omaha on May 18:

Mr. Gillette and I understood, in talking with you in Denver, that you would not be ready to decide upon doing anything in Alaska until too late for work this season. As it is important for our enterprise that surveys should be completed further into the interior and work of construction started this year, we have thought best to make an agreement with Messrs. Abbott and Helm under which our company will put two locating parties in the field for the necessary engineering work at once and under which they are expected to commence construction of the road this year.

I hope, that under the arrangement made, the railroad facilities you may need can be satisfactorily furnished. If not, it may not be too late next autumn or winter to talk with you about some joint arrangement. [2]

Holdrege was not the only railroad man interested in building at Valdez. In early 1902, Valdez papers had speculated about other railroad and mining interests that might be planning construction. M.J. Heney, who built the White Pass and Yukon Route with funding from Close Brothers of London, had traveled from Valdez to Eagle in 1901 and was frequently mentioned as a possible builder of a railroad from Valdez. [3] Capt. John Healy had dreams of a railroad link from Valdez to the Seward Peninsula and then across the Bering Straits to Siberia. [4] A group of Portland financiers, represented by Alfred B. Iles, was also reported to be investigating a rail route starting at Valdez. [5]

Late in June 1902, *The Alaska Prospector* reported that active construction was about to commence on the Valdez, Copper River and Yukon Railroad, with Gillette heading a corps of 25 surveyor and assistants. The article further explained: "Gillette now holds a responsible position with the Burlington railroad in Montana, and that stamps him as a competent railroad man. Mr. Gillette, in speaking of the new road in which he is interested, is careful to say that it is not a Burlington project, though some of the men financially interested in the latter corporation may be behind the new venture..." [6]

Soon surveyors were running angle lines from both the Hazelet townsite and Bloomerville to a point on the government trail near the foot of the mountains. [7] Although they were surveying both locations, Gillette and Holdrege favored the Hazelet site. Before leaving Sheriden, Wyoming, for Alaska, Gillette wrote Holdrege: "I hope the scrip is all right. I instructed Deyo to locate from our townsite, and also to run a line down to Abercrombie's land. This townsite question ought to be settled in the next month as the gold strike will bring in lots of new people and the town will build rapidly." [8]

A subsequent letter described the stock distribution for the Hazelet townsite as proposed by F.C. Helm, the agent for the English investors. Gillette speculated that "the townsite if properly handled would be worth more than $1,000,000," but expressed some reservation about whether "Helm's promise is good." [9]

Throughout the summer of 1902, railroad plans appeared to be progressing on schedule. F.C. Helm arrived in Valdez in mid-July with O.P. Hubbard. They conferred with B.F. Millard, their Valdez representative, and took a brief trip to the summit before leaving for Juneau. Helm was vague about specific plans but assured Valdezians that the work of actual construction on the road would be commenced that year, and that the work would be continued all winter with a view to being able to run trains across the summit by spring. He announced that the construction contract had been awarded to J.P. McDonald, "one of the most noted railroad contractors in the United States," who was currently enroute to Valdez. [10]

As the summer dragged on, Valdez awaited the arrival of contractor McDonald, but he never got farther than Seattle. In spite of rumors that equipment was on the way, [11] that large buildings were planned for the Hazelet townsite, [12] and that laborers were being recruited, [13] nothing more happened. While enroute back to Omaha from Alaska, Hazelet wrote T.J. Donohoe from Seattle on September 26:

> Helm is not here. No one knows anything at this end — or rather in Seattle. Had wire from Gillette saying he'd meet me on way east. ... I do not understand Millard, except that he wants to prove himself an all around S.B. and a bigger damned fool than he was taken for. I presume it is a hold-up figured out by Hubbard. I don't think they can win though. I only got the scrip filed Oct. 20, but guess that is plenty of time. ...
>
> Nothing known here about the copper deal except that a telegram came for Warner last night asking him to come to N.Y.C. at once to close on a cash basis. Will see Amy today. [14]

Valdez, Copper River, and Yukon Railroad officials, 1902.
PHOTO COURTESY OF VALDEZ MUSEUM

The copper deal referred to in this letter was the purchase of the Bonanza copper claims by Stephen Birch, representing New York financeers H.O.

Havemeyer and James Ralph. Once Birch had succeeded in purchasing the Bonanza claims, development of the mine and a railroad would probably have followed immediately had it not been for the previously described lawsuit, which was instigated by Helm in an effort to acquire the Bonanza claims.

When Helm's Copper River Mining Company, which had purchased the alleged interest in the Bonanza claims from the Chittyna Exploration Company, tried to sell stock in the claims, James Ralph, president of Alaska Copper and Coal, started legal proceedings against Helm, revealing that he had failed to abide by the provisions of his agreement with Holdrege and Gillette to start actual railroad construction and, thereby, had lost his claim to the right of way through Keystone Canyon. Gillette then secured passage through Congress of a bill extending the Akron, Sterling and Northern franchise for another two years. (15)

Hazelet, who was spending the winter in Omaha, informed Donohoe in a January 15, 1903, letter that he was considering selling his Mineral Creek property for $10,000. "I think the railroad is a go," he stated. "McDonald, the big railroad contractor of New York, is in the deal now and Abbott is out. It looks to me that Helm will also be out." (16)

Hazelet's information was correct. On February 13, 1903, Holdrege and Gillette gave James P. McDonald an option on all the property of the Akron, Sterling and Northern Railroad Company, including the right of way through Keystone Canyon, Gillette's survey data, and the Mineral Creek townsite, with the stipulation that $51,000 be paid before August 15, 1903. (17)

With the townsite apparently sold and the Chisna gold mine temporarily abandoned, Hazelet had no definite plan for the future. Since he was convinced that his best prospects lay in Alaska and did not wish to spend any more time away from home, he decided to move his family to Valdez for the summer. In May of 1903, the Valdez newspaper noted:

> G.C. Hazelet returned on the Excelsior from a trip to his home at Omaha, Neb. He also visited a number of the eastern cities during his absence. In speaking of the interest manifested in this country in the states, Mr. Hazelet says Valdez is the best advertised town in Alaska and is drawing the attention of people and capital from everywhere. ... Mr. Hazelet was accompanied by his wife and children, and will reside here. (18)

When he arrived back in Alaska, Hazelet discovered that the railroad situation in Valdez had become more complicated. Early that spring, Alfred B. Iles had presented the Valdez Chamber of Commerce with a new proposition to build the Valdez, Copper River and Tanana Railroad. An article in *The Valdez News* on March 21, 1903 stated that "Mr. Iles would agree to construct a railroad from

Valdez to the summit, said road to cost $550,000, provided the people of Valdez would subscribe $50,000 of that amount, payable in four payments, or as each five miles of the road was completed." The citizens of Valdez, anxious to see action on their long-awaited railroad, subscribed 125,000 shares of stock in the Iles company with the understanding that construction would begin by July 1. [19]

Trestle for Valdez, Copper River and Tanana, 1903.
PHOTO COURTESY VALDEZ MUSEUM

In May, while the Seattle Chamber of Commerce was debating the merits of the two railroad schemes, some Valdez citizens spoke in favor of the Iles plan, which would start tracks from old Valdez, where their businesses were located, rather than Hazelet's Mineral Creek townsite. [20] Furthermore, the Valdez, Copper River and Yukon company had lost favor with Valdezians because it had run short of money and left many bills unpaid. [21]

Although *The Valdez News* reported on June 6, 1903, that some of the Valdez, Copper River and Tanana crews were building a trestle from Front Street to the dock, little actual work was completed that summer on either railroad. Construction had undoubtedly been postponed pending a decision in the Bonanza lawsuit, which was to be heard in Valdez District Court the following November.

While awaiting further railroad developments, Hazelet needed money to support his family, so he spent the summer guiding the Anaconda mining experts who were assessing gold and copper prospects in the Nizina region. Upon their return *The Alaska Prospector* reported:

> For the purpose of investigating the quantity and quality of the minerals of the Copper River country, Messr. H.V. Winchell, D. Hay Stivers, J. Audley Smith and L.A. Levinsaler arrived here early this spring. While the snow was still heavy on the divide they went to the interior assisted by J.P. Roberts and Son, and Geo. Hazelet. Most of the locations were visited and examined, even the Nizina placer diggings. After two months in the interior they returned and departed on the SANTA ANA. They refused to say anything regarding the minerals, but speak well of the country in general. Their intentions could not be learned, but it is a rather significant fact that their horses and outfit are left here for safe keeping and are not for sale. [22]

The Winchell party reported favorably on some Nizina gold placer claims that were being worked by Hazelet's former partner, Arthur McNeer. On February 6, 1904, *The Valdez News* carried news that Hazelet had arranged a sale:

> Word was received Thursday by wire that the Carvey McNeer group of bench claims in the Nizina country had been sold, the purchase price being $100,000.
>
> The deal was consumated by Geo. Hazelet for the owners of the property and H.V. Winchell, the mining expert for the purchasers.

Further details were provided the following month:

> At least $50,000 will be spent this year in the Nizina country in testing and opening up the ground bonded to eastern capitalists through G.C. Hazelet and H.V. Winchell. The steamer JAMES DOLLAR brought up an outfit consisting of ten horses and sixty tons of freight which has already been started toward the interior. Mr. G.C. Hazelet has general superintendence of the company operations and accompanied the outfit on the DOLLAR. ...
>
> It is not the intention to attempt to take out any great amount of money from the company's properties this year, but simply to thoroughly test them and ascertain their value as near as possible. ...
>
> The company has 45 claims, all of which will be thoroughly tested. The mining operations will be under the direction of a competent placer mining engineer who will be sent up later in the spring. The company is taking in 15 men and from 15 to 25 more will be employed after the season opens up. Mr. Hazelet says work will be guaranteed to this number at $5 per day and board.

Mr. Hazelet will probably remain in Valdez the greater part of the summer though he may take a trip in later in the season. His brother, J.A. Hazelet, has charge of the trail work and has already left with the outfit. [23]

George Hazelet leading Anaconda Expedition.
ALASKA STATE LIBRARY. PAC 159-2

While working on the Nizina River placer claims in the summer of 1904, Hazelet had an opportunity to talk with Stephen Birch, who was working at the nearby Bonanza claims. Although Judge James Wickersham had decided the lawsuit in favor of the McClellan group, full-scale development of the Bonanza mine and a connecting railroad still awaited an appeal of Wickersham's decision. In a July 10, 1904, letter from Nizina to his lawyer, Thomas Donohoe, in Valdez, Hazelet affirmed that Birch was working with him in planning for future railroad development. He mentioned that Birch had just left for the Dan Creek gold mines and assured Donohoe: "Don't get excited about the railroad. We will be in time to make some money if it is built. It takes long hard work to do that thing." [24]

Throughout the summer of 1904, Valdez abounded with railroad rumors but saw little action. A new group of engineers, possibly associated with the Union Pacific, were making surveys for the Valdez and Northern Railroad Co., which apparently was an outgrowth of the Iles project. [25] Responsible financiers, including Judge W.F. Bay Stewart of New York, were rumored to have taken over the Helm project. [26] Interest in a Valdez railroad even took on an international flavor in September when M. Delabel of Paris explained his railroad undertakings to the International Geographical Congress in St. Louis. He claimed to have secured approbation of the Czar, President Roosevelt, and several European sovereigns, and would complete plans as soon as he could arrange for neutralization of the Bering Straits. [27]

When Hazelet and his family returned to Omaha for the winter, he attempted to arrive at some resolution of the railroad situation. On December 31, he wrote Donohoe: "I am trying to get to the bottom of the Railroad matter, but find it rather complicated. If it were not for that old crowd of horse thieves, I could pull the deal off, as I explained to you, through Bratnober. It is too bad things are as they are, but I hope to be able to break them loose yet." [28] Hazelet had now added Henry Bratnober, a weathy Californian who had extensive copper mining interests in Alaska, to his other backers. His new plan for the Trans-Alaskan Railroad was described in *The Alaska Prospector* on February 23:

> ... A Bill providing for the incorporation of a railroad from Valdez to Eagle has been introduced in the Senate by Senator Dietrich. The Bill proposed a government guarantee of 4% on its bonds up to $40,000 a mile. The incorporators are: Henry Bratnober, a well-known California capitalist; Chas. F. Manderson, ex-senator from Nebraska; George W. Holdrege of Nebraska, a prominent railroad man; George C. Hazelet of Alaska; Wm. Todd of New York; James E. Kelby of Nebraska; and Edward Gillette of Wyoming. The capital stock is fixed at $10,000,000. A right of way 200 ft. wide on each side of the track is granted by the bill, and the right to take from the adjacent public lands earth, stone and timber necessary for construction. ... The bill provides that construction begin within 2 years from the approval of this act; that at least 50 miles must be completed within 8 years. ...
>
> A deed transferring the Hazelet Townsite below Valdez from G.C. Hazelet to Henry Bratnober was filed for record this week in Commissioner Lyon's office.

The following month, at hearings before the House Committee on Territories, the complexities of the railroad situation were further revealed:

> The hearings before the Committee on Territories of the House disclosed a three corner fight between the Trans-Alaska Railroad Company, the Valdez and Yukon Company, and the Alaska Railroad Company. The first is the Hazelet-Bratnober Company and the Valdez and Yukon Company represents an assignment of all the railroad interests here, except Hazelet's from the Akron-Sterling and Northern down to the present time, including the Helm holdings. Edward P. Brown, who appeared for the Valdez and Yukon Company, stated that his company held the right of way originally granted to the Akron-Sterling, which

has had extentions of time carrying it to 2/16/05. ... He claims that Holdrege and Kelby, who are now interested in the Hazelet project, sold his clients the right of way grant and are acting in bad faith by working for another road over the same route. This statement brought Kelby to the floor with the statement that Stewart had never paid him and Holdrege for the interests turned over. Hazelet, Ivy, Bratnober, Ryan, Burleigh, Mercer and a number of others joined in the discussion, and the result of their testimony is so indefinite and so many charges of fraud and counter charges are made that it would take a corps of lawyers to decide which party was worthy of aid. Natural result of this fight was that the committee turned down all the railroad legislation. [29]

Staking Cordova townsite, 1905.
George Hazelet (facing camera)
ANCHORAGE MUSEUM OF HISTORY & ART. B62.1.2108

The Alaska Railroad Company, the third party in this trio of paper railroads, was the result of a desire to locate the port for a railroad closer to a source of coal that could be used to fuel the railroad and a copper-smelting industry. Coal had been discovered near the Bering Glacier, about 200 miles southeast of Valdez, in 1902. The Alaska Railroad Company organizers, Andrew Burleigh and Donald A. McKenzie, envisioned their railroad starting from a new port to be developed on the eastern side of Prince William Sound rather than from Valdez. In an effort to enlist the support of Senator Nelson, they proposed to name the new port city after him.

Although Hazelet was primarily concerned with development of the Mineral Creek townsite, he also recognized the desirability of a town nearer to the Bering River coal fields. As soon as he arrived back in Valdez in the spring of 1905, he joined a group of Valdez businessmen, which included T.J. Donohoe and his law partner John Y. Ostrander, John Goodell, A.J. Adams, and George Esterly, in putting up scrip to acquire a townsite on Orca Inlet. [30]

When McKenzie visited the area later that summer to determine where to locate a port for his Alaska Railroad, he found that the foresighted Valdezians already possessed the only good harbor on the east side of Prince William Sound with potential access to the Copper River delta and the Bering River coal fields.

Although Congress decided against providing financial aid to any of the projected railroads, Valdezians approached the summer of 1905 with optimism that something would be done that year. In March they speculated that the Valdez and Northern Railway Company would join the Bratnober-Holdrege-Hazelet group, [31] but it was several months before they realized that more new players were about to enter the field.

Anticipating a final decision in the appeal of the Bonanza lawsuit and anxious to see a railroad under construction, Stephen Birch approached John Rosene in New York City in the spring of 1905. Rosene had capitalized on the 1900 Nome gold rush, acquiring a fleet of steamships to transport miners to Nome, commercial outlets in Nome, and an 80-mile railroad between Nome and the Kougaruk gold fields. Rosene had dreams of a rail link to Siberia by tunneling under the Bering Straits, and had shared his international plans with the Frenchman Delabel. Birch's desire for a rail link from Valdez to his mining claims fitted in with Rosene's dreams, and Rosene could provide what Birch needed most — railroad experience and steamships to transport ore to Pacific coast smelters. [32]

Birch enlisted Hazelet's help in persuading Rosene that Valdez would be the best port for the railroad. Rosene, in his enthusiasm for development in Alaska, then agreed to add Birch's railroad and Hazelet's townsite, as well as Jarvis' canneries, to the holdings of his Northwestern Commercial Company.

As soon as the appeal on the Bonanza lawsuit was decided in Birch's favor, Rosene floated a bond issue to finance a railroad to the Bonanza mines. His plans were disclosed in the Valdez paper:

> A company known as the Copper River and Northwestern Railroad Co. has been organized in Seattle, with John Rosene as president and J.D. Trenholme as secretary, and John Rosene, Moritz Thomsen, D.H. Jarvis, J.D. Trenholme and Henry Bratnober as board of directors.
>
> It develops that this new organization is the preliminary company of what is locally known as the Hazelet railroad people, and that the surveyors who have been in the field for some time under Henry Deyo are working to the interest of these people.
>
> President Rosene makes the statement to the press that it is the intention of the company to proceed with construction work on the road within a very short time and that a number of miles of road will be built this summer.
>
> Geo. C. Hazelet, who went to the states about a month ago on business in connection with the railroad project returned on the EXCELSIOR this morning. [33]

In August, Rosene arrived in Valdez on the SANTA ANA to look over the potential railroad route with Birch and Deyo. Other railroad interests, however, were not content to leave the field uncontested. The same ship brought Colonel A.W. Swanitz, formerly chief engineer of the Alaska Central Railroad at Seward, with tools to begin grade work on the Valdez and Yukon Railroad, said to be a "consolidation of the Helm-Stewart and the Iles interests." [34]

Both railroad companies meant business this time. On August 19, *The Valdez News* announced that Rosene had definitely selected the Hazelet townsite for the terminal of the Copper River and Northwestern and had made final construction plans. In late September, the Valdez and Yukon Company was preparing the grade across the flats between Valdez and Keystone Canyon, while a gang of men under Deyo was doing rock work in Keystone Canyon for the Copper River and Northwestern. [35] The crew in the canyon continued working through most of the winter, and on February 17, 1906, *The Valdez News* speculated that "the first 20 miles will be actually constructed and in operation before the end of the summer."

The News continued to give optimistic reports. On April 17, 1906, it announced: "George C. Hazelet, who has charge of the company's affairs here, is now asking for bids for 50,000 railroad ties to be delivered during the summer." As the summer progressed, however, the pace of construction in Valdez slackened. The Valdez and Yukon Company abandoned the railroad grade it had been preparing and only token crews continued to work on the terminal site and Keystone Canyon rock work for the Copper River and Northwestern.

Rosene — The Dreamer

John Rosene's development schemes centered in Alaska, but his dreams were international in scope. Although he succeeded in building a significant commercial empire, his naivete in dealing with Russians, Frenchmen and New York business tycoons prevented the realization of his dreams.

Rosene, born on a Norwegian farm in 1861, went to sea as a teenager. After a disastrous shipwreck in 1880, he settled in the United States. Starting in Philadelphia, he gradually moved west, working in iron mills in Trenton and Pittsburg, and then running a grocery business in Chicago. Upon hearing of the Klondike gold strike in 1897, Rosene grubstaked a group of 11 loggers from Minnesota and accompanied them to Dawson by way of the Chilkoot Pass, Lake Bennett and the Yukon headwaters.

John Rosene—President of the Northwestern Commercial Company.
ALASKAN CARACITURES, TURN OF THE CENTURY CARTOONS FROM THE SEATTLE *ARGUS*

After spending several years in Dawson, Rosene heard of the gold strike at Nome and surmised that an ocean-going steamship to transport prospectors to the Seward Peninsula would be a more profitable investment than a Klondike gold mine. Upon returning to Seattle, he persuaded J.D. Trenholme and George T.

Williams to join him, and chartered the steamship CENTENNIAL from Charles Nelson and Company for $20,000 to make one voyage from Seattle to Nome. On May 30, 1900, the CENTENNIAL left Puget Sound for Nome with 636 paying passengers, more than a dozen stowaways, a crew of 116 and 100 horses. The ship also towed two barges with merchandise for a store at Nome, to be operated by Williams. The CENTENNIAL made $60,000 profit on the first sailing. After three more voyages that season, Rosene's newly-chartered Northwestern Commercial Company had brought in five times the original investment.

The following year the company built a store and lumber yard at Teller on Alaska's Seward Peninsula, added several more vessels to the fleet, and agreed to do lightering for the government at St. Michael near the mouth of the Yukon River. Acting on the suggestion of a prospector, Rosene met a Count Podhorsky in Nome to discuss establishing trade connections with Siberia. Podhorsky then contacted General Wonlarlasky, a personal friend of the Czar, and Wonlarlasky, in turn, obtained a mining and trading concession for the Ichutkotsk Peninsula on the east coast of Siberia, an area larger than the state of Washington. Rosene and Count Podhorsky traveled to St. Petersburg in December, 1901, to make plans for the creation of the Northeast Siberian Company, Ltd., with an authorized capitalization of 3,000,000 rubles.

As soon as the preliminary arrangements were made, the Russians arranged to send a mining engineer and 125 prospectors to the area, and Rosene chartered the steamer MANAUENSE to transport the miners from Vladivostock to Nome, where 50 additional American miners joined the expedition. In early July 1902, they sailed with lumber, coal and general merchandise to establish trading stations in eastern Siberia at St. Lawrence Bay, Plover Bay and East Cape.

Rosene spent two months of the 1902 season on the Siberian coast and was encouraged by reports of a gold strike at East Cape. In January, 1903, he returned to St. Petersburg and arranged to purchase the MANAUENSE to supply the miners at East Cape and establish fisheries in the area. Observers returning from Siberia expressed optimism that "under proper management the Northeast Siberian Company will be a richer corporation than the Hudson Bay Company."

The summer of 1903 was a disappointment, however. The gold discovery did not prove significant, development of fisheries was slower than anticipated, and the MANAUENSE sank off the coast of Japan. When war between Russia and Japan closed the port of Vladivostock and threatened the Siberian ventures, Rosene decided to concentrate on developing steamship trade in northwestern Alaska. He arranged to purchase the luxury liners VICTORIA, OLYMPIA and TACOMA from the Northern Pacific Railroad for $225,000 and organized the Northwestern Steamship Company.

The steamship company was a success from the start, the liners were filled with passengers, and Rosene even began promoting cruises to Siberia. The 75 excursionists who returned to Nome in August 1904, gave the cruise mixed reviews. Dr. Ed. E. Hill, writing for the *Nome Nugget*, had little enthusiasm for Siberia, commenting: "In conclusion, Siberia may be rich in many things... but, as a place of residence give me Nome, sweet Nome, every time."

Rosene went to New York City in January of 1905 to sell more Northwestern Commercial Company stock to pay for the purchase of the steamers SANTA CLARA, SANTA ANNA, EXCELSIOR, and DORA. While in the East he met men who persuaded him to add additional enterprises to his fast-growing empire. Capt. David Jarvis, customs collector for Alaska, introduced him to officials of the J.P. Morgan banking house, who talked him into adding to his growing empire. With the financial backing of the Morgan bank, he succeeded in purchasing the canneries, boats and other equipment of the bankrupt Pacific Packing and Navigation Company for $235,000 and formed Northwestern Fisheries.

While in New York, other promoters approached Rosene with proposals that would guarantee business for his steamships if he joined them in building railroads from tidewater ports in southern Alaska to the interior where copper mines were being developed. These proposals intrigued Rosene, who had already built a railroad on the Seward Peninsula and dreamed of a rail connection with Siberia.

Stephen Birch and George Hazelet convinced Rosene that Valdez would be the best port for a railroad, so Rosene acquired a franchise to build the Copper River and Northwestern Railroad from Valdez to Eagle, with a spur to Birch's Bonanza copper mine.

In the summer of 1906, Birch succeeded in convincing Guggenheim mining interests to join the Morgan bank and create the Alaska Syndicate. The Syndicate purchased 46.2% of the stock in Rosene's enterprises.

The New York managers of the Syndicate and Rosene had different objectives. Rosene, the dreamer, envisioned a railroad extending from Valdez to Nome and then under the Bering Straits to Siberia, while the Morgans and Guggenheims were primarily committed to developing the copper mines. In order to finance further expansion of his mining interests on Alaska's Seward Peninsula and in the Anadyr region of Siberia, Rosene borrowed money from the Morgan bank, with more stock in the Northwestern Commercial Company as collateral.

Before he realized what was happening, Rosene lost control of his enterprises because the New York financeers had acquired a majority of the stock. The Syndicate directors, who objected to Rosene using ships to support his Siberian enterprises, removed him from the presidency at a board of director's meeting in New York in 1907.

Within a year Rosene was no longer associated with any of the companies he had organized, but he continued to dream. In 1909, he was in France trying to raise money for the Trans-Alaska railway from Valdez to Siberia, but the Frenchmen Delonde and Lobel failed to make good on their promises.

Rosene dreamed on and formed the Alaska Exploration and Development Company, whose first project was to be the building of the Controller Bay and Bering Coal Railroad. When he died in 1919, Rosene was actively promoting the Alaska Midland Railway, which he planned to start at the port of Haines.

Alaska Syndicate

While Stephen Birch was enjoying success in his plans for development of the copper mine and access railroad, his friend Judge Wickersham continued to have problems. Wickersham returned to Washington, D.C., in early 1906 in order to continue fighting for confirmation of his judicial reappointment. On February 4, he recorded in his diary: "Steve Birch came over last night. He is greatly elated over getting his Bonanza mines railroad from Valdez into shape and it now seems a success." Birch and Wickersham saw each other socially and Birch again volunteered to contact congressmen on Wickersham's behalf. On March 5, Wickersham wrote in the diary:

> Steve Birch came over from New York last night and took breakfast with me this morning. He urges me to go over to New York and remain a few days as his and Mr. Ralph's friend, and I am going. He also suggests that personally he hopes I won't be confirmed as then they can employ me as the attorney for their Copper River Ry. and mining schemes.

While in New York, Birch and Wickersham visited the Morgan bank and met W.P. Hamilton, son-in-law of J.P. Morgan, J.P. Morgan, Jr. and Charles Steele.

At the end of March, Wickersham still had not been confirmed so Birch wrote offering help:

> My dear Judge:
> I returned to New York this A.M. Mr. Ralph has informed me of the situation in Washington as best he knows. ... I saw the Morgans this morning, and they told me they had done all they possibly could for you and they felt assured you would be confirmed. Of course I don't know the situation, but my suggestion is to keep a stiff upper lip and stay in Washington. Nelson is probably trying to delay all he can. Will you kindly drop me a line as to the situation. I will necessarily be delayed here for a few days, but if you think it necessary for me to come to Washington, let me know and I will come.
> Send me word of any particular Senator that you wish to reach. [1]

Wickersham recorded that Birch contacted several senators to urge confirmation. On May 4, he wrote in the diary:

> Had dinner at New Willard with Birch tonight — he suggested that if I wished
> to resign next fall after they were certain about their enterprises in Alaska, they
> would like to have me take charge of their legal business. I told him I would be
> willing to make some arrangement on that line.

Several days later Wickersham visited New York and went with Birch to meet Daniel Guggenheim, whom he referred to in his diary as "Dan Guggenheimer." Guggenheim was planning to go to the Yukon to look over mining property. Wickersham also mentions that he met a Mr. Steele, legal counsel for the Guggenheims and brother of Charles Steele of the Morgan bank. After spending the rest of the week attending plays with Birch and James Ralph, and riding around New York in Ralph's new electric automobile, Wickersham returned to Alaska. He had not been confirmed but had another interim appointment from President Roosevelt.

The men that Wickersham met in New York were the ones Birch was hoping to enlist for additional financial support in the development of his mine and access railroad. George Hazelet and the other Valdez railroad promoters had assumed that Congress would utilize private railroads to open Alaska for development with generous land grants and other concessions as it had previously in many western states. At the dawn of the twentieth century, however, the political climate was changing. Private railroads had reaped great profit and become too powerful in the minds of many citizens. The Populist movement, in particular, blamed railroad monopolies for luring settlers into arid lands and then charging unfair rates.

Since Congress was beginning to doubt the wisdom of granting public land to private corporations to assure the building of railroads, Alaska developers were not receiving the concessions given to early developers in the West. If private railroads were to be built in Alaska, a large amount of capital investment would be necessary before any return could be expected. H.O. Havemeyer and James Ralph had provided Birch with funds to acquire the Bonanza claims and John Rosene had acquired the railroad franchise but Birch knew he needed additional financial help to assure completion of the railroad.

Daniel Guggenheim was already convinced of Alaska's development potential, as shown in an interview quoted in the April 3, 1906, issue of *The New York Times*:

> Alaska is a new country. I should like to be one of those to bring it to its
> destined place in American affairs. It is not altogether a matter of money: there is
> some sentiment in an enormous undertaking of this sort.

> We want to go into the territory and build railroads and smelters and mining towns and bring men there and populate the country where it is habitable, and do for it what the earlier figures in American railroad building did for sections of the great West.
>
> Some of the copper districts of Alaska have already been prospected, and sections, the Copper River, for instance, have seen some development. But the mines in that country cannot be worked until railroads have put them within the reach of the seacoast and until smelters and concentrating plants are in the field to turn the ore into metal for its economical transportation to the consumer.
>
> If the plans we have made tentatively for the building of a road into the Copper River district go through, the American Smelting and Refining Company will build works at some point on the coast, probably Valdez.

Guggenheim's enthusiasm was reinforced by his trip to the north. Upon his return to New York in June of 1906, he joined the Morgan bank to form the Alaska Syndicate with the specific goal of developing Birch's copper mine and an access railroad. In testimony before the Senate Committee on Territories in February 1910, John N. Steele, one of the managing directors, gave the following description of the Alaska Syndicate:

> It was an agreement made in July, 1906, in the nature of a partnership, for a particular venture which they called the Alaska Syndicate. The amount of the venture was limited in that agreement to $10,000,000, but that amount could be exceeded with the consent of both parties. The particular things which were in mind at the time the syndicate was formed were the acquisition of certain stock in the Northwestern Commercial Company, the acquisition from Mr. Rosene of the entire stock interest of the Copper River and Northwestern railway, and the acquisition from the Alaska Copper and Coal Company of an interest in the Bonanza mine. [2]

The Alaska Syndicate purchased a 40% interest in Alaska Copper and Coal, the Copper River and Northwestern railway franchise, and a 46.2% interest in the Northwestern Commercial Company, which could provide the steamships to transport ore to a smelter in Tacoma, already owned by Guggenheim interests. Stephen Birch, John H. Steele, and Silas Eccles were named managing directors of the Alaska Syndicate, with offices in New York. John Rosene, David H. Jarvis, and William R. Rust, former owner of the Tacoma smelter, were designated as west coast managers.

Formation of the Alaska Syndicate made ample financial resources available, but also brought together a group of powerful men with differing allegiances, expertise and interests. The three New York-based managing directors represented the

Guggenheim interests and had the power of final approval on all development plans and expenditures. Stephen Birch's agenda was the easiest to understand. He had, from the beginning, been committed to developing the copper mines. S.W. Eccles, from Utah, provided expertise in construction and management of railroads. John Steele, not to be confused with his brother Charles, an officer in the Morgan bank, was the Guggenheim attorney.

The west coast managers were more intimately involved in the day-to-day operation of all the enterprises except the mine, which was Birch's domain. Although Rosene was responsible for the railroad construction, his primary interest was still in Siberian trade and he planned to use the steamships to supply his Asian outposts. Capt. Jarvis was primarily interested in fisheries and also had expertise in the management of steamships. Jarvis, who had demonstrated his executive ability as head of the custom service in Alaska, was made treasurer. Executives of the Morgan bank had such faith in Jarvis that they gave him proxies to vote the Morgan stock. W.R. Rust had sold his Tacoma smelter to Daniel Guggenheim in 1905 for $5,000,000, with the stipulation that he remain as president for at least five years at a salary of $25,000 yearly. [3]

The Morgans and Guggenheims added an overall interest in the eventual industrial development of Alaska to the specific agenda of the six directors. Foreseeing the value of a readily available supply of coal for the railroad and a potential smelter in Alaska, they insisted that the railroad port be close to the Bering River coal fields, several hundred miles east of Valdez. With this in mind, the financiers hired M.K. Rodgers, a well-respected railroad engineer, to study potential railroad routes. On July 17, 1906, *The Alaska Prospector* reported to the citizens of Valdez:

> If the route is found practicable the Copper River and Northwestern Railroad will move its terminus from Valdez to Catalla (sic), on Controller bay. M.K. Rogers (sic), representing eastern financiers interested in the road, has returned from Catalla, where he has been for six weeks with a party of twenty surveyors in the field. The route of the proposed line will be along the Catalla river, and across the Copper river, with a view to tapping the copper fields. Rogers has secured options on most of the waterfront property at Catalla. In an interview with John Rosene, he admitted the truth of the story. Heney, who has started a road from Orca, is here (Seattle) watching developments. He is also securing options on property at Controller bay. Both parties intend to rush construction this summer.

M.J. Heney, the contractor who built the White Pass and Yukon Route from Skagway to Whitehorse in 1899, had obtained a right of way for a railroad from Orca, the site of the current town of Cordova, up the Copper River. George Hazelet and Stephen Birch had also surveyed the route up the Copper River, but had not filed for that right of way because they did not believe a railroad could be built between the Miles and Childs glaciers. (4)

Heney, however, had studied reports of the Allen Expedition, which had succeeded in ascending the Copper River in 1885, and realized that the glaciers were not directly across the river from each other. Late in the fall of 1905, Heney had sent his associate Sam Murchison with Jack Dalton and J.L. McPherson to Alaska to ascertain whether it would be possible to pass the Childs Glacier by running tracks on the east bank of the Copper River and then cross the river to pass the Miles Glacier with tracks along the west bank. When Murchison reported that such a route might be possible, Heney filed for the right of way in Juneau and approached Daniel Guggenheim, who had expressed his interest in building a railroad in Alaska. (5)

Driving first spike on the Copper River Railway.
PHOTO COURTESY OF COROVA HISTORICAL SOCIETY

Heney was unable to persuade Guggenheim to use his route, but went ahead and started to build the Copper River Railway, using a million dollars of his own and a similar amount from Close Brothers, the English bank that had financed the White Pass and Yukon. Heney realized that he did not have sufficient financial resources to complete his railroad, but planned to force the Alaska Syndicate to buy him out in order to obtain the right of way through Abercrombie Canyon, which was too narrow to accommodate more than one railroad. Since a railroad starting at Katalla would have to pass through this canyon, Heney threatened to set off dynamite charges if any other railroad builders entered the canyon. The threat worked. In October 1906, the Syndicate purchased Heney's Copper River Railroad for the amount already spent plus $250,000 in Copper River and Northwestern Railway stock.

Before starting to build his railroad up the Copper River, Heney had to choose a location for the port city. His old friend, Capt. Johnny O'Brien, advised strongly against Katalla because it lacked a sheltered harbor. The Orca Inlet townsite, which Hazelet and his Valdez associates had staked the previous spring, provided the best harbor on the east side of Prince William Sound, so Heney purchased half of that townsite for his railroad terminal and christened the new town "Cordova." (6) During the summer of 1906, buildings started springing up in Cordova, but when Heney sold his railroad to the Syndicate that new town was temporarily abandoned.

The Irish Prince

Nature richly endowed Michael James Heney for the times in which he lived. Known as "Big Mike" to his railroad crews in Washington, Canada, and Alaska, he was at home in front-line construction tents. In the financial and social circles of Seattle, San Francisco, New York and London he was called the "Irish Prince." To his many friends he was simply "M.J."

Heney had those qualities that assured success on the western frontier at the turn of the century. Vision of the future prompted him to undertake projects shunned by less daring men. Although he lived only 45 years, he founded a city, amassed a fortune, and inspired a best-selling novel. Without technical training, Heney built two railroads considered impossible by the leading engineers of his day. A ready Irish smile drew people to him and they became his friends for life. Wherever "M.J." led, his workers followed, each proud to be one of Heney's men.

Heney was born to build railroads. As a boy of 14, this son of Irish immigrant farmers ran away from his Pembroke, Ontario, home to work on building the Canadian Pacific Railroad. He moved west with the railroad, driving mules and laying rails. In March of 1888 he joined John Stevens' survey crew and helped chart a path for the railroad through the Selkirk Mountains. While working on the right of way along the Fraser River in British Columbia he learned to measure grades, blast cliffs, build tunnels and estimate costs. By the time he was 21 years old, Heney had established himself as a railroad contractor with a natural talent to inspire working men.

After several contracts upgrading and revising tracks on the Canadian Pacific, Heney moved to Seattle where he built a 40 mile section of railroad between Sedro-Woolley and Sumas. He prospered in western Washington, where he was known as the "boy contractor," until the crash of 1893. Work was hard to find in the Seattle area during the ensuing depression so Heney accepted a contract to build a hydraulic line for a placer mining operation on Alaska's Kenai Peninsula. He arrived back in Seattle just in time to greet the PORTLAND on July 17, 1897, when it brought news of the Klondike gold strike. That summer Heney watched as thousands of stampeders left Seattle with horses and dogs to flood the mountain passes into the Yukon or to travel thousands of miles by boat up the Yukon River from St. Michaels. He was convinced that he could build a railroad from the coast to the gold fields.

Early in the spring of 1898, Heney borrowed money and booked passage with his friend, Capt. Johnny O'Brien, on the UTOPIA for Skagway. He shouldered a pack and set out to see the country for himself. After three weeks studying the

Chilkoot and White Pass routes, he arrived at the St. James Hotel in Skagway, where he met an engineering party sent to Skagway by the Close Brothers' Bank of London. Sir Thomas Tancrede and Erastus C. Hawkins, both noted engineers, had studied the passes and were about to concede that building a railroad from Skagway was impossible, but Heney persuaded them that he could do it.

Heney's crew arrived in Skagway on May 27, 1898, and began laying tracks down the main street of town on June 16. When the tracks reached Rocky Point, 10 miles out of town, Heney entertained 150 townspeople, transporting them "comfortably seated" on temporary seats on three box cars and then serving a hearty meal garnished with chutney and caviar. When the tracks reached the summit of the White Pass in mid-winter, he entertained again with a "banquet at twenty below."

Working summer and winter with men recruited from among the gold seekers, Heney's crews completed the 110.4-mile narrow gauge railway from Skagway to Whitehorse in two years. After a final banquet, Heney sold his teams of horses and most of his equipment, announcing that he was getting ready to show the world that he could rest as well as work.

M.J. Heney "presented a commanding and conspicuous figure midst gatherings of the social whirl," according to his associate Dr. Fenton Whiting, but Seattle social life and world travel did not satisfy the "Irish Prince" — he still wanted to build railroads. When Daniel Guggenheim announced interest in developing a copper industry in Alaska, Heney began careful study of a railroad route up the Copper River. Although he failed to convince the Morgan-Guggenheim Syndicate to use this route, he went ahead anyway, using his personal fortune. Heney's crews moved into an abandoned cannery on Orca Inlet on April Fool's Day in 1906 and began constructing the Copper River Railway.

After a busy summer of construction, Heney sold out to the Morgan-Guggenheim Syndicate and spent the next year traveling around Alaska with Governor Wilfred Hoggatt. While in Nome, he pondered whether a railroad should cross the Bering Straits by bridge or tunnel. In the meantime, the Syndicate decided that Heney was the best man to build their railroad to the Kennecott copper mines and that Heney's route from Cordova should be used.

Pressure to complete his contracts on schedule forced Heney to work summer and winter, personally participating in all phases of the work. Heney never asked men to do work that he would not undertake himself. He enjoyed close contact with his workers, inspiring the following verse during the building of the White Pass and Yukon:

There's our friend Mr. Heney, who's probably as brainy,
As any in Skagway, I think,
Whose bright pleasant smile shortens many a mile,
As he hands you his flask with a wink.

Heney's railroad workers ate well and his guests dined sumptuously. During the building of the Copper River and Northwestern he entertained United States senators and cabinet officers, newspaper editors and writers. His most notable guest, the author Rex Beach, used Heney as the prototype for the hero of his novel *The Iron Trail*, which gives a fictional account of the building of the Copper River and Northwestern.

Heney did not live to see the completion of the Copper River and Northwestern Railway. He contracted pneumonia after swimming to shore when the steamship OHIO sank in August 1909. His health was further compromised while he pushed ahead with railroad construction until well into the Alaskan winter. He was unable to return to Alaska in 1910 to observe the successful completion of the Million Dollar Bridge across the Copper River. Heney died of pulmonary tuberculosis on October 11, 1910, a week before his 46th birthday.

Officials of the Copper River & Northwestern.
M. J. Heney (front row, fourth from left)
ANCHORAGE MUSUEM OF HISTORY & ART. B72.104.3

Fairbanks Weekly Times   September 28, 1907

BLOODSHED RESULT OF RIGHT-OF-WAY ROW

SIX UNARMED EMPLOYEES OF THE VALDEZ HOME RAILWAY SHOT DOWN IN COLD BLOOD BY PARTY OF GUGGENHEIM MEN IN KEYSTONE CANYON NEAR VALDEZ

The Katalla Herald   August 31, 1907

GRASP OF REYNOLDS

REYNOLDS BUYS OUT SEWARD BUSINESS
HOUSE FORMS TRUST AT VALDEZ AND
SOON WILL OWN EVERYTHING IN SIGHT
INCLUDING THE CHURCHES

*Has an Extreme Fondness for Banks,
Grocery Stores, Etc., Etc.*

Daily Alaska Dispatch   September 26, 1907

ABANDON KATALLA

ENGINEER HAWKINS REPORT BAD FOR NEW RAILROAD TOWN

Daily Alaska Dispatch   November 14, 1907

HUGE STEAMSHIP MERGER AND REORGANIZATION UNDERWAY

NORTHWESTERN COMPANIES AND ALASKA STEAMSHIP COMPANY CONSOLIDATE

Fairbanks Weekly Times   May 2, 1908

Jury Acquits Hasey of Charge of Murder

*Man Accused of Killing Reinhardt in
the Keystone Canyon is Found "Not
Guilty" by Juneau Jury*

Daily Alaska Dispatch   July 17, 1908

WICKERSHAM FOR DELEGATE

Wickersham Backed by Leading
Businessmen and Miners to Save
Alaska from Guggenheims
Telegrams from All Parts of Alaska
Urge Him to Run

The Katalla Herald   August 31, 1907

NO WORK AT VALDEZ

Daily Alaska Dispatch   October 28, 1907

VALDEZ APPEALS FOR IMMEDIATE REMOVAL OF GOVERNOR HOGGATT

Railroad Warfare

XVI

The Alaska Syndicate decision to use Katalla as the railroad port was another defeat for George Hazelet. He had financial interests in townsites at both Valdez and Cordova, but in the fall of 1906 it appeared that neither one would be developed by the Copper River and Northwestern Railway. The Alaska Syndicate formed the Katalla Company to serve as contractor for the railroad construction and hired M.K. Rodgers to be the chief engineer. Although most of the railroad workers were moved from Valdez to Katalla or to camps along the Copper River, the Katalla Company had a new job for Hazelet.

Firebox for the first Copper River steamer CHITTYNA—weight 5700 pounds.
George Hazelet (left), George Meals (second from left)

In order to facilitate roadbed construction along the Copper River above the glaciers, the Seattle-based managers arranged to have a 70-ton river steamer, the CHITTYNA, built in sections that could be freighted on sleds from Valdez to the Copper River over Tasnuna Pass during the winter of 1906-1907. Hazelet was placed in charge of hauling the boat sections to the Copper River where Capt. George Hill could assemble the steamer. Among the men that Hazelet hired to do the packing were A.J. Meals and his son, George, who gave the following account:

> In February 1907 the riverboat CHITTYNA arrived in bundles, also some 20 or more horses... I left March 12th with the boiler. It weighed 5,700 pounds. ... Going up the switchback I used a block and tackle in order for the horses to stay on the trail. ... Used six horses on the cable and one in the staves. Took three or four days to reach the summit.
>
> Going down the river in places had to rough-lock (hitch ropes to the trees, hauling back on the sled) to keep it from breaking loose and running over the horses pulling it. [1].

The river steamer CHITTYNA in Tasnuna Pass.
THE HINCHEY-ALAGCO COLLECTION, ANCHORAGE MUSEUM OF HISTORY & ART. B62.1A.136

By August 1907, the CHITTYNA was assembled and hauling supplies to the upriver camps while the bridges over the Copper River were still under construction.

The people back in Valdez hailed Hazelet's success in transporting the steamship over the mountain pass as proof that the route from Valdez was the best way to reach Alaska's interior. On April 25, 1907, *The Alaska Prospector* commented:

> The expeditious and economical manner in which the Steamer CHITTYNA has been transported from here to the Copper river is the greatest object lesson there has ever been as to the practicability of a railroad from this point. ... This steamer, 110 feet long, 23 feet beam, weighing over one hundred tons, with one single piece weighing four tons, was taken by horses, without a dollars worth of work being done to reduce the grades as nature made them.
>
> Through policies adopted in ignorance of conditions as they really exist we may be sidetracked for a while but we have the natural metropolis and railroad center of Alaska and must eventually win out.
>
> The pluck of Geo. Hazelet in tackling this apparently difficult task is something to be proud of and his success will make a great many people sit up and take notice.

With this job successfully completed, Hazelet and his son, Calvin, left Valdez with Stephen Birch to spend the summer visiting the Bonanza mine and other portions of the copper district. (2)

The Katalla Company's other construction efforts during 1907 were not as successful as the transport of the CHITTYNA. M.K. Rodgers spent lavishly on building a breakwater at Katalla even though development work on Bering River coal mines was suspended when President Theodore Roosevelt withdrew Alaskan coal fields from entry in November of 1906, pending passage of new federal regulations. Over 900 coal claims had already been staked in the Bering River field under the provisions of the Coal Law of 1904, which stipulated that a claim could contain no more than 160 acres and that no more than four claims could be combined for mine development prior to the granting of patents. (3) Since development of a profitable mine on such small acreage was unlikely, claimants hoped for a new law with more generous land provisions.

Members of the Roosevelt administration led by Chief Forester Gifford Pinchot, however, were opposed to releasing more federal lands to private ownership. The problem of obtaining patents for the coal claims was further complicated in 1907 when the Bering River coal fields were included in the newly created Chugach National Forest. (4) The claimants, many of whom were influencial western businessmen, still had faith that they would get their patents, particularly since Richard Ballinger, a former mayor of Seattle, was heading the Interior Department's Land Office and helping to develop the new legislation. In order to assure a supply of coal for the railroad once patents were issued, officials of the Alaska Syndicate purchased an option on a half-interest in a group of 33 claims managed by Clarence Cunningham, a mining engineer from Idaho. [5]

Katalla Company engine and crew at Bruner Crossing, July 14, 1907.
ANCHORAGE MUSUEM OF HISTORY & ART. B89.14.41

In the expectation that coal would soon be mined, both the Copper River and Northwestern and the Alaska Pacific and Terminal Railway, known as the Bruner line, hastened construction at Katalla. Provisions of the Homestead Act of 1898 allowed competing railroads to utilize simular routes, but since Copper River and Northwestern tracks, running in from the breakwater, had to cross the Bruner line's right of way, conflict was inevitable. On July 4, a news dispatch from Valdez carried the following account of bloodshed at Katalla:

> Under the protection of fire from detachments of armed men, a party of Guggenheim laborers succeeded in laying track over the disputed Bruner right-of-way at Catalla yesterday, but one man is dead, another will die, and nine more are seriously wounded by bullets from the Bruner blockhouses.
>
> Tony de Pascal led the construction party and received $1,000 reward offered by Guggenheim to the man who would lead the attacking forces. Soon after he was shot dead by one of his own men, who mistook him for a member of the opposing force.

Men who arrived here on the BERTHA today say the Bruner forces are gathering reinforcements and that another conflict is momentarily expected.

The men were wounded while capturing the big steel go-devil, upon which the Bruner forces relied to keep the men off the right-of-way. The men stormed the machine, which was swung viciously back and forth by a donkey engine, while the Bruner contingent in the blockhouses kept up a brisk fire. This was returned from a half dozen camps which the Guggenheim people had stationed in a radius of several hundred yards, commanding a view of the disputed grounds. The go-devil was finally captured.

The representative of the Bruner company here is making every endeavor to have the territorial government cable Washington for troops to prevent further bloodshed. In this he is backed up by the residents of the town, who are sure of a continuation of hostilities. [6]

This account is an example of the exaggerated reports circulated throughout Alaska from Valdez, and of the tendency to blame everything on the Guggenheims. The details given in this news release were not accurate. Jack McCord, who was a participant in the confrontation, contended that Bruner workers actually were paid off and that the shooting was for show. [7] Tony de Pascal was the only man wounded. He recovered, but was drowned in a rescue attempt at Katalla the following year. [8] The two rival railroads continued working through the summer with no further fighting and Judge James Wickersham decided the right of way controversy in favor of the Copper River and Northwestern.

While railroad workers were fighting at Katalla, officials of the Alaska Syndicate in New York and Seattle continued to argue about the best place for the railway terminal. In spite of the pressure from New York, John Rosene still favored Valdez and Capt. Jarvis was well aware of the difficulty in landing ships at Katalla after watching Revenue Marine shipmates drown while trying to land on Gulf of Alaska shores in 1891. [9] In order to get another opinion, the Katalla Company hired Erastus C. Hawkins, the railroad engineer who had worked with Heney on the White Pass and Yukon, to study the railway routes and recommend the best location for the terminal. [10]

Before Hazelet left for the Bonanza mine in June, he was aware that Hawkins would be studying the railway routes and left word that he should be apprised immediately if any word should come from Hawkins. The expected message arrived in mid-July and Hazelet returned immediately to Valdez to prepare for Hawkins' arrival. A letter from John Rosene reached him in Valdez with the following instructions:

Mr. E.C. Hawkins has been appointed Chief Engineer of the C.R. and will leave here on the S.S. SARATOGA about the 18th and will be due in Katalla about the 23rd or 24th of this month. When he leaves here I will give him a letter of introduction to you. Mr. Hawkins will undoubtedly stop over several days at Katalla for the purpose of examining the line there. What I would advise him to do will be to make his examination at Katalla as far up as the Martin River, and then go to Valdez and go in from there over the Tasnuna route to the Copper River, and take the steamer down as far as the canyon and then small boats from there, which will enable him to examine the river route quicker than he can by making his way up the river from Katalla.

What I expect of you and particularly of Mr. Deyo, is to show Mr. Hawkins all the advantages of the Valdez route as compared with the Katalla route. To show them fairly and squarely and to make no statements that will not be corroborated by the facts as they actually exist; that is to say, that I want Mr. Hawkins to be possessed of all the information possible concerning the proposition of railway construction in the Copper River Valley; both from Katalla and Valdez, with a view of enabling him to have a correct opinion as to what really is the best thing to do. ... I expect you to consider the contents of this letter absolutely confidential and make no statements or remarks to anyone that would lead them to think that there is any possibility of changing the railroad back to Valdez, and that the whole thing is simply a question of showing the advantages of the Valdez route over that from Katalla. [11]

Hawkins then wrote Hazelet that he would be delayed, and sent his assistant, Alfred Williams, to help in making necessary arrangements and to "have the opportunity to go over the harbor situation and terminal tracks and other parts of the line in the vicinity of Valdez."

Early in August 1907, Hazelet was approached by Henry Durr Reynolds, an entrepeneur from Boston who owned a copper mine on Prince William Sound. Reynolds announced his intention to build a 34-mile electric railroad to the summit and offered to buy the rock work in Keystone Canyon on which the Copper River and Northwestern had spent about $85,000. Hazelet told him that any such decision would have to be made by his employers and refused the suggestion that he join or invest in the Reynolds enterprise. Reynolds then sent a telegram to Daniel Guggenheim in New York offering to buy the right of way.

On the evening of August 10, Reynolds convened a mass meeting at which he challenged the people of Valdez to subscribe money for his project, the Alaska Home Railway. Alaska's former governor, John G. Brady, chaired the meeting with

Reynolds. Even though Brady's involvement in promoting the Reynolds development projects had cost him the governorship in 1906 when it was determined to be in conflict with his official duties, the presence of this white-haired Presbyterian missionary lent an aura of respectability to Reynolds' proposals. By the end of the evening the citizens of Valdez had pledged $106,000 of the $340,000 necessary to construct the road to the summit. (12)

Valdez City Council passing franchise of the Alaska Home Railway, August 12, 1907. Reynolds (seated center of front row), Brady (seated third from right)
ALASKA STATE LIBRARY. PCA277.7.7

Judge James Wickersham, who was holding court in Valdez at the time, wrote the following account in his diary on August 11:

> People are out staking lots this morning, and the rosy dawn is just dawning. However, it is an interesting proposition. Reynolds and his company have just purchased the Alaska Steamship Co. — the PORTLAND, BERTHA, JEANNIE, etc. and have declared rate war on the Northwestern Co., and now this Ry. project is launched just at a time when Hawkins is expected here to change the Northwestern Ry. back from Katalla to Valdez. The N.W. people admit the Katalla terminal to be error after spending nearly half a million dollars on it and when they turn back to look at this old Valdez project Reynolds jumps in with his scheme, and binds the businessmen in 3-year rate contracts, takes possession of strategic points, gathers a

large popular subscription, and is in possession of much that is vital and will cost the N.W. large amounts of money if they attempt to dislodge.

Wickersham did not explain the source of his knowledge about the plans for the Copper River and Northwestern Railway, but at this time he was still on friendly terms with Stephen Birch and probably had confidential information from him. Birch had returned to Valdez shortly after Hazelet. Wickersham's diary entry continued:

> They presented a franchise to the town for a 99 year right-of-way, agreeing to protect the town from the inroads of the glacial stream for that time as a consideration!! Foxy! ... Reynolds has also bought half interest in the *Prospector* and will install a first class newspaper plant— so he told me. They have their newspaper people with them and they have certainly gone to shouting "before the snow flies."
>
> Gov. Brady opened the mass meeting last night **by reading from the Bible!** the story from Nehemiah about the valiant young man who gathered a few resolute souls around him and rebuilt the walls of Jerusalem — and they took Reynolds for the young and ardent soul...

Reynolds continued buying up properties and businesses in Valdez for exorbitant sums until he controlled the banks, the utilities, the stores and hotels, and even had investments in laundries and music stores. On August 14, the town turned out en masse with picks and shovels to grade the first mile of the Home Railway grade. *The Alaska Prospector* commented with enthusiasm:

> ... Every available team in the vicinity of Valdez was pressed into service. Work was given to all applicants. With steady efficiency the work progressed and before nightfall a splendid start had been made on the long journey to the interior. The town is dazed by the rapidity with which each move is made. Only four days ago the proposition was laid before the people by Brady and Reynolds and here we are with the long hoped for railroad actually under construction. Obviously Reynolds outfit is as efficient in railroading as in mining and no one doubts the success of the project. Subscriptions continue to roll in. The other sections of Alaska are beginning to add their contributions and hourly the movement gains strengths. The resourcefulness of Valdez is demonstrated in the high character of the men who have lined up with Reynolds and in the way every requisite for immediate construction work is promptly forthcoming. It is as though a wizard's wand had aroused the dormant energies of a mighty people.
>
> The town is united as never before and every petty difference is buried beneath a whirlwind of enthusiastic activity. Every local business is undergoing rapid

reorganization in preparation for the big boom. Lots have been filed upon to the far outskirts of the city. New buildings are being planned. Rush orders are going out for new supplies. The harbor fleet is scattering to the various Sound ports to bring men and timber. Thanks to the policy of utilizing to the utmost local resources there is work for everyone and new business for all established concerns. Never has there been such a spirit of hopefulness and enterprise in Valdez. [13]

Valdez citizens grading Alaska Home Railway, August 13, 1907.
ALASKA STATE LIBRARY. PCA277.7.8

Wickersham still had doubts. On August 18, as he prepared to leave Valdez, he commented in his diary: "Reynolds is exhibiting signs of greater genius or ranker insanity in his 'plunging' in real estate and other schemes here. The town is greatly excited in a speculative way — and the end is not yet."

When Wickersham arrived at Katalla, he observed that Reynolds and his agents were there "gathering up men — snatching them from the other roads." Mark Morrisey, an agent for the Home Railway who had previously worked with many of the railroad workers at Seward on the defunct Alaska Central Railway, plied them with drinks and promises of increased wages and succeeded in luring several hundred to Valdez. [14]

As boatloads of railway workers poured into Valdez to work on the Alaska Home Railway, George Hazelet, fearing for the safety of the 40 to 50 men he had engaged to work on the Copper River and Northwestern grade in Keystone Canyon, requested that United States Marshal Perry provide a deputy marshal to protect the grade at no cost to the government. It apparently had been a common practice of Marshal Perry to appoint additional deputy marshals when a breach of the peace was imminent. [15] The specific man that Hazelet requested was not available, but Duncan Dickson was deputized on August 22. Several days later, Edward C. Hasey, who had previously been a deputy marshal in Valdez, arrived back from Southeastern Alaska and was deputized by Deputy Marshal James Lathrop at the suggestion of Marshal Perry. [16]

The first rail for the Alaska Home Railway, September 16, 1907.
ALASKA STATE LIBRARY. PCA192.17

Hazelet's resolve to protect the Keystone Canyon rock work was fortified by a letter from M.K. Rodgers, written on August 23 from Katalla, which stated:

> Please take the necessary steps to protect the rights of the Copper River and N.W. Ry. line in Keystone Canyon and around Valdez. Mr. E.C. Hawkins is going up on this boat and he will confer with you about the matter, and any arrangements you enter into under advisement with him will be all right. We wish to protect the right of way of the C.R. & N.W. Ry. from trespass by any other

railway, until you are advised to the contrary. If you require any funds for this, please advise and we will supply you with the same for any necessary expenses.

When Hawkins arrived in Valdez, he instructed Hazelet to post "No Trespassing" signs along the Copper River and Northwestern grade in Keystone Canyon. Conflict in Keystone Canyon was predicted in *The Katalla Herald* on September 14:

> The Alaska Home Railway people threaten to do things to the Copper River and Northwestern Railroad Company because the latter is doing some work on its right-of-way through Keystone Canyon. The Valdez Company declares that the work is being done only for the purpose of impeding work on the Reynolds-Brady electric tram car project and predict that a pick-handle fight, or worse, will result as soon as Reynolds returns from Seattle, where he is now sojourning.

The Home Railway promoters claimed that the Copper River and Northwestern Railway had relinquished rights to the Keystone Canyon right of way because they had not completed construction within the two year period allowed. However, the Homestead Act of 1898 stipulated that Congressional action was necessary to revoke rights of way that had been granted.

In late August, when James O'Reilly, a foreman for the Home Railway, confronted Hazelet and Dickson on the canyon grade, they warned him; "You go in at your peril. We will defend that place like a man would defend his home." [17] Shortly thereafter Hazelet sent the following letter to Hasey:

> Dear Sir. I expected to come out this AM but find I cannot. I may get out tonight. Have tried all day to get in touch and have a talk with Mr. Stevens (Blamey Stevens, Chief Engineer for the Home Railway) but have been unable to do so up to this time, 9 PM. I feel that if he would meet me halfway we could get along without any trouble out there. I simply want to impress on you and Dickson to be patient and not get excited. Take it cool, but I look to you boys to protect our rights. The right-of-way is ours until Congress declares otherwise and we are wholly within our rights in protecting it. Stay by the thing until I see you. [18]

At first, Stevens refused to talk to Hazelet, but later in the day he tried to arrange a meeting in order to present a proposal that the Home Railway build a spur to the Hazelet townsite and promote a city there in return for the Keystone Canyon right of way. [19]

Hazelet wrote Hasey again on September 6: "Dear Sir. All of your requests will be looked after by me." [20] This letter undoubtedly refers to Hasey's request for firearms and ammunition, which Hasey later claimed he had requested in order to hunt bear that were molesting the camps. [21]

Some of the messages between Hasey and Hazelet were delivered by R.J. Boryer, an attorney for the Katalla Company. On September 18, when Boryer apprised Syndicate officials in Seattle of the impending trouble, Jarvis wired Hazelet: "Have no trouble with Reynolds outfit under any circumstance. Wait." The same day Syndicate attorney Bogle sent Hawkins the following telegram: "Think maintenance force of men on Valdez line unnecessary expense. Conflicting claims will be determined by priority filings." [22]

When Hazelet received the Jarvis telegram, Hawkins had already left for Seattle to make his report, but Stephen Birch happened to be dining with Hazelet. [23] After discussing the situation with Birch, Hazelet wired Jarvis on September 19: "Do not anticipate any trouble, but will hold canyon under instructions from Rodgers, Hawkins and of Stephen Birch. Use Bedford-McNeil." [24] This last reference was to the code that Syndicate officials used in many of their telegrams. Hazelet felt that the Jarvis telegram might have been read by other parties and weakened his position.

Northwestern Railway "cut" in which the Home Railway men were shot, showing the marshal's tent and barricade, September 25, 1907.
ALASKA STATE LIBRARY. PCA192.26

Upon receiving reports of a potential conflict, Marshal Perry, who was in Fairbanks, requested information from Deputy Marshal Lathrop in Valdez. Lathrop responded on September 19:

In regard to Hasey, reports conflict, but I am satisfied he has overstepped his authority. Hazelet is not trying to hold the canyon but only his grade in it. Advise that you wire Hasey and Dickson to be careful and involve this office in no way. Also wire Hazelet to same effect. Also wire Stevens that they have been instructed to confine their authority to proper limits. I look for no trouble out there of any nature. It is a simple bluff. (25)

The Homestead Act of 1898 clearly stated that no railway could restrict passage through a narrow defile to another railway, but Keystone Canyon was considered to be wide enough for two railroads. The old right of way for the Alaska Yukon Railroad, which the Home Railroad was following, actually ran along the south side of Keystone Canyon rather than the north side where the Copper River and Northwestern crews had done their rock work. Colonel Swanitz, the former Alaska Yukon engineer who was consulting for the Home Railway, still strongly favored the route along the south side and wanted the Home Railway engineer, Blamey Stevens, to abandon any hopes of using the Copper River and Northwestern rock work. (26)

Deputy Marshal Lathrop was unduly optimistic in his assessment that there would be no trouble when the Home Railway workers approached Keystone Canyon. Early in the morning of September 25, 1907, watchmen at a barricade

Rearview of marshal's tent and barricade on Northwestern Railway grade, September 25, 1907.
ALASKA STATE LIBRARY. PCA277.7.127

that Hasey had erected on the Copper River and Northwestern grade realized that Home Railway workers were gathering near the entrance to the canyon. When about 260 men carrying picks and shovels had arrived, Charles Ingersoll, an attorney from Ketchikan, stood on a tree stump and gave a rousing speech, telling the workmen: "The only way to get any money or anything is to jump this cut and take possession of it." Ingersoll told the assembled men that he had been to Juneau and found that the Copper River and Northwestern no longer had rights in the canyon. Mark Morrisey, who had recruited many of the men at Katalla with promises of increased wages, then led a group, carrying stones, shovels, clubs and pick handles, toward the Copper River and Northwestern barricade.

Bringing in the wounded Home Railway men shot in Keystone Canyon, September 25, 1907.
ALASKA STATE LIBRARY. PCA192.24

Even after Hasey, who was stationed behind the barricade, ordered them to stop, the Home Railway men kept coming. In an effort to prevent bloodshed, Copper River and Northwestern Superintendent O'Neill ran out to the approaching mob, shouting, "Go back! Someone is going to get hurt." Morrisey and some of the other men grabbed O'Neill and carried him ahead of them as a hostage. About this time, Hasey realized that men with dynamite were climbing up on the summer trail above the barricade. He fired in the air but the men kept coming. Then he fired low at the ground in front of the approaching men. Bullets ricocheted off the stones and several men fell with wounds in their legs and feet.

[27] Some of the advancing Home Railway men turned and fled, while others stopped to care for their fallen comrades. Word of the conflict spread quickly and ambulance wagons soon arrived from Valdez to carry the wounded men to the local hospitals. Deputy marshals arrested the men that did the shooting. [28]

The confrontation in Keystone Canyon was over almost as soon as it had started, but it lasted long enough to have a profound effect on the careers of Hazelet, Jarvis and Birch.

Manic Manipulater

In many ways Henry Durr Reynolds epitomized the early 20th century Alaska boomer. A natural salesman with boundless energy, he had complete faith in his ability to perform miracles. Eastern investors and Alaskan sourdoughs believed in him and eagerly invested their life savings in his Alaskan enterprises, but the tall, handsome Bostonian was too good to be true — too visionary and too energetic.

Reynolds came north early in the summer of 1902 to take over the Aurora Gold Mining Company on Kachemak Bay, in which he had invested on the assumption that the property would be as rich as any mine in Alaska. The New York promoters of the Aurora Company had erected 15 or 20 buildings, an expensive stamp mill and an electric plant on the property. These improvements impressed investors, but, upon arrival in Alaska, Reynolds found the Aurora property to be worthless. While being swindled himself, however, he became aware of what it would take to entice investors with schemes of his own.

Realizing the potential for profit in combining mining, town growth and railroad construction, Reynolds concentrated on the port of Valdez, which he envisioned might become Alaska's future San Francisco. Enroute back to New York to report on the failure of Aurora, he acquired property on Latouche Island in Prince William Sound near the Beatson copper mine.

The young, energetic Easterner mesmerized Alaska Governor Brady, a former Presbyterian missionary with naive faith in the goodness of his fellow man. During the summer of 1903 Reynolds worked with Brady to revitalize the governor's Sitka Sawmill Company, and incorporated the Reynolds-Alaskan Development Company with Governor Brady as a trustee. The following year Reynolds circulated promotional literature in the eastern United States, which stated that the Reynolds-Alaskan Development Company was organized under the resident directorship of the governor of Alaska to combine under one management valuable properties on the southern Alaska coast, principally gold and copper mines, and oil, coal and timber lands.

Although the use of Brady's name lent credibility to the Reynolds enterprises, it did not sit well with Interior Secretary Hitchcock, who thought it inappropriate for the governor to use his office to promote a private enterprise. Brady resigned under pressure, and then the very mention of the fact that Alaska's governor was resigning to participate more actively in the Reynolds Development Company impressed eastern investors.

Reynolds reported that he was starting development work again at Aurora with his British brother-in-law, Blamey Stevens, as chief engineer. He moved ahead elsewhere in a flamboyant manner, renting office space in Boston's tallest building and constructing a model town, called Reynolds, on Latouche Island. He built a tramway there for show but never actually operated a mine. Eastern investors visited the Latouche Island property with ex-Governor Brady as tour guide, and Reynolds invited a number of prominent Valdezians to the inauguration of his new power plant in November 1906.

The "Reynolds System" was building to a climax in the summer of 1907. In a flurry of activity, Reynolds, with Brady by his side, descended upon Valdez with a proposal to build an electric railway to the summit of Thompson Pass and subscribed a third of the necessary money from donations by townspeople during a mass meeting that resembled a religious revival. He then proceeded to secure options on most of the leading commercial interests in town and paid $47,000 for an option on a steamship line. He bought the local newspaper and offered to buy an interest in the *Alaska-Yukon Magazine*, which printed a glowing description of "Renascent Valdez." His plans included rebuilding the business district with beautifully designed buildings having wide porch roofs to protect pedestrians from rain and snow. He promised to provide libraries, museums, a school of mines, and eventually a university. Reynolds appeared to believe in the reality of his grandiose plans, and Valdez believed in Reynolds.

Reynolds left Valdez shortly after the mass meeting to raise more money in the Pacific Northwest. Wickersham, who was on the same boat, described Reynolds' aberrant behavior during the voyage in his diary.

When Reynolds failed in Seattle to raise the money necessary to exercise his options to purchase Valdez property, he tried Tacoma, but that city wasn't buying either. Then Reynolds disappeared.

Within two weeks the Reynolds empire collapsed. The bank in Valdez closed and railroad workers, lured to Valdez on promises of increased pay, were left penniless, many not even receiving pay for their work in August.

Ex-Governor Brady faced financial ruin and the censure of friends who had invested in the Reynolds empire, while Reynolds, his blond "messiah", took refuge in an insane asylum, reported to have suffered a complete nervous breakdown.

Reynolds recovered sufficiently in a year to suggest recovery plans to his stockholders and congratulate Wickersham on his election as Alaska delegate to Congress. He did not return to Alaska until 1916 when he appeared in Seward and tried to raise $15,000 in local subscriptions to establish a smelter. Some of his former Valdez associates backed him but most Alaskans still remembered the 1907 debacle, so Reynolds disappeared again.

In 1928, the Reynolds name appeared again in newspapers, this time in New York City, where he was arrested for vagrancy after wandering away from the psychopathic pavilion of Philadelphia General Hospital where he had been under treatment for a year and a half. He was 54 years old and claimed to be head of the non-existent Reynolds Publishing Company at No.1 Park Avenue. His son and daughter-in-law appeared at the Centre Street court to take care of him.

⁂

Whether H.D. Reynolds was an unprincipled confidence man or a victim of psychotic mood swings — or both — his infectious enthusiasm during two months in the summer of 1907 altered the course of Alaska's history.

Trials and Tribulations

The shots that rang out in Keystone Canyon reverberated throughout Alaska, reinforcing the populist outcry against the "Guggenheims" for attempting to monopolize railroad construction. The news media in Valdez, controlled by Reynolds' associates, sent the following dispatches:

VALDEZ, Sept. 25 — Valdez was shocked as never before when it became known that half a dozen surveyors and workmen employed on the Alaska Home railway had been shot down in cold blood this morning by men employed by the Guggenheims to guard the right of way through Keystone canyon, fifteen miles from here.

The Home railway party started in this morning to make a preliminary survey of the Keystone canyon. They were unarmed and anticipated no trouble of any description. When they were about one hundred yards up the canyon they were met with a rifle fire from men concealed behind a barricade on the side of the canyon.

As the party advanced the Guggenheim foreman told the surveyors to stop or be shot. Thinking that it was only a bluff the men continued to work, when suddenly they were met with a fusillade from the guns of the concealed men. The casualties were as follows:

E. CHRISTY, shot in the foot.
THAYNE HACKMAN, Seattle, shot in the thigh.
FRED REINHARDT, shot in the left knee.
JOHN PHILLIPS, shot in hip.
CHRIS OLSEN, shot in breast, near heart.
V. HUTCHINS, shot in the hand.

The Alaska Home men could offer no resistance and left the canyon as soon as the wounded could be carried out. Word was at once sent into Valdez and ambulances were dispatched for the wounded men, and they are expected to reach town late this evening. A score of deputy marshals armed with rifles have been dispatched to the scene to arrest the men who did the shooting.

Feeling in town is running very high and it is feared that the citizens will handle the culprits roughly if they get their hands on them. The feeling is particularly bitter against Ed Hasey, a former United States deputy marshal, who is said to be the leader of the Guggenheim forces.

The Guggenheims are endeavoring to prevent the Alaska Home Railway company, recently organized by the citizens of Valdez, from building their railroad through Keystone canyon, claiming that they have the exclusive right thereto, in spite of the fact that they abandoned it last year and moved to Katalla. [1]

VALDEZ, Sept. 26 — Intense indignation is still felt over the brutal shooting down yesterday in Keystone canyon by Guggenheim men of six employees of the Alaska Home railway. Ex-Deputy Marshal Ed Hasey and R. Dickson, who did the shooting, have been arrested, but as yet have had no preliminary hearing, as the authorities are afraid to take action in the present state of public opinion.

Five of the victims of the shooting are in the hospital here, and it is feared that at least one may die. The latter is John Phillips, who was shot through the hip and groin with a soft-nosed bullet. The wound is a terrible one and it will be almost a miracle if it does not have a fatal result.

Chris Olsen, who was shot in the breast, is also very seriously hurt, and the doctors say that he can not be pronounced out of danger for some time yet.

Ed Hasey has confessed to doing the shooting and appears to be proud of it. He has a record as a bad man in Southeastern Alaska. The Guggenheim officials say that they did not order the men to shoot, and that they exceeded their authority. People here, however, find it hard to reconcile this statement with the fact that all the Guggenheim men were heavily armed.

In the canyon all is quiet. There are still some Guggenheim men in the camp, but all Alaska Home people are camped below the scene of the trouble.

Officials of the Alaska Home company today say that it is far from their intention to take any offensive steps, and that such has never been their intention. They maintain that they are anxious for a peaceful settlement of the dispute and will bring the matter into the courts, but they are determined to proceed with the construction of the road. [2]

John Phillips did not die, as predicted above, but Fred Reinhardt succumbed to blood poisoning in Valdez several days later, following amputation. The wounds sustained by Phillips and Reinhardt were jagged and contaminated, not from soft-nosed bullets, but from bullets that had ricochetted off the ground. [3] Olsen left the following day for Seattle and was not heard from thereafter. [4]

The telegram that Hazelet sent to Governor W.B. Hoggatt in Juneau carried a differing version of the incident:

> A mob headed by officials of the Alaska Home Railway attacked employees of Copper River and Northwestern Railway who were in peaceable possession of grade in Keystone Canyon. A fight ensued and six wounded. Preparations are being made to renew attack, which will result in loss of life. Ask department to order troops to scene to prevent further riot. [5]

The Seattle papers that printed news of the Keystone Canyon shooting also carried accounts of an interview with Hawkins, who had just arrived in Seattle after experiencing delays and witnessing difficulty in unloading supplies at Katalla. Although Hawkins refused to give a positive statement without conferring with Syndicate officials, the articles speculated that Katalla would be abandoned as the harbor, although work on a railroad spur to the coal fields would continue. [6]

District Attorney Nathaniel Harlan, who was in Valdez at the time of the shooting, took charge and assured Governor Hoggatt that he could control the situation. [7] Harlan then arrested George Hazelet, in addition to Hasey and Dickson, and jailed them under heavy bond. [8] Hazelet, who was charged as an accessory before the fact because he had supplied the guns, was freed after posting $30,000 bond. Remembering the fate of Barrett Scott back in O'Neill, Nebraska, Hazelet feared for his life and the safety of his family. A local doctor allowed the family to take refuge temporarily in the hospital because public opinion in Valdez was strong against the "Guggenheims." [9] Harlan had a "well known enmity" towards Hazelet and stated publicly that he was responsible for the armed conflict. [10]

Governor Hoggatt arrived in Valdez several days after the shooting to make his own investigation of the situation. He criticized Harlan for not having also charged the Home Railway officials with instigating a riot, but soon had other problems that took priority. On October 9, the Reynolds Bank in Valdez closed its door, not having sufficient funds to meet its liabilities. Hoggatt wired Jarvis, who was in charge of Syndicate activites in Seattle: "400 idle men Valdez without funds account collapse Home Railway. Can you employ any Katalla. If so how many." Jarvis responded immediately: "Believe we can employ all idle men. Hold men until you hear from me." The following day Silas Eccles, president of the Copper River and Northwestern, confirmed by telegram from New York: "Hawkins here.

Can employ all men. Will transport to Katalla." About 75 workers took advantage of the offer and left for Katalla on October 15. [11]

The extent of Reynolds' defaults were summarized in *The Katalla Herald* on October 19:

> ... 406 men were employed by the company and the total sum due them amounted to $30,000, of which $12,000 was for the August labor account. There is also due local Valdez merchants about $20,000, and Reynolds' Seattle liabilities are placed at $75,000 besides the bank's liabilities which are estimated at $85,000.

A month earlier the same paper had described Reynolds' business ventures: "That is to say Reynolds buys a $1,200 Valdez business for $2,500 and forthwith capitalizes it at $250,000, sells stock and promises dividends out of the water. Which reminds one of the line of the old song, 'I may be crazy.'" [12] This description turned out to be prophetic. After he had been unsuccessful in trying to raise more money in Seattle and Tacoma, Reynolds disappeared around October 19. He failed to use tickets he had purchased on the YUCATAN to return to Valdez, and was last seen in Seattle boarding a Northern Pacific train, whistling "When Johnny Comes Marching Home." [13] Subsequently he was confined to a mental hospital for the first of several admissions. [14]

⁂

After preliminary hearings, Hazelet and Dickson were released, but Hasey was charged with manslaughter. [15] Governor Hoggatt, still upset that District Attorney Harlan had not prosecuted the Home Railway employees, wrote the Secretary of Interior on October 26 requesting the removal of Harlan on the grounds that he was unfit to assume the burden of responsibility because of indulgence in alcohol. [16] The citizens of Valdez, already polarized by the railroad issue, took sides in the Hoggatt versus Harlan controversy and bombarded the Interior Secretary with testimonials either for or against the district attorney. The territorial Republican convention, held in Valdez, endorsed a resolution asking President Roosevelt to make a thorough investigation of the Keystone Canyon shooting and Hoggatt's "unwarranted interference with the United States marshal's office and also that of the district attorney in the prosecution of the parties charged with the shooting of railroad laborers." [17]

Governor Hoggatt was not the only official who questioned Harlan's competence. Judge James Wickersham of Alaska's Third Judicial District commented several times in his diary about Harlan's decline and increasing alcoholism following the death of a son. [18] Eventually Wickersham himself wrote Attorney

General Bonaparte requesting Harlan's removal, [19] and Harlan was forced to resign on the grounds of poor health.

Before resigning, Harlan sent Attorney General Bonaparte a lengthy diatribe accusing Hoggatt of favoring the Guggenheim interests, which contained the following reference to Hazelet:

> Gov. Hoggatt was continually associated with Mr. Blum, Hazelet, and the friends of Hazelet during all the time he spent in Valdez, and it is perfectly natural that he was influenced by them and he became more radical and rabid in his position in favor of the defendants, except Hasey, and it seemed to be agreed by the defendants and their immediate friends that Hasey should by sacrificed for the good of Hazelet and company, and inasmuch as Hasey was an appointed Deputy Marshal and had a commission at the time, the odium of the shooting and killing might rest on the offices of the Government. ... The Copper River and Northwestern does not want the odium of murder to rest upon their manager at Valdez, or upon any of their men if they can avoid it, hence they are going to bend every energy and employ every means possible to have their employees acquitted. [20]

Early in 1908, the grand jury convened in Valdez to consider the Hasey case. From the beginning of the trouble with the Keystone Canyon right of way, Hazelet relied on the local law firm of Donahoe and Ostrander to defend him, but Syndicate officials engaged the Seattle-based firm of Bogle and Spooner to represent Hasey. At the insistence of Stephen Birch, John A.Carson, a trial lawyer from Salem, Oregon, was added to the defense team. [21]

The grand jury indicted Hasey for second degree murder in the death of Reinhardt and several counts of shooting with the intent to kill the other victims. The defense succeeded in getting a change of venue to Juneau for the Hasey trial. In answer to a request from District Attorney Harlan, Attorney General Bonaparte assigned U.S. Secret Service Agent Eugene McAdams to watch the trial for any evidence of tampering with witnesses or jurymen. [22]

McAdams communicated frequently with his associates in the Justice Department during March and April of 1908 while the trial was taking place in Juneau. He recognized that the trial was a "contest between Hoggatt and Harlan," and was unhappy because he was "practically isolated so far as social amenities are concerned." [23]

More than 70 witnesses for both the prosecution and defense arrived from Valdez and other Alaskan ports. Upon arrival in Juneau, the prosecution discharged some of their presumptive witnesses because their testimony actually favored the defense. Ironically, M.R. Morrisey, who had led the Home Railway workers into Keystone Canyon on the day of the shooting, was among the men who were then retained as defense witnesses. Morrisey was the Home Railway agent who had visited Katalla the previous August to lure railway workers to Valdez with promises of better pay, and then had urged the same men to advance on the Copper River and Northwestern grade, in order to assure that they would be paid.

After the shooting, Morrisey was one of the men who accepted employment with Copper River and Northwestern Railway. During the trial, he continued to be a leader of the railroad workers and took charge of housing and feeding the defense witnesses.

Although Bogle and Spooner retained a Valdez attorney, Fred Brown, to examine witnesses during the trial, John A. Carson also went to Juneau and assumed the responsibility for taking care of the expenses of the witnesses. Syndicate Treasurer Jarvis, who remained in Seattle, repeatedly complained of the expense, and Carson responded by describing the problems he was encountering with the witnesses:

> ... those witnesses are a troublesome lot. We have to exert ourselves to the utmost to see that they present a half decent appearance in the court room, and yet they are running around town, fighting and drinking at night, and generally making a nuisance of themselves. I have had experience in the past with railroad navvies, but this bunch is certainly unique. It is no light task to endeavor to have such men come into the court, and by their conduct and testimony, impress the court favorably for their client. Their conduct and habits on the outside of the courtroom, if known, would most prejudicially affect their testimony, and as I say, we have to exert ourselves to the utmost to uphold them in order to get the benefit of their testimony. [24]

In spite of concern that the trial would be bitter, no violence occurred. At the end of April *The Alaska Dispatch* reported that Hasey had been acquitted and gave the following report about the ease with which the verdict was reached:

> It took the Hasey jury less than two hours to eat dinner and secure the verdict. It is probable that the jury spent more minutes deliberating over their dinner than they did in arriving at a verdict. When the baliff notified Judge Gunnison at 8:30 that the jury was ready to report, it caused some anxiety on the part of the defense as they never in their most visionary moment expected the jury to acquit on practically the first ballot. When the verdict was read there was little or no demonstration. Hasey being deaf did not know that he was free man until told so by his attorney. The defense stood on self defense, protecting property entrusted to his care, exercising his right as a deputy U.S. Marshal in quelling a riot and protecting the life of O'Neill and Biggs.

The case took twenty-eight days of the federal court's time and was perhaps the freest case from personal bickering between council ever conducted in the federal court here. The attorneys on both sides left nothing undone but kept free from violent entanglements.

Another remarkable thing in connection with the case was the excellent deportment of the witnesses on both sides. Several were accused of throwing down their friends, but whatever bad feeling existed was concealed from the public. [25]

Hasey was a free man, at least while the prosecution considered whether to try him again on the lesser charges of shooting with the intent to kill. Although the trial had been peaceful on the surface, it further divided Alaskans in their support or opposition to "the Guggenheims." Alaskan newspapers tended to support one side or the other. *The Daily Alaska Dispatch* in Juneau blamed the Home Railway promoters for provoking the unfortunate affair:

> The excitement and visions attending the spectacular career of promoter Reynolds as a western Alaska railroad magnate has been apparent all through the famous trial just closed in the federal court. That a man like Reynolds, supported by Governor Brady, could enthuse a body of men like he did the Alaska Home railroad people is beyond belief. Juneau has stood for many false alarms, but never in her palmiest days could a Reynolds or Brady stampede the camp or loosen any coin from the proverbial iron vest which is characteristic of some of her wealthiest citizens.
>
> The Keystone canyon shooting was the climax of the Reynolds operations. It was the last rally of the promoter in securing a right of way to the interior for a railroad on paper, backed by the subscription of a few deluded victims in the far east. ... Now that the case is over what is the government going to do with these promoters? Is the grave of Fred Rhinehart no reminder that there was a swindle perpetrated in the name of the Alaska Home railroad? ... He (Hasey) has been forced to stand trial for his liberty. In the meantime Reynolds and Brady, men who are responsible to a great extent for the shooting, are allowed their liberty. They should be taken before a jury of their peers and prosecuted for fraud. [26]

The *Fairbanks Weekly Times*, on the other hand, claimed that "The government's case was poorly handled, even to such an extent as to cause much adverse criticism." The article pointed out that the prosecution had much trouble procuring evidence because the witnesses they were counting on had been given employment in lucrative positions by the Guggenheims and thereby "their mouths were closed." [27] At this time, however, there were no accusations of bribery of witnesses or jurors. Many Valdez citizens, who had lost heavily, continued to blame "the Guggenheims" for the collapse of the Reynolds empire.

— ·◦⊱⚶⊰◦· —

While the Hasey trial was taking place, the managers of the Copper River and Northwestern Railway were still debating where the port for the railroad should be located. Katalla was definitely out — autumn storms had completely destroyed the breakwater. The choice now was between Valdez and Cordova, where M.J. Heney had started his Copper River Railway in 1906. Although John Rosene, the main proponent of the Valdez port, was no longer in charge of the railroad construction, E.C. Hawkins, the consulting engineer, favored Valdez and did not want to stake his reputation on trying to build a railroad across the mud flats from Cordova. [28]

Had Valdezians not been so hostile to the Copper River and Northwestern, the railroad might well have returned to their town. The Alaska Syndicate, however, had to move quickly because the agreement with Stephen Birch and H.O. Havemeyer of Alaska Copper and Coal stipulated that the railroad had to be constructed so that copper ore could be moved from the Bonanza mine in 1910. [29] M.J. Heney still favored the Cordova route. Since he was confident that he could move fill into the mud flats in the winter on tracks laid over frozen mud, he contracted with the Alaska Syndicate to build the Copper River and Northwestern Railway from Cordova to the Bonanza mine. Hawkins, as chief engineer for the Katalla Company, assumed responsibilty for designing and constructing the three major bridges. [30]

Frontier Politics — 1908

Although Stephen Birch was moving ahead on developing the mine and railroad, he was encountering problems in persuading associates to employ his friend Judge Wickersham as an attorney for the Alaska Syndicate. Had he been more successful, the next several years would have been more pleasant for the Syndicate and the history of Alaska might have been profoundly altered.

A series of letters between Birch and Wickersham highlight the fickle nature of Alaska politics. In an April 8, 1907, letter to Wickersham, Birch explained that other directors of the Syndicate had different legal commitments:

> The consolidation of the Alaska S.S. Co. and the Northwestern S.S. Co. will not go through, any how for the present. Peabody wants too much cash. We are all good friends however and will work in harmony. I do not think this will interfere with my plans about employing general counsel but it will be necessary for me to work on our people in N.Y. Young Mr. Morgan has instructed Jarvis and Rosene to employ the law firm that young Spooner is in, so you can see where the work will have to be done. ...Spooner wants to make a yearly arrangement, but I have told Jarvis to hold him off. [1]

On June 3, Birch further explained the status in a letter to Wickersham:

> The situation is not clear as I would want it. As I wrote you some time ago, we did not purchase the Peabody line, and as a result the N.W. Commercial Co. is still managed about the same as in the past. Hartman has been acting as attorney for the N.W. Co. and Bogle for the R.R. Co.
>
> The Morgans had because of Spooner practically engaged Bogle for this year, and I am looking up the minutes of the N.W. Co. Found that Hartman had been engaged for another year at six thousand dollars per year. Bogle has not a fixed fee,

so I guess the attorney bills will be large enough by the end of the year to show good reason for a General Counsel.

I talked with all my people and they would like to have you, so I hope you plan so that you and I can get together with our people this fall and settle the matter before it comes time to renew the arrangements with Bogle and Hartman.

Am sorry we cannot have a talk now. It is so much more satisfactory than writing. ... I want you with us and, if you will help me, can do the trick. I leave tomorrow on the SARATOGA for Katalla, and expect to go inside all summer.

Saw Gov. Hoggatt. He says you are very busy. Trusting you are well. [2]

Wickersham and Alaska's territorial governor, Wilfred Hoggatt, were good friends until June 1907, when Wickersham refused to disbar a young Juneau attorney who Hoggatt felt had committed legal malpractice by representing both plaintiff and defendant in a legal case. [3] On July 1, Wickersham expressed this new antagonism to Hoggatt in his diary:

Well. Gov. Hoggatt, Shackleford and others of their — and my — friends are tearing their hair and rending their garments because I did not disbar Cobb. ...

I am as greatly disappointed as they are, for I expected decent treatment from them and did not get it. Well, they can go to the devil. I never have tempered my legal duties to suit either friends or enemies and don't intend to do so.

Finis. Governor!

Hoggatt was just as strong in his reaction to the episode. On September 13, he sent letters to both President Roosevelt and Secretary of the Interior James Garfield advising against "the longer continuance of Judge Wickersham on the bench." [4] These letters from Hoggatt were partially responsible for Wickersham's decision to resign from the bench and enter private law practice in Fairbanks. Birch responded from New York on November 15, 1907, to the news of Wickersham's resignation, and reiterated his desire to employ Wickersham:.

Dear Judge:

Your letter of October the 3rd, written from Fairbanks, received. ... I regret very much indeed that there should have arisen any unpleasantness between yourself and the Governor. I do not know all the circumstances, but think I realize how you feel, and while I am sorry that you resigned without having it understood who was to be your successor, I nevertheless feel that it is better for your own personal interest to resign from office. I am fond of Hoggatt and know that he is headstrong, but am surprised that he should undertake to interfere or take exception to your decision. I have not seen Hoggatt, but understand from others that he was disappointed with your decision. I thought Hoggatt was too big a man to be spiteful. I note that you are going to stay in Fairbanks until spring and practice law, and hope by the time you get out that the Seattle Companies will be in a position to avail themselves of your services. No change has been made other than what I wrote you last spring. Bogle is the attorney for the Company.

I leave here tomorrow for Seattle, expecting to remain there several months. I hope it can be brought about so that our people can make you a satisfactory proposition. [5]

Dr. Fenton Whiting (left), Governor Wilfred Hoggatt (center), M.J. Heney (right)
PHOTO COURTESY OF WASHINGTON STATE HISTORICAL SOCITY, TACOMA, WA.

Capt. Jarvis also wrote to Wickersham upon learning of the resignation, stating that he could not respond to the political implications of the move since he had "dropped out of the political field altogether." Instead, Jarvis, who had stood by Wickersham for years while the Judge battled for confirmation, responded sympathetically on a personal level:

I was both glad and sorry when I heard of your resignation, but I think now you know that the trouble of resigning and getting over the feeling in the matter was not half so bad as it appeared before you took the step. Surely you have lost nothing as far as I can see in the estimation of right thinking people. ... You surely have relieved yourself of a great deal of trouble and nasty disagreeable backbiting, and should have a great deal more peace of mind and a great deal more benefit to your pocket-book. [6]

In a December 19, 1907, letter to Birch, Wickersham provided some indication of his future plans:

My dear Birch:

I am in receipt of your kind letter of November 15, from New York, saying that you are coming out to Seattle to remain several months. I was very glad to hear from you and pleased to know through the newspapers that your enterprise at Cordova is under way. ...

I am going to practice law as soon as the new judge gets here, though when that will be the Lord only knows. ... I am getting very nervous about the delay, and anxious to get out of office. Just as Captain Jarvis wrote to me, the actual effort to get out when I got up courage enough to do so, was nothing at all when compared to what it seemed to be and now that the effort has been made and my resignation accepted I am anxious for my successor to get here so that I may take up the effort to make some money. I am going to forget my enemies, even if I don't forgive them. I am not going to try to get even with anybody but I am going to work. [7]

On February 1, 1908, Wickersham wrote Birch an update on his plans and indicated continued interest in the success of Birch's enterprises in the Copper River country. [8]

Since Wickersham was now in private practice and potentially available for hire, Birch hoped to pushed for his employment at the next annual meeting of the Syndicate in Seattle. On March 17, 1908, he wrote Wickersham:

Dear Judge:

I still call you Judge, and expect that name will remain with you for the rest of your days although you do not now hold that office. ... I wish you would advise me as to what your future plans are. If you are going to be out, I should like very much to have you meet Mr. Eccles, who will also be in Seattle at the same time I am there. Will probably return to New York again before going to Alaska for the summer.

Mr. Bogle is still the General Counsel for the Northwestern Commercial Company and subsidiaries. Whether he will be General Counsel after the annual meeting I cannot say at this time. My people are beginning to realize that the Company should have a General Counsel whose entire time shall be given up to them. If I can get them to take action at the annual meeting, a change might be made. I wish you could advise me, and address me care Northwestern Commercial Company, Lowman Building, Seattle, if you would care to become the General Counsel for the Company in Seattle, and what compensation you would wish. Please address me personally. If you do not care to come to Seattle, will you let me know what your plans are, and where you are going to make your headquarters. (9)

Wickersham answered promptly from Fairbanks on April 8, 1908, expressing his interest in employment with the Syndicate:

My dear Mr. Birch:

Your letter of March 17th has been received and I hasten my answer that it may catch the last mail out over the ice.

I regret that I cannot meet you in Seattle the latter part of the month, because one can make one's ideas plainer in conversation than by writing, but since the opening of the April term of courts prevents it, I shall briefly state the matter by letter.

I have entered upon the practice of law here, and represent some of the most important interests in the territory, and the outlook for returns is satisfactory, still I long for the flesh pots of the "outside", and would accept an offer from your allied Alaska interests to act as their General Counsel, but not in any subordinate capacity. I will accept a three years contract at $15,000 per annum with offices in Seattle and office force and maintenance. Upon that sort of arrangement I would devote my time exclusively to their interests, and give them the best service possible. My opportunities here, however, are so good that I could not afford to give them up for less than a three years contract with you. Please advise me by wire if anything is done in connection with this offer and it may be thus arranged.

Remember me kindly to Captain Jarvis. (10)

Wickersham's letter did not reach Birch prior to the Syndicate directors' meeting at which Eccles was elected president and Jarvis secretary-treasurer. Birch wrote Wickersham on May 6, 1908, from New York, on stationery that reflected the new name, Kennecott Mines Company. In this letter Birch indicates that S.W. Eccles had become the dominant force in the Syndicate, but that he still had control over the mine business:

Dear Judge:

Your letters of December 19th, 1907, and April 8th, 1908, have been forwarded to me here in New York. ...

We held the annual meetings and the firm of Bogle and Spooner were employed as General Counsel for the Railroad and Commercial Company at a salary of $1,000 per month. The Kennecott Mines Company have not joined in this, nor will they do so. Bogle seems to have been giving satisfaction to the Morgan people, and old man Spooner has been pulling for the Bogle and Spooner firm with the Morgan people.

In a talk I had with Jarvis regarding you, he suggested that you become one of the firm of Bogle and Spooner, and stated to me that he had some talk with you in regard to this, but since receiving your letter I do not think that this would be satisfactory to you. You are right in wanting a contract of at least three years, for I am satisfied that you can make as much as you mentioned in Alaska, if not more. I really think that there are greater opportunities in Alaska than there would be in devoting your entire time to the allied interests of the Alaska Syndicate in Seattle. When I wrote to you I wanted your own ideas regarding this proposition, so that I could be in position to bring you in touch with Mr. Eccles, provided you wished me to do so. Now my conclusion, Judge, is this, personally, I want to do for you that which is the best for your interest, and after reviewing the entire situation, believe that at this time the General Counselship of the Alaska Syndicate has not as good a future in it, nor the opportunity of making money, as a free lance like yourself will have in Alaska.

Faithfully yours, Stephen Birch. [11]

Birch did not give up easily. On May 11, 1908, he again wrote Wickersham from New York, implying continued interest in making some arrangement for legal employment of Wickersham. [12] The letters apparently took a long time in reaching Wickersham because he did not record his reaction in the diary until July 8:

Received letter from Stephen Birch about his desires that I be employed as the general counsel for the N.W. Ry. and Steamship Co. and the Guggenheim-Morgan exploiters of copper in Alaska. Nothing done yet and I am satisfied that nothing can be. He tells me that Bogle and Spooner are serving the company for $1,000 per month — I asked $15,000 a year! I am glad I did ask that amount. Things may come around in time so that I can assist Birch — but I am not inclined to hurry the situation for I can make more money as I am. My business here is good and it will bring me as much or more than that Co. pays B.& S. at Seattle and I am, as Birch says, a free lance!

We can only speculate whether the outcome might have been different if the directors of the Alaska Syndicate had received Wickersham's proposal for employment prior to their annual meeting. As it happened, Wickersham had already made a momentous decision regarding his own future when he received Birch's letters explaining the lack of response to his terms for employment by the Syndicate. On June 23, 1908, Wickersham telegraphed Jarvis in Seattle: "I intend to run for Congress. Where is Birch?" Jarvis immediately wired back: "Birch in New York. Leaves tomorrow. Due here July first. Don't you think little late?" Jarvis then wrote Wickersham that, although he was reluctant to mix in politics, he had already expressed himself in favor of John W. Corson, the Republican candidate. He went on to state:

> Of course you must have some good reason for announcing your candidacy, or it may seem to you inside there that you can obtain enough votes to carry you through; but Judge don't break away from your party unless you feel sure you are strong enough to win. A winning fight will leave you with a party or following of your own in the country that will probably last for some time, but a losing fight placing you outside of the lines of your own party surely looks like it will not benefit you any. Advice is easy, and I do not know how you see the thing from your position; but if I had been near you, and could have talked with you before you made this announcement, I would have said just exactly what I have written above. I will give your cable to Birch when he arrives and he may be able to assist you. It looks like the thing will be very much split up, as there appear now five candidates in the field, so all I can say is sail in and let the best man win. [13]

In the past, as evidenced in his diary entries, Wickersham had sought advice from Jarvis and acted accordingly. However, upon receipt of the above letter on July 17, Wickersham wrote in his diary:

> Letter from Jarvis, Mgr. of the Guggenheims from Seattle and he strongly advised me to keep out of the race and announced his intention to support Corson. Immediately revised my address — then almost done, and put in a strong plank against Guggenheim domination in mining and transportation matters in Alaska.

This is the first mention in the Wickersham diary of any opposition to the Alaska Syndicate or the Guggenheims, and the turning point in his relationship with Jarvis.

When Birch reached Seattle and learned of Wickersham's proposed candidacy for delegate, he responded in much the same manner as Jarvis had:

Dear Judge:

Have just returned to Seattle from the east and expect to leave here on the 8th for Cordova to go in to the interior for the summer. Capt. Jarvis showed me your telegram stating that you intended to run for Congress and asking where I was.

Capt. Jarvis seems to be of the opinion, and I feel the same, that we would have liked very much indeed to have had you announce your candidacy before the Republican convention was held in Alaska and before Corson was nominated, and believe you would have received the nomination had you wished it and would have received the strongest support. It is unfortunate that the distance is so great that we cannot keep better in touch with one another so that we could know what was going on. It does seem to me as being late for you to announce your candidacy. I had no idea that you cared for any more political positions and was somewhat surprised to hear that you had decided to again get into politics.

Am very sorry indeed that there should be any misunderstanding between Governor Hoggatt and yourself. Personally I desire harmony and think for the best interests of Alaska and for all her good citizens that the least strife we have amongst ourselves the better.

It seems to me that if you should lay low this election and come out strong in advance of the next election and run on the Republican ticket that you could win out very easily.

Of course, Judge, I do not wish to assume to dictate what your actions shall be but only wish to convey to you my own impressions. I wish to be your friend and want you to consider me as such and hope you will take my suggestions in the spirit in which they are offered. [14]

Wickersham was more concerned with his political future than with the friendship of Birch and Jarvis. For years he had used their friendship to foster his ambition, but now, since it was apparent that he would not receive their endorsement for his candidacy, he was quick to turn against them and look elsewhere for political support. From that time on he made every possible effort to renounce any connection with his former friends.

Wickersham realized that public opinion in Alaska still blamed the Alaska Syndicate for the bloodshed at Keystone Canyon, and that independent Alaskan miners feared domination by Eastern financiers. The Democratic candidate for delegate tried to emphasize that Wickersham had always been friendly to the Guggenheim interests — which indeed had been the case up to that point. When Jarvis tried to see Wickersham on July 17, several days before the August election, Wickersham wrote in his diary:

Capt. Jarvis came in this afternoon on the NORTHWESTERN and has been trying to see me, but I have purposely avoided him — he is the Pacific coast manager of the Guggenheim interests — and since I am loudly called a Guggenheim man, I am at a loss to understand his action. He can not assist me — he can only do me an injury by even inquiring for me and exhibiting an interest in my presence here. I will not permit him to assist my candidacy and I hesitate to act discourteously toward him. I wish he would leave me alone.

"HIS MASTER'S VOICE."

Front page cartoon in July 6, 1908, Fairbanks Daily Times.

Wickersham understood Alaskan voters. His anti-Guggenheim campaign paid off. He was elected delegate to Congress on August 11, 1908, despite M.J. Heney's attempts to get out the Corson vote in Cordova by transporting railway workers to the polls on special trains.

In spite of Wickersham's attacks on the Syndicate's Alaska operations, Birch attempted to preserve his friendship with the new delegate. On September 9, 1908, he wrote Wickersham from his office at the Kennecott mines:

My dear Judge:

Am advised that you have been elected Delegate, and wish to congratulate you on your election. It takes some time for news to get in here, hence this delay in sending my congratulations.

As I wrote you from Seattle, I was surprised to hear that you again desired public office. ... While I do not know Corson personally, I had been advised by men whom I considered your friends that he was all right, and the Governor pledged my support last June, which, as a matter of fact amounts to very little, and as you know, I am not a very popular man in politics myself. I was further advised that you would make a mistake to run at this time, as an independent candidate would complicate matters. However, your election shows that I have been ill advised, and am really glad that it is so, and hope that when you go to Washington all this wrangling over Alaska Legislation will be stopped, and that we can all expect more harmony in the future.

Wishing you success, and trusting that you will look me up when you come east, I am very faithfully yours, Stephen Birch. [15]

Upon receipt of this letter, Wickersham wrote in his diary on October 16, 1908: "This letter gives me a chance to give Birch and his crowd a good `roast' and I sure intend to do it, and try and get them to break away from the Governor in Territorial politics."

When Wickersham went to Washington in 1909, the feud with Governor Hoggatt continued. Wickersham insisted that Hoggatt was acting as a lobbyist for the Guggenheims and demanded that Richard A. Ballinger, the new Secretary of the Interior in William Howard Taft's administration, order Hoggatt to leave Washington and return to Alaska. Wickersham and Birch continued to correspond, primarily about some gold mining claims that Wickersham hoped to interest the Guggenheims in developing. On March 26, 1909, Wickersham wrote in his diary:

Have had a long consultation with Stephen Birch, Eccles and Steele of the Copper River Ry. Co. this afternoon, and I told them with brutal frankness about the Cordova election frauds, the fight their people made against me in the last election. They listened with interest. I explained that I wanted a law passed giving Alaska a local legislature and that I wanted them to help me and that I wanted Gov. Hoggatt to go home and attend to his duties as governor, etc. The conversation covered the conditions in Alaska very fully and I think some good will come of it. I explained very frankly to them that I only asked fair consideration for the people of Alaska and wanted nothing from them politically. That their support politically would do me more harm than good, etc.

When Governor Hoggatt resigned in May 1909, to accept a position with the Northwestern Commercial Company, President Taft appointed Walter E. Clark, the newspaper correspondant who had worked hard in support of Wickersham's judicial confirmation. Taft hoped that this would heal the feud between Alaska's delegate and governor. Rather than being pleased, Wickersham was offended that his advice had not been sought. In his diary he referred to Clark as a "subservient servant of Jarvis, the Guggenheim Trust, etc.," but decided against actively opposing the appointment. Clark left Washington to spend all of his time attending to gubernatorial duties in Juneau. Peace reigned in Alaska politics for a brief time, at least.

Fairbanks Weekly Times January 29, 1910

WICKERSHAM SLANDERS TAFT AND ROOSEVELT

Our Delegate Intimates the President and His Predecessor Helped Maintain a Lobby at Washington in the Interest of Hoggett

HALLEY'S COMET

DUE TODAY
Superstitious
Alarmed

NOTICE

It has come to the notice of the Power Company that certain people are tapping wires and connecting electric heaters, flat irons, etc. This practice not only endangers property but is a theft under the statutes, and will be prosecuted to the full extent of the law. – G.C. Hazelet, Manager

---

Seattle Post-Intelligencer   October 12, 1910

M.J. HENEY DIES

HIS BIGGEST FEAT NOT QUITE DONE

Seattle Post Intelligencer   March 8, 1910

Birch Describes Alaska Activities of Guggenheims

PINCHOT IS DAFFY OVER CONSERVATION

IN HIS TESTIMONY BEFORE COMMITTEE GIVES AS REASON FOR ATTACKING BALLINGER THAT LATTER IS UNTRUE TO THE DEPOSED OFFICIAL'S POLICY

Cordova Daily Alaskan   August 13, 1909

GIGANTIC COAL FRAUDS

U.S. Land Office Has Had Secret Agents Working For Months on Alaska Coal Land Entries–Many Prominent Coal Companies Involved

Cordova Daily Alaskan   November 2, 1909

Cordova Bear to go to Zoo

The Park Board of the zoo at Woodland park, Seattle, received a communication from M.J. Heney, stating that he would like to make the board a present of a sixty-pound black bear which he had at Cordova. Mr. Heney said that the bear was as playful as a kitten, and he believed that it would be a valuable addition to the zoo at Woodland park.

Cordova
The New Railroad Town

As soon as the Hasey trial in Juneau was over, George Hazelet returned to Valdez and promptly went to Cordova with Thomas Donohoe "to make selection of lots and get that thing going." [1] Now that the new town of Cordova was designated as the port for the Copper River and Northwestern Railway, Hazelet had business of his own to attend to. Although the Valdez businessmen who staked the Cordova townsite in 1905 had sold some of the land to the railroad, they still owned ample ground to promote development of the town.

Cordova, 1908
ANCHORAGE MUSEUM OF HISTORY & ART. B62.1.2049

Hazelet remained on friendly terms with the Alaska Syndicate and the Katalla Company, but ceased to work for them and became the manager of the Cordova Townsite Company. Hazelet stayed in Cordova and corresponded frequently with Donohoe, who returned to Valdez to continue his law practice.

Hazelet reported on May 21 that he had sold 12 to 14 lots and was considering raising the price. (2) The first major problem arose in July when the noted trail-blazer, Jack Dalton, claimed a tract of land adjoining the railroad and threatened to interfere with access to the small dock Hazelet was constructing to receive freight. (3) After obtaining an injunction against Dalton, the matter was resolved favorably for the railroad and the townsite company. Hazelet was also concerned about means for assuring light and power for the town since the townsite owners did not have enough money to install them. On August 15, he wrote Donohoe that he hoped Henry Bratnober, his wealthy California friend, would take up that franchise. (4)

Townsite development problems, however, were minor compared to the political storm that brewed when James Wickersham ran for delegate to Congress against John W. Corson in the 1908 Republican primary election on an anti-big-business platform, reminiscent of the Populist movement that Hazelet had encountered back in Nebraska before coming to Alaska.

Prior to the election, newspapers throughout Alaska ran articles claiming that there was a Guggenheim plot to have 1,500 illegal votes cast in Cordova by railroad workers. In Juneau the *Daily Alaska Dispatch* announced that Wickersham's managers were "busy all day wiring to head officials of the Third Judicial District asking that steps be taken to prosecute those at Cordova impli-cated in the plot." They also sent an appeal to Washington asking that several special agents of the U.S. Department of Justice be sent to Cordova to gather evidence that could later be presented before the Valdez grand jury to secure indictments. (5) In spite of these warnings, M.J. Heney, the railroad construction contractor, suspended work on election day so that the workers could vote, claiming that the workers had been Alaska residents long enough to qualify as voters even if they did not reside in Cordova.

When Wickersham won the election in spite of the Cordova paper's continued blistering attacks on the new delegate. Donohoe and his law partner, John Y. Ostrander, cautioned Hazelet: "We believe these criticisms or attacks very ill-advised. ... To accomplish results, he (Wickersham) will require the cooperation of all those now interested and expending their money in opening up the country. ... We want his assistance and he will require ours. ... Such articles as those contained in the *Alaskan* of the 22nd will, if continued, make it impossible for him to support any form of legislation favored by the Morgan or Guggenheim interests. ... This is a good time to switch — the paper is about to pass into new hands and may very well change its tactics." (6) If Hazelet did indeed attempt to alter the editorial policy, it apparently did no good. The battle lines were drawn. Wickersham continued to rely upon anti-Guggenheim sentiment for his political support. Whenever he attacked the "Guggs", the *Cordova Daily Alaskan* retaliated.

Before the end of summer, the newspaper happily announced that, despite anti-Guggenheim rumors to the contrary, Cordova would soon have light and water at rates "lower than that of any other city in Alaska." The townsite company had granted Bratnober a franchise to install a water system, an electric light plant and a telephone system for Cordova. (7) Bratnober appointed Hazelet general manager to supervise the installation of the water, light and telephone plants, and Hazelet promptly contracted with his old partner, A.J. Meals, to do the actual digging. On September 28, Hazelet reported to Donohoe that they would have the lights on in 60 days and water in 15 days.

Officers of the cableship BURNSIDE *with officials of the
Copper River and Northwestern Railway, August 21, 1908.
Hazelet (seated third from left), Hawkins (seated fourth from left),
Heney (seated fifth from left), Bratnober (seated second from right)*
PHOTO COURTESY OF WASHINGTON STATE HISTORICAL SOCIETY, TACOMA, WA.

After years of separation and financial insecurity, the Hazelets were finally in a position to enjoy social life the way they had years before in O'Neill, Nebraska.

Hazelet assumed the responsibility of preparing Cordova's exhibit at the Alaska-Yukon Exhibition, to be held the following year in Seattle, and Harriet Hazelet was elected president of the ladies' auxiliary even before she moved permanently to Cordova. The Hazelets lived in one of the railroad cottages during the summer, but moved into the new Burke Hotel as soon as it was finished. The Burke was the center of their social life the following winter. They enjoyed the dining room, where they frequently hosted small dinner parties; the parlors, where the ladies held meetings; and attended regular weekly dances.

Harriet Hazelet
PHOTO COURTESY OF HAZELET GRANDCHILDREN

Harriet displayed her musical talent by leading a group of local ladies who sang at a banquet hosted by the Chamber of Commerce for railroad builders Heney and Hawkins on November 11. [8] As an encore the ladies sang a parody on the popular song, "So Long Mary," that ended with the chorus, "So long Heney, don't forget to come back soon." Heney responded by sending his Cordova lady friends carnations, chrysanthemums, ferns and holly for Christmas. [9] The Hazelets entertained Judge and Mrs. Ostrander from Valdez at the Burke Hotel over the holiday season and hosted several small dinner parties for their visiting friends.

Following the Christmas season, Hazelet had to leave for Juneau to testify at another Hasey trial. Although Edward C. Hasey had been acquitted of the charge of second degree murder the previous spring, he still faced the lesser charges of assault with a dangerous weapon and shooting with intent to kill during the Keystone Canyon encounter. The Valdez legal office of Ostrander and Donohoe was no longer involved in Hasey's defense. In their letters, Hazelet and Donohoe frequently referred to the difficulty the Valdez lawyers were having in getting full payment from the Katalla Company's Seattle office for the services that Ostrander and Donohoe had performed during the previous trial. [10] As treasurer for the Katalla Company and representative of the Morgan bank, Jarvis felt responsible for the prudent use of money. He believed that too many lawyers had been involved in the first Hasey trial and that expenses had been excessive. This time a Juneau law office had the full responsibility for handling Hasey's defense.

After testifying as the final defense witness, Hazelet went to Seattle and returned to Cordova on March 14 with Hawkins and 50 Katalla Company employees. [11] A.J. Adams had covered the townsite office in his absence. Cordova real estate was booming and Hazelet was forced to resign as agent for the Alaska Steamship Company. In the meantime the verdict in the second Keystone Canyon trial was announced. Hasey was convicted of assault with a dangerous weapon and sentenced to 18 months in the McNeil Island Penitentiary, which some anti-Guggenheim activists felt was too lenient a sentence. When Hasey was released on bail awaiting appeal of the verdict, he was attacked in Juneau and found wounded in the bay. [12]

Back in early February, Hazelet had met with a group of Cordova citizens who were pushing for incorporation of the town. Although the railroad company, which owned half of the townsite, was opposed to incorporation, Hazelet wrote Ostrander on April 3: "The people are very anxious to incorporate as soon as possible, and I think it is better to have it come off early than late." [13]

Both Hazelet and Ostrander were planning to build on their Cordova lots, as was A.J. Adams, another one of the townsite owners. On May 24, *The Cordova Daily Alaskan* announced that work had started on Hazelet's two-story building on First Street. The entire building was rented before construction began, and the new Eagles' hall on the upper floor was dedicated in mid-July. Hazelet was eager to encourage construction of private homes in addition to new business and social buildings. The newspaper regularly carried the following announcement:

WHAT CORDOVA NEEDS

Now more than anything else is a number of substantial residences.

Here is a chance for an investment that will pay large returns.

Resident lots sold at large discount for immediate building.

See Geo. Hazelet, Trustee, for terms.

In late May, Hazelet informed Ostrander that notices had been posted announcing the voting on incorporation, and detailed his plan to have the old school board make its report to the governor as required, and ask for funds so that "we could have that money to use for school purposes even though we incorporated." (14) On June 23, 1909, the *Cordova Daily Alaskan* announced that incorporation had passed 227 to 17, and that George Hazelet had received the largest number of votes for city council. When the seven new councilmen met on July 14, they unanimously elected Hazelet the first mayor of Cordova. (15)

Hazelet family home in Cordova built in 1910.
PHOTO © 1996 ELIZABETH TOWER

Muckraking — 1910

The summer of 1909 was a peaceful and productive one for Cordova and the Alaska Syndicate. With Governor Clark minding his business in Juneau, Wickersham suspended his attacks on the Guggenheims and set to work preparing a bill to provide Alaska with an elected legislature. Railroad construction on the Copper River and Northwestern was finally progressing satisfactorily, although the railroad still would not be completed in time to meet a deadline set by Birch and his original backers. In order to protect their 40% interest in the mine, the Alaska Syndicate purchased the remaining 60% from Alaska Copper and Coal for $3,000,000 and retained Birch as manager.

Million dollar bridge under construction.
ANCHORAGE MUSEUM OF HISTORY & ART. B83.159.35

In preparation for shipping copper ore out over the railroad, Birch assembled an able core of assistants to run the mines. Lewis Levensaler left the Anaconda Company and went to work for Birch in 1908, first mapping the gold placer claims at Dan Creek, and then going to Kennecott in 1909 to prepare the Bonanza and Jumbo claims for mining. Later that year, Birch sent Levensaler to LaTouche Island in Prince William Sound to survey and sample the Beatson mine. Levensaler forwarded his data to Birch in New York, and in 1910 Birch purchased the Beatson mine.

Steamer in canyon on Copper River.
ANCHORAGE MUSEUM OF HISTORY & ART. B64.1.137

The New York financiers sent some more mining and transportation experts to look over their Alaska projects in 1909. Pope Yeatman, who assessed the mines for the Guggenheims, was favorably impressed and confirmed previous optimistic reports. The Morgans sent A.H. Gray to look over the railroad situation. While Gray and Birch were touring Alaska looking for a feasible route for an extension of the railroad to the Tanana valley and the thriving gold mining district near Fairbanks, they met with Falcon Joslin and Martin Harrais, builders of the Tanana Valley Railway.

At this meeting, Birch told Harrais that J.P. Morgan had given him the following instructions: "Steve, when you go into that Tanana country, I want you to pay particular attention to the agricultural possibilities. If they can raise stuff like that man Joslin brought out two years ago, and those pioneers want to stay there after the gold is mined out, I'll build a railroad in there for them. I don't care a damn what it costs me, or whether I get a cent of the investment back! I'd like to help those pioneers, who had the courage to go in there. I'd like to make it possible for them to remain. John D. Rockefeller has built churches and Andrew Carnegie, libraries, as their monuments — I am going to build a railroad to benefit those Alaska pioneers as my monument!" [1]

Meeting on board, SS YUCATAN, 1909.
Hazelet (eighth from right), Heney (fourth from right), Birch (fifth from right)
PHOTO COURTESY OF WASHINGTON STATE HISTORICAL SOCIETY, TACOMA, WA.

Birch contacted Wickersham in Fairbanks during one of these trips and spent time photographing gardens, perhaps to reassure J.P. Morgan about the agricultural potential of the Tanana Valley. Wickersham also took Birch to see some of his own mining prospects, and reported in his diary on August 3, 1909:

> Birch is not strongly impressed with the quartz showings on Cleary. He says, and I think correctly, that it is a "good prospect," but not a mine. He also said to me (privately) that it was too small for his people to invest in, and I think nothing can be done about selling these mines before more extensive work is done in developing the same.

The entire country was optimistic about Alaska's development prospects during the summer of 1909. Huge crowds were attending the Alaska-Yukon Exposition in Seattle and learning that the great northern territory was ready for settlement. Richard Ballinger, the new secretary of interior, was a westerner from Seattle and far more receptive to development than his conservationist predecessor, James Garfield. There was even hope that, with Ballinger in the Interior Department, the coal fields in Alaska might finally be opened. When President Taft visited the Exposition in September to speak on his plans for Alaska, many people expected him to advocate more self-government for the territory. Instead he proposed a military commission government, similar to one that he had set up as governor of the Philippines. This proposal of Taft's did not bode well for Wickersham's bill to create an elected legislature in Alaska, and suggested trouble ahead.

Jarvis at his desk reading Collier's.
PHOTO COURTESY OF MARY JARVIS COCKE

The trouble started on November 13, 1909, when *Collier's Weekly* carried a front page story with the headline: "The Whitewashing of Ballinger: Are the Guggenheims in Charge of the Interior Department." This article was the culmination of a feud between Ballinger and Gifford Pinchot, head of the National Forest Service in the Department of Agriculture.

Pinchot was upset that Taft had not retained Garfield as head of the Interior Department. Ballinger was amenable to transferring land into private ownership for development while Pinchot wished to reserve federal land. When Pinchot found out that Ballinger had tentatively cleared the Cunningham claims in the Bering River coal field for patents, he realized that he might have a way of getting rid of Ballinger. Since the Alaska Syndicate had taken an option on a half-interest in the Cunningham claims, he invoked the Guggenheim monster and accused the Syndicate of trying to control the Taft administration. The muckraking press printed derogatory articles about Ballinger that prompted him to sue *Collier's* for libel. The feud drew so much public attention that Congress decided to hold a special investigation of both the Interior and Agriculture departments.

Cartoon from LaFollette's Weekly Magazine, *March 19, 1910.*

Just as the Pinchot-Ballinger hearings were about to start in Washington, President Taft arranged to have Senator Albert Beveridge of Indiana introduce a bill creating a military-style commission to govern Alaska. Since this legislation was in direct opposition to his bill to authorize an elected legislature for Alaska, Wickersham was furious. To make matters worse, the delegate was barred from attending hearings on the bill before the Senate Committee on Territories. Wickersham accused everyone who favored the Beveridge bill, including Major Wilds Richardson, head of the Alaska Road Commission, of being controlled by the Guggenheims.

A January 16, 1910, entry in his diary revealed a plan through which Wickersham hoped to discredit the Taft administration and defeat the Beveridge bill:

> Today, however, a ray of hope comes from a visit which I received from Mr. Ben B. Hampton, the owner and proprietor of *Hampton's Magazine*. This is one of the great magazines of New York — a muckraker of the most virulent type — a fighter of Apacheland, and one which can reach millions of readers. ... I gave them facts and exhibited evidence in my possession and told them how more could be obtained — and, in short, an arrangement was entered into that Mr. Lyle, of *Hampton's*, is to begin the story at once and *Hampton's Magazine* will immediately enter upon a campaign of indictment, arraignment, and trial of the Administration's scheme of a Guggenheim Commission government for Alaska. I see no other way to fight it, and they are anxious and willing to take up the fight, and I expressed perfect willingness to assist them. So the Battle for a government by the People in Alaska is on and I may no longer hope for any thing from the Administration but War — but thank God I will now be able to reach an audience — the Public, and the Echo will get into Congress even if my voice cannot.
>
> For myself, I shall be as discrete as I can — smile and be a still villain until the Administration shall find out that I am furnishing the facts — evidence — and then I'll fight openly. We begin the War tomorrow and I am delighted. I do not anticipate an easy victory — maybe not a victory at all — but as to that one takes the chances in War, and I can no longer refuse the risk — and will go armed with the spear and javelin for whatever enemy appears.

The facts that Wickersham presented to the magazine and to the Committee on Territories were calculated to exaggerate the influence of the Alaska Syndicate. For example, he accused the Syndicate of trying to control the Bering River coal field, when, in truth, it only had an option that was never exercised on 33 out of 900 claims. He also claimed that the Syndicate controlled the White Pass and Yukon Route, although the only connection was a small amount of Copper River and Northwestern stock given to Samuel Graves of Close Brothers Bank when the Syndicate bought Heney's fledgling Copper River Railway in 1906.

In mid-February, Stephen Birch and John N. Steele asked to testify at hearings before the Senate Committee on Territories to tell the true story of the Syndicate's Alaska activities. The testimony, given by Birch, with Steele acting as the questioning attorney, was simple and factual. Wickersham's reaction was shown by his diary entry on February 18:

> Birch is before the Senate Committee on Territories today — he and Steele have slid in quietly and gave testimony to show that the Guggenheims are real

good people and do not own Alaska and its resources. Of course their statements are prepared to minimize their efforts in Alaska — and they gave me no notice. I did not find out until they had finished, but I intend to be present tomorrow morning when they are to be cross examined.

The following day Wickersham did attend the hearings, but was told that he could not cross-examine Birch. That day he wrote in the diary:

> At the last of his testimony, Birch did a very untruthful and ungentlemanly thing in saying that I had — after I was no longer on the bench and before I was elected delegate — applied to them for employment as attorney, but that I had not been retained. I then said to the Com. that Mr. Birch had stated the fact unfairly since the truth was that he wrote me a letter suggesting my employment and then I read to the Com. from my letter press copybook the three or four paragraphs saying that in answer to his letter I would accept employment if it was desired by them. ...
>
> Their refusal to permit a cross examination of Birch and Steele ought to create a decided impression against the Guggenheims and anything the Beveridge Committee may do in their aid and assistance.

One part of Birch's testimony that aroused nationwide interest was his estimation of the potential worth of the coal in the Bering River coal fields. Experts, such as Arthur H. Brooks of the United States Geological Survey, corroborated Birch's estimates. This emphasis on the mineral wealth of Alaska, coupled with Wickersham's exaggerated accounts of Alaska Syndicate holdings, served to increase suspicion of the Guggenheims.

The following month Birch and Steele appeared before the Pinchot-Ballinger hearings at their own request in order to refute statements made to the press by Wickersham in which he claimed that the Guggenheims "owned all the fish, the mines, the railroads, the steamship lines, and the rivers — all of Alaska." Steele testified as follows:

> We ought to have encouragement in the building of our Copper River railroad. It is the only enterprise of its kind in that country.
>
> Now as to the Wickersham charges — he said we own all the fish — well, we only have $300,000 worth out of about $3,000,000, which is the total production. We only own 12 out of about 28 of the steamers running to Alaska; we own one railroad, and have no coal, nor interest in any claims except the Cunningham group.
>
> We want equal rights under the law with all others in developing the country. We have never attempted to shut out any others or tried to stifle competition. We ought to receive any encouragement Congress can give us. [2]

Articles began appearing in the April issue of *Hampton's Magazine* and other muckraking magazines distorting Birch's testimony and amplifying Wickersham's claims of Syndicate domination. On April 30, Wickersham received a surprise visit from Birch, which he described in his diary:

> I was greatly surprised this morning when Stephen Birch, the managing director of the Alaska Syndicate called me up at breakfast and wanted to see me. He came to my office at 9:30 and remained till 12, and then went over with me to the New Varnum and took dinner with Debbie and me. ... Birch begged me to quit the fight and to give them terms of peace. He said: "What do you want us to do? We will do anything you say. Just say it, and it will be done.", etc. He wanted the fight against them stopped — but I said: "Can you stop a prairie fire when the whole great grassy plain is ablaze and driven before a 50-mile gale?" I denounced their Cordova paper, the stuffing of the Cordova ballot box, the fixing of the Valdez grand jury and the bribery of the Deputy District Attorney and then showed him the Douglas copies of John A. Carson's letter to Jarvis, and the accompanying account, when the bribery of jurors and witnesses in the Hasey case was admitted, and approved by Bogle and paid by Jarvis. He certainly was perturbed by these photographic copies of their criminality, and begged me to quit. Plainly I told him I would when his people would quit their criminal practices and support my efforts to give a popular legislative government to Alaska. He went away unhappy, and I then filed my letters and charges including a copy of the two photographic exhibits with the Senate Committee and Judiciary. ... I may be defeated finally on my fight against the Taft appointive military legislative bill, but they will know that Alaska has a Delegate at any rate.

This diary entry refers to another Wickersham plan to force the Taft administration to support his bill for an elected legislature. Several months before, H.J. Douglas, a former Syndicate auditor whom Jarvis had fired, approached Wickersham with two documents that he had removed from the Katalla Company files in the hope that he could use them against Jarvis. The papers consisted of a letter from John A. Carson, one of the attorneys in the first Hasey trial, to Jarvis explaining a bill from M.P. Morrisey for the lodging and feeding of some of the witnesses during the trial.

Wickersham's Scapegoat

Wickersham's April 30, 1910, diary entry is the only documentation of his meeting with Stephen Birch but during that discussion Wickersham apparently agreed not to attack Birch directly as long as Birch and his associates did not interfer with Wickersham's political agenda. Wickersham subsequently directed all of his accusations toward his former friend, Capt. David Jarvis, although Birch, through his lawyer, John A. Carson, was probably more involved than Jarvis if there was any bribery of witnesses during the Hasey trial.

Jarvis with children, David, William and Anna.

Both Wickersham and Birch had reasons for picking on Jarvis. Wickersham had never forgiven Jarvis for declining the Alaska governorship and then siding with Hoggatt in the confrontation between delegate and governor. Birch, who was allied with the Guggenheim faction in the Syndicate, probably resented Jarvis' concern for financial accountability to protect the investment of the Morgan bank.

On January 6, Wickersham had received the following telegram from H.J. Douglas, a former auditor for the Katalla Company: "Please advise when and where I can discuss with you plans and ideas suggested by Judge Hartman." [1] John P. Hartman had been counsel for the Northwestern Commercial Company before it was taken over by the Alaska Syndicate, which then engaged the Seattle law firm of Bogle and Spooner at the insistance of J.P. Morgan. [2] Hartman and Wickersham met in Seattle the previous month, and presumably discussed the Hasey defense. [3]

Selection of lawyers to defend Hasey had already caused considerable controversy among the managers of the Alaska Syndicate and Jarvis had repeatedly complained about legal expenses during the Hasey defense. George Hazelet had engaged the Valdez firm of Donohoe and Ostrander to defend him immediately after the Keystone canyon shooting and during the grand jury arraignment. Bogle initially suggested that Hasey be given a sum of money to hire his own attorney, but the Syndicate's New York managers insisted that the Seattle law firm of Bogle and Spooner handle the defense. Birch, whom Hazelet had listed along with Hawkins and Rodgers as his advisers in holding the canyon, demanded that John A. Carson from Salem, Oregon, be added to the defense team. [4] Carson had been Birch's lawyer in the 1903 Bonanza lawsuit.

Carson did not get along well with Donohoe and Ostrander so he recommended that Bogle retain Fred Brown, another Valdez lawyer, to be Hasey's lead defender during the first Juneau trial. [5] Bogle suggested that Donohoe and Ostrander retire from the case, but they refused to do so at the insistence of Hazelet. [6]

During the first Hasey trial, therefore, Brown was Hasey's primary lawyer while Carson was on the sidelines looking out for Birch's interests. Ostrander also went to Juneau to make sure that Hazelet was not further implicated. Jarvis, as treasurer for the Katalla Company in Seattle, was responsible for paying all of these legal bills once they were approved by Bogle. Jarvis and Bogle both felt that too many lawyers were involved and that the defense was too costly. Furthermore, they were displeased with the whole situation because they both had specifically warned against any use of force in Keystone Canyon.

The auditor Douglas, who had been sent to Seattle by the New York managers to look out for their interests, clashed with Jarvis over payment of bills for the Hasey defense. As a result, Jarvis fired Douglas.

Before Douglas left the Katalla Company, he removed from the files some papers that he planned to use against Bogle and Jarvis, including a bill from M.B. Morrisey to reimburse him for taking care of witnesses during the first Hasey trial. The bill, which had been approved by Bogle and Jarvis, was accompanied by the following cover letter from Carson to Jarvis:

My Dear Captain:

The inclosed account of Mr. M.B. Morrisey has been submitted to me by him. I do not claim to have personal knowledge of all of the items therein mentioned —necessarily I could not have such, but I do know that Mr. Morrisey was taking care of several of the Government's witnesses. I saw him take them into restaurants very many times (it was generally rumored around Juneau that the majority of the Government's witnesses were broke) and I have not the least doubt that Mr. Morrisey cared for them in the manner shown in his account.

In addition to this I wish to express my appreciation of the services rendered by Mr. Morrisey, not only in Juneau but also at Valdez during the session of the grand jury there. I found him very efficent and competent and his acquaintance with many of the Government's witnesses and control over them placed him in a position to be of the greatest possible service in defending this action.

I scarcely need tell you that Mr. Morrisey is an expert accountant employed by Mr. Heney at Cordova. He is anxious to return there promptly to resume his duties, and I trust that you will treat him in a very liberal manner.

Wickersham had Douglas photograph these papers and send him several copies that he could send to the attorney general and supply to the muckraking press, which was at that time giving nationwide coverage to the Pinchot-Ballinger controversy. [7]

Wickersham also sent copies of these papers to U.S. Marshal Dan Sutherland in Juneau with the suggestion that he prosecute Jarvis and the lawyers for bribing the witnesses in the first Hasey trial. Wickersham, who had awarded Sutherland, his former campaign manager, with the Juneau appointment, discovered on April 23 that President Taft had removed Sutherland from his position on the recommendation of Alaska's Governor Walter E. Clark. Clark readily admitted that he was a friend of Jarvis', but presented evidence that his action had been taken as a result of Sutherland's incompetence in an unrelated matter. Sutherland, on the other hand, claimed that Clark had recommended his removal to prevent him from following Wickersham's suggestion to indict Jarvis. [8]

Wickersham then intensified his attack on Jarvis although the Syndicate treasurer had not been directly involved in either the Keystone Canyon shooting or the trials. Jarvis was well-known in Washington, D.C., and had antagonized some senators during his lobbying efforts for the Copper River and Northwestern Railway and Northwestern Fisheries in 1905 and 1906, before they became part of the Alaska Syndicate. After Sutherland appeared before the Senate Judiciary Committee to protest his removal, Wickersham indicated in his diary that Senators Lodge and Borah were prepared "to expose the scandal" and "cry Guggenheim." [9]

Cartoon published in 1910 during Pinchot-Ballinger hearings.

In order to get more ammunition to use against Jarvis, Wickersham again summoned Douglas and obtained from him "a strong affidavit that in 1908 Jarvis, in collusion with another bidder, robbed the government of large sums by false and collusive bids for coal." [10] Although he had no proof to support the Douglas affidavit, Wickersham filed it with the Senate Judiciary Committee and sent copies to the attorney general and the secretary of war, again demanding prosecution of Jarvis.

Colonel Dick

Wilds Preston Richardson was a very large man from a large state. This 300-pound, Texas-born army officer graduated from West Point in 1884 and spent the next 13 years fighting Apaches and teaching cadets at his alma mater.

In August, 1897, "Lieutenant Dick" welcomed an assignment to accompany Capt. Patrick Henry Ray on a fact-finding trip to Alaska. For the next 20 years that immense territory provided an appropriately large theater of operation for a man of his stature. As he rose through the ranks, "Captain Dick" requested service in the Philippines during the Spanish American War, but the War Department considered his continued presence in Alaska to be essential.

While helping prospectors at Circle and Rampart during the winter of 1897-8, Ray and Richardson foresaw the need to improve trails for gold-seekers heading to the Klondike. Their recommendations resulted in the assignment of Capt. W.R. Abercrombie and Capt. Edward Glenn to lead expeditions to explore and map the Copper River and Susitna River routes to Alaska's interior during 1898 and 1899. The War Department then assigned Richardson to help keep order at Nome during the subsequent gold rush and smallpox epidemic there.

When President Theodore Roosevelt established the Alaska Road Commission on January 27, 1905, he named Richardson, to be its first president. Richardson proposed a main transportation corridor from Haines to the Yukon. Being a good soldier, however, he followed orders and concentrated on the route from Valdez that had been established to supply and maintain the government telegraph line.

Every winter when construction ended, the War Department ordered Richardson to Washington, D.C., to undertake various assignments. Congressmen liked "Major Dick" and came to depend on his first-hand knowledge of the exotic, far-off territory. The gregarious army officer was a good friend of Alaska Governor Wilfred Hoggatt and usually agreed politically with the governor, a retired Navy officer, who also spent the winter in Washington while Congress was in session.

After Alaskans elected their first delegate to Congress in 1906, a conflict arose as to who should be asked to advise on Alaskan matters. The rift between delegate and governor deepened in 1908 when Judge James Wickersham was elected delegate. Wickersham came to Washington intent on fulfilling a campaign promise to have Congress endorse a locally elected territorial legislature for Alaska.

President William Howard Taft had other plans for governing Alaska. As governor of the Philippines, Taft had successfully established a military-style commission there and he proposed to use a similar type of governing body in Alaska. Senator Albert Beveridge of Indiana agreed to sponsor a bill to establish such a commission. President Taft called upon Richardson to help him draft the bill, which contained the provision that one or more of the commissioners could be Army officers.

Delegate Wickersham was furious when he found out that he had not been invited to attend a session of the Senate Committee on Territories that was discussing the Beveridge bill on January 20, 1910. When Wickersham forced his way into the meeting and accused "Major Dick" of developing the bill for his own personal gain, he almost came to blows with the huge Army officer. The animosity between the two men lasted for years, sparked by Wickersham's repeated denunciation of both Richardson and Governor Hoggatt as lobbyists for the Guggenheims.

By helping muckraking journalists attack the Guggenheim interests during the Pinchot-Ballinger controversy, Wickersham succeeded in defeating the Beveridge bill, but he never forgave Richardson for his association with that hated legislation. The delegate repeatedly complained to the Secretary of War, demanding that "Major Dick" be sent back to Alaska. Among other accusations, Wickersham asserted that Richardson had aided the Alaska Syndicate in efforts to prevent his re-election in 1910.

Even after passage of the Organic Act of 1912, which gave Alaska a territorial legislature, Wickersham continued to complain about almost everything that Richardson, who had been promoted to colonel, did and even attempted to block funding for the Alaska Road Commission. Investigators, sent to Alaska by the War Department during the Wilson administration in response to the delegate's complaints, found no grounds for the accusations, and returned with high praise for "Colonel Dick's" work and his fine rapport with Alaskans. Richardson, who believed that Wickersham was intent on ruining his military career, commented to the secretary of war about the delegate's vendetta: "It has disclosed to me a character the moral quality of which was heretofore utterly beyond the horizon of my experience, a character which would apparently without hesitation destroy, if possible, the good name and reputation of any man whom he thought in the smallest degree in the way of his own plans, regardless of any obligation to truth or sentiment of fair dealing between men." [1]

Richardson did not lobby against the building of the Alaska Railroad although he felt that the money would be better used in developing Alaska if spent on roads and trails. When accused of preventing the railroad from fulfilling expectations by not building sufficient feeder roads, Richardson requested transfer to Washington.

Soon after Richardson had resigned from the Alaska Road Commission on December 29, 1917, he was promoted to brigadier general and placed in command of the 78th Infantry Brigade 39th Division. "General Dick" served with distinction in France and then commanded American forces at Murmansk. He retired from the Army on October 31, 1920, with the permanent rank of colonel, and received the Distinguished Service Medal for his capable leadership in Siberia.

Richardson was mentioned as a potential candidate for governor of Alaska in 1921, but President Warren G. Harding dismissed the idea upon learning that Richardson was a life-long Democrat.

Shortly before his death in 1929, Richardson wrote an article for the *Atlantic Monthly* that was considered controversial at the time but has since proved prophetic. In the article Richardson advocated self-government for Alaska, quasi-private ownership for the Alaska Railroad, and a spur line to Portage Bay (Whittier). He criticized the motivation for building the Alaska Railroad, pointing out that the hoped-for agricultural development could not be stimulated until sufficient population growth demanded it. He blamed the conservation mania of the Pinchot era for locking up Alaska's natural resources when they could have been used to promote healthly population growth. Furthermore, Richardson foresaw that Alaska scenery would be a great resource which "grips the public mind with a romantic interest which is not readily displaced by talk of material development." "This sentiment," he concluded, "is of substantial value and may be utilized for the benefit of Alaska and for the pleasure and happiness of a great number of people." [2]

Richardson is remembered in Alaska for the highway that bears his name and the Army post near Anchorage. In later years even James Wickersham paid tribute to his old enemy when he stated in his book *Old Yukon*, "the Richardson Highway from Valdez to Fairbanks is a fitting monument to the first great road-builder, General Wilds P. Richardson."

ALASKA HAS ENOUGH COAL TO HEAT THE WORLD INDEFINITELY

The Chitina Leader   April 1, 1911

Railroad Completed to the Copper Belt

ERUPTION IS LOCATED

Mount Katmai is belching fire, smoke, and lava. Kodiak and all surrounding towns are cut off from communication.

Cordova Daily Alaskan   June 8, 1912

LEASING BILL DEFEATED IN THE HOUSE

'During the discussion of Alaska coal measure delegate Wickersham assaults congressman Mondell and Speaker calls upon sergeant to preserve order.'

WICKERSHAM CONVENTION ENDORSES ROOSEVELT

LOCAL JOTTINGS FROM CHITINA

A report from the steamer on which Dr. Whiting shipped a few Alaska squirrels to his wife in Seattle is to the effect that the little fellows gnawed their way out of the wooden cage and are now the real mascots of the ship. The doctor shipped two more this week, but not in a wooden cage, putting them in an oil can so there is no chance for them to get away.

Cordova Daily Alaskan   June 8, 1912

ALASKA IS A ZOOLOGICAL PARK

This Northland Empire Now One Vast Game Preserve

Cordova's Coal Party

The citizens of Cordova watched procedings in Washington, D.C., closely in hopes that the Bering River coal fields would soon be opened for development. George Hazelet introduced the matter at a Chamber of Commerce meeting in October and in February 1910, the Chamber petitioned Congress for a speedy adjustment of the coal controversy so that Alaskans could use local fuel instead of paying an exhorbitant price for poor quality foreign coal. [1] Cordova was experiencing an unusually cold winter and the early freeze-up had resulted in shortages of both power and water. While Hazelet was in Seattle securing additional machinery for the power plant, he visited Ed Hasey at the McNeil Island Penitentiary. [2]

Hasey's attorneys had initially planned to appeal the conviction, but in October the Juneau paper announced that Hasey would drop the appeal and agree to serve his 18-month sentence. [3] Hasey decided to go to prison because he was afraid that the Alaska Syndicate would not continue to fund his appeal and he could not afford it himself. [4] W.H. Bogle, the Katalla Company attorney, realized it would be less expensive to pay Hasey while serving his sentence than to assume financial responsibility for the appeal. Although Hasey refused Bogle's initial offer of $1,800, he eventually negotiated with the Syndicate's New York office and agreed on terms to be mediated through E.C. Hawkins. [5]

Among other things, Hawkins agreed to assist in obtaining a pardon for Hasey. On November 29, 1909, he wrote John A. Carson:

> Dear Sir:
>
> In the matter of the verdict and sentence of Edward C. Hasey at Juneau last spring for assault with deadly weapons in the Keystone Canyon troubles, I wish to say that I believe this was a mistaken verdict and was given under peculiar conditions and prejudice. I think you are also satisfied as to this. I believe we should do all what is in our power to secure a pardon for Mr. Hasey. ...

Can you advise me as to the best steps to take, particularly in initiating the proceedings. I am going to New York and can take the matter up with some friends in Washington if you think such course would be advisable. ... I am taking this up simply in order to have justice done Mr. Hasey, and is not a Company business affair.

Neither the attempts to get a pardon nor Hasey's request to be jailed in Juneau rather than McNeil Island were successful. When Hazelet visited him in February, Hasey was tending cattle at the penitentiary farm. Hazelet wrote Donohoe: "I dislike very much to see him lay there in jail for the next 14 months and what he wants as much as anything else is the restoration of his citizenship." [6] The Alaska Syndicate had agreed to pay Hasey $150 a month during his imprisonment to be used to support his wife.

Although almost three years had passed since the unfortunate shooting in Keystone Canyon, litigation was still pending in the summer of 1910. John Phillips, one of the injured men, had filed a civil suit against the Copper River and Northwestern Railway Company, George C. Hazelet and Edward Hasey asking judgment for $25,000 damages. [7] Phillips contended that he had been permanently crippled by the leg wound and was awarded $15,000 after a trial in Seward. [8] When Hazelet testified at this trial, he expressed his continued anguish over results of the canyon shooting. [9]

The legacy of Keystone Canyon and Wickersham's persistent attacks on the Alaska Syndicate did not damage Hazelet's political position in Cordova. The *Cordova Daily Alaskan* supported Hazelet with the following editorial on the day prior to the April, 1910, city council election:

Geo. C. Hazelet, whose name heads the Taxpayers' ticket, came to Prince William Sound, Alaska, in the spring of 1898, since which time he has been ever active in all enterprises for opening up the country and developing its resources. Every prospector who goes into and explores the Copper river country necessarily travels over trails constructed by Hazelet. He has been a pioneer of pioneers. The Slate creek country, which has turned out many thousands of dollars, was first discovered by him. When the history of Central Alaska comes to be written by those familiar with the facts, Hazelet's name will appear near the top of the list of men who have contributed their means and muscle and the best years of their life to bringing the country to a stage of justifying the founding of the prosperous young City of Cordova.

About two years ago when Mr. Hazelet came to this community he found the present townsite of Cordova in its primitive state — a succession of hills and ravines covered with timber, about as unpromising a townsite proposition as can well be imagined. Nothing daunted by conditions, he went to work, and since then has devoted his time and energy to building up the town, and in every way possible advancing and promoting the welfare and best interests of the inhabitants. As trustee of the people owning the townsite, he has more than fulfilled every promise made to the people and has expended thousands of dollars on public improvements of the same. Not a dollar of taxation has been imposed to bring the town to its present condition. It is true that, during his residence here and elsewhere in Alaska, he has from time to time represented capitalists who were exploiting, investigating, and developing the country. He may, possibly, have been guilty at one time or another, of inducing capital to come to the country. Indeed, it may be truthfully said that he has never been a knocker, but has been consistently, and at all times, a booster for the Copper river and Prince William Sound districts.

He now pleads guilty to the charge of being friendly to the C.R. & N.W. Ry. Co. hoping that they may carry out their gigantic enterprises, the inevitable consequence of which will be the up-building of the town of Cordova into a thriving young city of many thousands of population. His private character is above reproach. His business ability and integrity are necessarily admitted. His interests in Cordova are considerable. His career as a public servant is in all respects commendible and challenges adverse criticism. There should be no question of his re-election by an overwhelming vote. [10]

Copper River and Northwestern Train on Flag Point bridge.
ANCHORAGE MUSEUM OF HISTORY & ART. B64.1.121

The newspaper eulogy may have helped Hazelet to continue on the council but did not convince the Cordova electorate to elect the rest of his ticket. On April 7, 1910, Hazelet lamented in a letter to Donohoe: "We got licked like Hell in the election. Guess the people of Cordova have no use for the railway and the townsite company." Dr. Will Chase received the largest number of votes and succeeded Hazelet as mayor. Soon the citizens of Cordova and the absentee land owners were assessed property taxes to pay for a school and a larger jail. [11]

Hazelet continued to be active in the Republican party and was elected as a delegate to the nominating convention in Douglas in June 1910. The Cordova delegates joined in endorsing Ed Orr as a compromise candidate who would be independent of both factions of the party. [12] Wickersham subsequently convened his own rival convention which nominated him to run against Orr in the Republican primary. Cordova supported Orr, but Wickersham prevailed in both the primary and the general election, winning a second two-year term as delegate to Congress. Hazelet and the other Cordova councilmen welcomed Wickersham to their city. The delegate, aware of his unpopularity in that part of Alaska, usually by-passed Cordova when recommending federal projects and appointments.

The Copper River and Northwestern Railway was completed between the Kennecott mines and Cordova in November of 1910, but the proposed extension to the interior rivers and the spur to the coal fields were postponed. Since the Bering River coal fields remained closed, the town of Cordova was not growing as fast as the townsite company had anticipated. On February 17, 1911, Hazelet wrote E.C. Hawkins of the railway company that about $15,000 was overdue on lots but that he was not forcing foreclosure because "lots are almost impossible to sell in Cordova at the present time." The townsite company still had over 400 lots to sell. [13]

Hazelet and Donohoe were soon involved in promoting their other townsite. On April 26, Hazelet returned to Cordova after attending a court session in Valdez at which Judge Cushman dissolved an injunction against development of the townsite along Mineral Creek near Valdez that Hazelet had acquired back in 1902 for a railroad terminus. John Rosene had been issued 65% of the capital stock in that property, known as Hazeletville, in 1905 with the provision that he construct a railroad from Hazeletville to the interior of Alaska. Abandonment of Valdez as terminus for the Copper River and Northwestern Railway made Hazeletville a dead issue for the next four years, but when gold was discovered in the area, a man named H.R. Robbins appeared with an assignment of the Rosene stock. Hazelet refused to transfer the stock because Rosene had not fulfilled the original agreement. Robbins then brought suit and tied up the property with the injunction. [14]

After the injunction was lifted, Donohoe and Hazelet made an abortive attempt to develop the Mineral Creek townsite. Hazelet immediately suggested that Jack Meals put up a tent and live on the land to keep squatters off pending arrangments with B.F. Millard and James Lathrop to handle the sale of land in the townsite. [15] Hazelet requested that Donohoe send him blueprints of the new town and price lists so that he could try to sell lots over in Cordova. [16] Within a month Hazelet had reached an agreement with Millard and Lathrop, stating in a letter to Millard: "I want to say that I desire to have you satisfied in every way so long as it is consistent with good business on my part, and do not want any misunderstanding in anything." [17]

On June 12, Hazelet received the following telegram from Rosene, who had just arrived back in Seattle from Europe: "Suit commenced by Robbins based on misapprehension. If you will consent to dismissal without prejudice or postpone until fall and come here at my expense, we can undoubtedly come to amicable satisfactory understanding." [18] Donohoe advised that they go ahead with the trial rather than delaying because Rosene still had an impractical idea of building a monorail up Mineral Creek. [19] On July 6, the case was decided in Hazelet's favor and Rosene was ordered to turn over his stock, stated to be worth $97,500. [20]

Shortly after settlement of the lawsuit, Mother Nature appeared to be taking a hand in promoting development of the Mineral Creek townsite. The original townsite of Valdez was frequently threatened by flooding from glacial streams, and, in late July, a torrent of water rushed through the town, washing away cabins and undermining several houses, including one owned by Ostrander. [21] Hazelet immediately wrote Millard to cut the price on business lots temporarily in order to induce businesses to move to the new townsite while the glacier was on rampage. [22] On July 27, Hazelet wrote Donohoe that he would be willing to sell lots for 33% if building was started within 60 days. "If we could get 8 to 10 businesses established we would have the thing going and finally succeed. ... I don't want to give all the property away to have a town built there but am willing to allow the good people of Valdez a chance to get in on the ground floor." [23] Although the glacial streams repeatedly broke the dikes and flooded Valdez that summer, the good people of Valdez did not take advantage of Hazelet's offer. On August 22, he again wrote Donohoe: "See Mayor Cavanaugh and offer him any lot in the townsite. It would cost much less to move government buildings than to try to fix the glacier streams." [24] Valdez still refused to move.

Before making all these efforts to develop the townsite near Valdez, Hazelet had attempted to get rid of some of his responsibilities in Cordova. Back in March he had announced his desire not to seek re-election to the Cordova city council. Throughout the year he had opposed spending and taxation and had watched a $3,000 city surplus evaporate and a deficit accumulate. The voters nominated him anyway and Hazelet agreed to stand for re-election.

Hazelet was re-elected and the new city council adopted his retrenchment policy, promising to lop off unnecessary expenditures. A new councilman, Captain Austin E. Lathrop, received the largest number of votes and was proclaimed mayor. [26]

The financial outlook for Cordova improved in April of 1911 when the first load of copper ore arrived in town from the Bonanza mine, but the Bering River coal fields remained closed. Steamers, railroads and utilities were being altered to burn California crude oil rather than continuing to bear the expense of importing coal from Canada. On May 4, 1911, the citizens of Cordova took matters in their own hands by dumping tons of the imported coal into the harbor.

The Cordova Coal Party was carefully planned by local businessmen as a protest to resemble the Boston Tea Party. They secreted shovels in a dockside warehouse and arranged for all federal law enforcement officials to be called away from town on business. Mayor Lathrop and the city police chief made only token efforts to stop the attack on the imported coal by hundreds of Cordovans.

"Tired and Worn Out"

The dumping of coal into Cordova Bay focused nationwide attention on the Prince William Sound community and on the dilemma that closure of the coal fields was causing in Alaska. Sentiment in Congress began to swing towards giving Alaskans more voice in the governing of their country. Delegate Wickersham succeeded in defeating the Beveridge bill that would have created a military commission to govern Alaska. Wickersham's own bill authorizing a territorial legislature was sure of Congressional approval but supportive west coast senators still feared a presidential veto. An article in Juneau's *Daily Alaska Dispatch* announced: "The allied commercial bodies of the Pacific Coast are already planning a campaign to bring President Taft into line for the bill when it reaches his hands." [1]

Cordova Coal party, throwing foreign coal into bay.
ALASKA STATE MUSEUM. PCA277.8.88

Early in June of 1911, Wickersham wrote in his diary about a meeting with Senator Wesley Jones of Washington at which they discussed means by which to put more pressure on the Taft administration. They agreed to keep attacking "the Attorney General for condoning, concealing and protecting Jarvis and other Syndicate criminals from punishment for admitted crimes against the United States in Alaska matters." Wickersham's diary entry concluded:

> After a long discussion and careful examination of all of the Attorney General's letters, he (Senator Jones) advised that I go into a public investigation of the Attorney General and his attitude favoring the Alaska Syndicate in Alaska. ... He frankly said that he thought the Attorney General and the Taft administration had pushed their efforts to aid the Guggenheims to the point that left me nothing else to do than to fight — and the harder and more public I did it the more credit would be mine. [2]

Wickersham was aware that the U.S. Department of Justice had already made an extensive investigation of his charges of bribery of witnesses during the first Keystone Canyon shooting trial, but felt that he could still accuse the attorney general of ignoring his charges that Jarvis had been involved in price fixing on the Nome coal contract back in 1908. On October 25, 1910, Wickersham mentioned in his diary that his friend H.J. Douglas, "accountant for the Guggenheims and the archenemy of Jarvis and that crowd," had informed him that the assistant attorney general and 12 or 15 secret service men were in Alaska checking on his allegations of corruption in the Hasey trials.

One of the Justice Department special agents, W.A. Bryan, spoke at length with Jarvis in his Seattle office between November 5 and December 1, 1910. These interviews were arranged by J.M. Lathrop, who was deputy U.S. marshal in Valdez at the time of the Keystone Canyon confrontation. Jarvis explained in detail the arrangements that had been made with the various lawyers involved in the Hasey defense and the ways in which they had been paid. He turned over to the special agent letters and telegrams that documented his admonitions against any violence in Keystone Canyon and his regret when it had occurred. The only documentation that he was unable to provide was the detailed account from John A. Carson, the lawyer that Stephen Birch had insisted on hiring to assist in the first Hasey trial. A copy of the Carson account was missing from the Seattle files because it had been sent to New York at Birch's request.

After his first interview with Jarvis, the special agent reported:

> There is a letter written by Captain Jarvis which makes the statement, "We are to blame." I asked the Captain for a copy of the letter and he said that personally he was willing to give it to me — but that he did not wish to put himself in a position

of protecting himself and placing the blame on some one else. That when the time came that the files of his office were wanted by the court or a Grand Jury, that they would be forthcoming — he said that he did not want to make trouble for Mr. Hazelet or anyone else as it would do no good, the harm is all done. That when he heard of the evidence which was going before the Congressional Committee in Washington last winter, he was tempted to go to Washington and request to be sworn, but later concluded that if they wanted him they would send for him.

It is impossible for me to recall all of the letters which were shown to me. If permitted to see more of the files I will take more time and care, but Captian Jarvis says that they are open to me at all times, and I am in duty bound to say, that so far, there is no reason why both Captain Jarvis and Mr. Bogle should not be more than willing to produce at any time what has been shown to me to date. So far as I am able to judge in my humble way, the correspondence redounds to the credit of both Captain Jarvis and Mr. Bogle. ...

Captain Jarvis takes the position that he had no alternative as Treasurer for the Company other than pay as directed any claim against the company which found its way to his office accompanied by voucher and approval of one authorized to incur expense. That he had no part in any of the Legal Department's plans for the defense of Hasey and that as Treasurer and a part of his duty, he at all times used due diligence to protect the company from exorbitant charges. In this matter his correspondence certainly bears him out. [3]

At a subsequent meeting with Jarvis, Special Agent Bryan reiterated his impression that "seemingly the Captain has no concern for himself, evidently believing that the files of his office constitute a complete defense for himself." [4] In a letter from Jarvis to John A. Carson in which he requested information on Carson's expense account, Jarvis explained: "You probably know what kind of a character Mr. H.J. Douglas is, and it is my belief that after he was discharged by the Company, or just before he was discharged, he abstracted everything possible from the files of the Company to make trouble for some of the people connected with it, yourself and Mr. Birch among the number. I presume I am included also, as well as Judge Bogle. These he no doubt has given to Mr. Wickersham, who also is not a very enviable character, and they probably will distort, twist, lie about and misrepresent the items contained in the statement. I would be very glad if you can furnish me any light on the matter so I can send it to Mr. Birch. The matter causes me no uneasiness, for it was one I always religiously abhorred, and would have nothing to do with except pay the bills, but I do not wish to be twisted in such shape as to reflect on the rest of you." [5]

During the meetings in Jarvis' office, Special Agent Bryan had an opportunity to listen in on conversations between James Lathrop and Jarvis regarding affairs in

Alaska. Lathrop indicated that Delegate Wickersham had expressed to him a desire to make peace with the Alaska Syndicate, and that Major Richardson of the Alaska Road Commission had reported to him that Stephen Birch had in some way aided Wickersham's 1910 campaign for delegate. They also discussed the dissension among the managers of the Guggenheim companies occasioned by Birch having received $90,000 over and above his salary as a commission on the sale to the Guggenheim company of the Beatson copper mine on Latouche Island. Jarvis, who was concerned with judicious use of funds from the Morgan bank, complained about waste of money and materials during construction of the Copper River and Northwestern Railway, which he referred to as "steals that could not go on without the consent of Hawkins and Eccles." [6]

Special Agent Bryan then reported on conversations he had with Hasey at the McNeil Island Penitentiary later in November. When he returned to Jarvis' office on December 1, Bryan found that Jarvis had still not received the information he had requested from Carson. In his report of that day's conversation he stated:

> In connection with the files of Captain Jarvis office, I wish to state that I have information from a reliable source, not Captain Jarvis, that it is possible that Captain Jarvis may enter the employ of a rival steamship company. That is to say plans are now under way for the formation of a company which will compete with the Guggenheim boats. The competitive company wishes to have Jarvis with them, Jarvis being the only sea man with the Guggenheim company. At present all other officials being Southern Pacific Railroad men, placed by Mr. S.W. Eccles of the New York office of the Guggenheims, and not competent ship men, or at least not so regarded.
>
> The action of Stephen Birch, who obtained from Jarvis the Carson account and failed to return same to Jarvis, has widened a breach that has existed for some time. Jarvis' recent action in giving out the information which he has in this investigation is expected to make matters still worse. And in the event Captain Jarvis leaves his present position **It Is Highly Probable That Further Information Will Be Denied. Mr. Jarvis Wants The Government To Have Full Information While Things Are Under His Control.** [7]

Captain Jarvis did not join a competitive steamship company as predicted, but disapproved of the business practices of his associates and persisted in his desire to leave the Alaska Syndicate. On April 1, 1911, an article in the *Cordova Daily Alaskan* announced that "all of the properties of the Northwestern Fisheries Company, including nine of the largest and best equipped canneries on the coast of Alaska, seven sailing vessels and numerous tugs, launches, fishing boats and machinery and equipment for its extensive operations, were taken over on April 1 by a new syndicate, a reorganization of the Booth Fish Company of Chicago, New York and Baltimore." Jarvis, whose primary interest was in Northwestern Fisheries, which he organized back in 1905, became the president of the new company.

Shortly before leaving the Alaska Syndicate, Jarvis wrote William Hamilton, vice president of the Morgan bank:

> Seattle, Wash., Nov. 25, 1910.
> My dear Mr. Hamilton:
> I have today sent to J.P. Morgan & Company drafts for $85,764.30, which completes payment on what this Company owed your firm. Since we began these payments November 1, 1907, they have amounted to $1,117,612.29 principal and $160,448.28 interest. During the same time we have paid about $600,000.00 other obligations here and in Alaska. This has all been done without issuing a stock, bond or other outside obligation except for temporary loans from local banks which have been promptly paid.
> I enclose summary of the outcome of the Fisheries Company for the year. If that Company pays the $350,000.00 dividend earned and recommended, it will have paid the Commercial Company a total of $900,000.00; increased its cash working capital from $500,000.00 to $644,780.62, and will show on its general statement a surplus of $160,831.77 and a depreciation account of $287,028.33. It has also built an entirely new cannery, added to and rebuilt a large part of its other property, installed a large part of its machinery new and taken a position at the head of the general business, second to none, for the character of its output and for the character of its dealings with employees, competitors and customers.
> Now that this is all done and the years business is practically wound up, I feel I am ready to be relieved at your convenience after the first of the year.

Jarvis was justly proud of the accomplishments of Northwestern Fisheries under his management. After paying off the money loaned by the Morgan bank when he and Rosene purchased the assets of the bankrupt Pacific Packing and Navigation Company, Jarvis felt free to leave the Syndicate. Hamilton answered, expressing his regrets that Jarvis was leaving:

> December 1st, 1910.
> My dear Captain:
> Yesterday the firm received your remittance closing the loan matter with the exception of a small matter of interest and today I am in receipt of your personal letter of the 25th.
> It is a source of great gratification to us all here to have had this matter work out so successfully. The splendid business that the Fisheries Company has done this year is also very gratifying and I feel much indebted to you and to those who

have looked after the affairs of the Company during several pretty trying years. I believe we have now started upon a firmer foundation than ever before and, unless all signs fail, should do a satisfactory business in the future. ...

I see from the end of your letter you still feel that you should retire and I am still in the dark as to why you wish to do so as I was in hopes that you would find your surroundings pleasant and the work agreeable. No one at this end wishes you to sever your association with us. Would not you like to come on and talk matters over before definitely making up your mind? You have shown that you would not desert a sinking ship so why leave her now that she is well corked and in smooth waters.

With kindest regards, believe me,

Yours very truly,

William P. Hamilton. [8]

Even though Jarvis was no longer working with the Alaska Syndicate when Wickersham and Senator Jones devised their plan for pressuring the Taft administration, Wickersham focused his new attack upon his former friend and demanded that Attorney General George Wickersham (no relation to the delegate) prosecute Jarvis for collusion in bidding for coal in 1908, as claimed in the Douglas affidavit. The final report of the McNamara investigation, submitted to the attorney general in April, did not include examination of this new allegation. McNamara suggested that further investigation of that charge should be undertaken although the "only evidence so far obtained is the statement of H.J. Douglas, formerly in the employ of the Northwestern Commercial Company, to the effect that he overheard a conversation between D.H. Jarvis of the Northwestern Company and John Bullock of the Sesnon Company, about the plan to submit the bids under an agreement to divide the profits." The McNamara report concluded that the investigation had failed to turn up any evidence of bribery of any juror or witness in the Hasey case upon which to base an indictment. [9]

—⁓◦⟨⊙⟩⊶⟨⊙⟩⊷◦⟨⊙⟩⊶◦⁓—

On June 22, 1911, newspapers in Seattle and Alaska carried the following story:

Washington, D.C., June 22. — Delegate James Wickersham opened a fight on the administration here today when he introduced a resolution in the House calling upon the attorney general and secretary of war to inform the House what had been done regarding irregularities in the letting of coal contracts at Fort Davis and Fort Liscum in 1908, the delegate claiming to hold documentary evidence that Captain Jarvis, treasurer of the Guggenheim corporation, robbed the government out of several thousand dollars on these contracts. [10]

When these new public allegations convinced Jarvis that Wickersham had singled him out as the target of his venomous attacks, this proud, reserved man chose to escape rather than endure the slings and arrows of outrageous fortune, not stopping to think that his escape might be interpreted as an admission of guilt. The day after Wickersham made these accusations in the House of Representatives, Jarvis shot himself in a room at the Seattle Athletic Club, where he was staying while his family was at their summer cottage. He left no explanation except a note saying, "Tired and worn out." As far as friends in Seattle and Alaska knew, Jarvis was in excellent health and had no family or financial problems.

News coverage of the suicide in Seattle and Alaska was complimentary to Jarvis in spite of Wickersham's recent accusations. An editorial in the *Nome Daily Nugget* concluded:

> Alaskans who know him, personally and otherwise, will always have great respect for the work he did to help develop the country. ... He was a builder and left monuments to perpetuate his name. Had the destiny which shaped his end allowed him to round out the full three score and ten, he would have reared other monuments to hand down to prosperity, for being a man of action, was able to accomplish much of a permanent nature. [11]

A contributing factor to the depression that apparently led Jarvis to end his life may have been the realization of what might have been his future had he remained in the Revenue Marine. Shortly before his suicide Jarvis learned that Elsworth F. Bertholf, the junior officer who had accompanied on the Overland Expedition of 1898, had been placed in charge of the Revenue Marine. The comments of Capt. Bertholf upon hearing of Jarvis' suicide offer insight into the man's life and his handling of Wickersham's attacks on him:

> The news has stunned me and I find it hard to realize what has happened. Years ago when Capt. Jarvis and I were brother officers in the same service, I lived with him in the same tent, was his comrade in times of hardship and danger and got to know him as a man of indomitable courage, unswerving in his devotion to duty and uncompromising in his honesty. Not many people really knew him well but no one who ever had the privilege of knowing him well ever failed to love and appreciate him. Being trained in military habits from his youth, he gave unquestioned obedience where it was due, and demanded the same when it was due him and rarely gave an explanation. Ever conscious of rectitude in his own actions, he seldom defended himself when criticized by those who misunderstood him, and the note he left on his desk when he passed into the great beyond is characteristic of the man —"tired and worn out," no explanation, no complaint and no bitterness, just a simple heartbreaking statement of the facts. [12]

Wickersham had no such kindly words for his former friend, supporter, and confidante. His diary entry on June 24, 1911, consists merely of a news clipping about the Jarvis suicide and the following underlined words: "**Poor Jarvis. Until he became the employee of the Guggenheim bunch of Jew thieves, he was a man of honor and courage.**" The next day the diary had a clipping of a newspaper article saying that Jarvis was distressed by the Douglas and Wickersham charges, under which Wickersham wrote the following comment, which he must have realized was not true: "Conscience makes cowards of us all. Possibly the fact he gave the order which caused Hasey to shoot an unarmed and innocent workman may have caused the remorse and shot."

Wickersham did not let Jarvis rest in peace, but seized the opportunity to make more accusations. A newspaper article, pasted in the diary and undoubtedly written after an interview with Wickersham, stated: "In his operations Jarvis was bold beyond the possible realization of people who do not know Alaska. Whether it was in lobbying legislation through Congress, in seizing a railroad right of way by power of Winchesters and stuffed clubs, in fighting the powers of business, in fixing juries or playing corrupt politics, Jarvis was of utmost boldness and resource."

The article exaggerated the Keystone Canyon injuries and concluded: "The death of Jarvis, it was explained today will not end the matter. It ends the trouble of Jarvis only. Why the Administration has failed so many times to proceed against Jarvis and his associates for the various alleged crimes marking their careers will be the subject of persistent inquiry, just as if Jarvis were still alive." [13]

Wickersham must have felt a need to justify his attacks on Jarvis because he kept referring to the Nome coal case for years. Diary enteries with newspaper clippings tell of the grand jury investigation, indictment, trial, and conviction of John Bullock and Charles Houston, the representatives of the other coal-bidding companies, for fraud in colluding to fix the price of coal. A clipping in the diary on August 17, 1912, gives Bullock's explanation that a coal shortage and transportation problems caused coal to be expensive in 1908, but that, as far as he knew, there had been three competitive bids. Articles in several Alaska newspapers confirm the coal shortage. [14] No evidence was ever produced to confirm the Douglas allegations but the Justice Department persisted in prosecuting Bullock and Houston because of pressure from Wickersham. When a group of western senators approached President Woodrow Wilson in 1913 to obtain pardons for Houston and Bullock, Wickersham sent the President a letter of protest against granting the pardons. The last mention of the case in the diary, on September, 1913, implied that a court of appeals might overturn the convictions of Bullock and Houston. [15]

The coal fraud case dragged on for years. A letter from Wickersham's secretary to an inquiring citizen in March 1915, indicated that the conviction had been upheld and that Bullock and Houston were serving short sentences. [16] Transcripts and exhibits from the case were removed from the federal court records in 1918 by a federal investigator without any explanation for their removal. [17]

Wickersham and the muckraking press made accusations, but gave little concrete evidence that Jarvis did anything that was either illegal or basely motivated. Wickersham's attacks on Jarvis and the Alaska Syndicate were designed to make full use of all scare tactics of the time. For the sake of political expediency, Alaska's congressional delegate was willing to sacrifice a friend who had always wished him well. Wickersham's preoccupation with the insignificant Nome coal-bidding case and his campaign to prevent pardons for Bullock and Houston must have been caused by a deep need to justify what he had done. Perhaps he was really speaking for himself when he wrote "conscience makes cowards of us all" in his diary on the day after he learned of the Jarvis suicide.

Stephen Birch, who was more directly involved than Jarvis in the Keystone Canyon shooting and the actions of his attorney, John A. Carson, during the first Hasey trial, escaped any of the fallout from the affair. Apparently Birch worked out a truce with Wickersham by agreeing not to oppose Wickersham's efforts to obtain more home rule for Alaska. Birch never spoke directly with Wickersham following their meeting in April 1910, but occasionally consulted the delegate through intermediaries, such as Donald McKenzie and Falcon Joslin, to avoid incurring Wickersham's wrath in political matters. [18]

Cordova Daily Alaskan August 1, 1914

GERMANY DECLARES WAR

AIRSHIP MAKES FIRST FLIGHT IN ALASKA

Valdez Daily Prospector August 4, 1913

Strange Race In Kuskokwim

Tribe of 1000-3000 People Living in Kuskokwim

They Do Not Cook Food

Live on Birds, Fish and Eggs Which Have Reached Stage of Decay

---

KATMAI BLAMED FOR POOR RUN

Recent eruption on coast is cause of poor salmon run this year

LOST MAN EATS PORCUPINE AND LIKES IT

PANAMA CANAL WONDER OF THE WORLD AT LAST A REALITY

WORLD'S GREATEST ENGINEERING FEAT WILL COST $400,000,000

SHELDON AUTOMOBILE RUNS FROM FAIRBANKS TO VALDEZ IN 54 HOURS

THREE ALASKAN TOWNS MAY GO DRY

Ketchikan, Sitka and Wrangell Will Take Vote On the Question of Granting Liquor Licenses.

Depression and Death

XXIV

The citizens of Cordova took little note of Jarvis' suicide — they had other problems to contend with in 1911 and 1912. When Delegate Wickersham returned to Alaska after Congress adjourned, he visited Cordova to plead for harmony. In a public address on November 27, 1911, he wooed Cordovans by stating his support for opening the coal fields and extending railroads to the interior rivers of Alaska.

After the Cordova Coal Party the previous spring, both Secretary of Interior Walter Fisher, the conservationist who succeeded Ballinger, and Gifford Pinchot visited Alaska. The frustrated people of Katalla, who blamed Pinchot for the closure of the coal fields, burned him in effigy. Fisher, on the other hand, was well received by Alaskans, hopeful for any measures that would open up the country. Fisher returned with suggestions that a leasing policy be established for the coal lands and that the federal government assume responsibility for construction of railroads in Alaska in order to prevent mining and transportation monopolies. Many of the Bering River coal claims, including Cunningham's, had already been cancelled as fraudulent and more litigation was pending.

Wickersham did not attack the Copper River and Northwestern Railway directly, suggesting rather: "Let's let the Guggenheims come in with us if they will be good. ... They have $20,000,000 invested in the railroad. ...I want to see it extended to Fairbanks. I want the railroad developed. From what I saw I am ready to quit fighting if they will quit and do right and all get together and counsel one with the other and do all we can to get the coal situation settled and the territory developed." [1]

In spite of Wickersham's pleas for unity, the split in Alaska's Republican party between Wickersham and the conservative faction headed by National Committeeman L.P. Shackleford continued. George Hazelet was still loyal to the Republican party, but was more concerned with local Cordova politics and attempted to steer an intermediate course without identifying with either side in statewide issues. He declared his support for a liberal leasing bill that would facilitate opening the coal fields with railroad access, [2] and joined in a reorganization of the Cordova Chamber of Commerce that emphasized "harmony without political or social frills." [3] Anticipating the busy political season, Hazelet wrote his friend Donohoe, who was a leader of the Democratic party in Alaska: "I don't believe that I have often known so many things to come all at once. You, with your Democratic convention in Valdez on the 29th, the Republican pow-wow in Cordova on the 30th, and the election of seven august councilmen for the town of Cordova on April 2 is too much for your humble servant. Now after this is all over with we will have nothing to do but sit around and growl at each other." [4] Hazelet was a delegate to the Republican convention in Cordova in April which nominated William Gilmore of Nome for delegate to Congress and endorsed the re-election of President Taft. [5]

Hazelet did not run again for city council in 1912, but was pleased with the results of the April 1 election. On April 9, he wrote Donohoe: "Several things make it gratifying. First, we will have no tax if it can be done without. Second, we have done up a few that deserved to be done, and third, Shackleford was very anxious to see our opponents win. I really think he felt worse than Dr. Chase or Thisted over the result and the funny part was that he could not help but show it." [6]

Soon there were more political developments to consider. Wickersham, who was not content with the Republican nominations, convened his own convention, which again named him as candidate for delegate and endorsed Theodore Roosevelt in his Bull Moose bid for the presidency. In late July of 1912, the Senate passed Wickersham's amended home rule, which became known as the Second Organic Act and gave Alaska official recognition as a territory with the right to elect its own legislature.

Wickersham, riding on the crest of popularity, was re-elected in August, but some Alaskans were not enthusiastic about the new legislature. The *Valdez Prospector* commented: "The Alaska home rule bill which has become a law and which Wickersham professes to be so jubilant about is chiefly noted for what the territorial legislature can not do, rather than what it can do." [7] However, as soon as President Taft signed the bill, Alaskans began considering whom to elect as representatives to send to Juneau for the new legislature. A non-partisan primary held in Cordova on September 14, 1912, nominated Hazelet to be their candidate for state senator in a 55 to 3 vote over Dr. Will Chase.

Hazelet was in Seattle attending to sad personal affairs when Cordovans gave him this vote of confidence. On August 22, banner headlines in the *Cordova Daily Alaskan* announced: "Death Angel Calls Mrs. G.C. Hazelet." Hazelet was devastated by the loss. His family had always been his greatest pleasure and for years both George and Harriet had hoped for more children. Already middle-aged, with Calvin and Craig attending college, their wishes were about to be fulfilled when Harriet and the baby died in childbirth. [8] Both sons were away from Cordova when their mother died, Calvin with his uncle John at the Chisna mine and Craig at the Kennecott mine. [9] When the boys returned to town, the family accompanied Harriet's body to Seattle for burial at the Mount Pleasant Cemetary.

Harriet Hazelet
PHOTO COURTESY OF HAZELET GRANDCHILDREN

Bishop Peter Trimble Rowe conducted graveside services and commented in a letter to the Rev. Eustace Ziegler in Cordova: "The boys at the fraternity house to which Calvin and Craig belong were the pall bearers. It is all so sad. I was shocked when I heard of her death. What a loss we have suffered, as you say, in the death of Mr. Hawkins and Mrs. Hazelet! What a friend and helper, true and tried, through these many years Mrs. Hazelet has been. And I am so sorry for Mr. Hazelet and the sons." [10] (Railroad manager, E.C. Hawkins, who left Cordova in October 1911, died suddenly in New York the spring of 1912.)

Upon his return to Cordova early in October, Hazelet called for a meeting of men of every political affiliation to discuss the nomination for state senator. At this meeting he declared that "in order that Cordova and the Copper river country might have a member in the Senate it is necessary that all elements in Cordova get together and give a practically unanimous endorsement, and then give that man a united support." Feeling that he might not be supported by all factions, Hazelet then declined the nomination and Cordovans voted to support T.B. Tansy, the announced candidate of the Home Rule party. [11]

The editor of the *Cordova Daily Alaskans* commented favorably on Hazelet's gesture and predicted victory for Cordova's candidates:

> And in deciding to rise superior to the ordinary methods of politics, the majority did a generous act that cannot help but bear the rich fruit of a closer friendship among neighbors and a united and more forceful effort upon the part of all the people for the future advancement, prosperity and happiness of the community. This only made possible because the minority have a deep sense of appreciation for the unusual and unexpected act, and a feeling of deep gratitude for the strong support extended a worthy man whose candidacy is now so fortified that his election will naturally follow. [12]

The editor was not correct in his prognostigation. The Tansy-Baldwin ticket lost to the Millard-Ray ticket. Since the elected men were from Valdez, the rival community across Prince William Sound, rather than Cordova, was represented in Alaska's first territorial legislature.

Cordova faced more economic problems during the winter of 1913. The Copper River and Northwestern Railway stopped running until spring and several businesses were forced to shut down. Hazelet wrote Donohoe when he received news that the local theater was closing:

> Times are hard enough down here without the loss of any more business. I don't see any immediate chance of business picking up either and that makes it still worse. The road don't seem to open up and don't think it will till there is an entire change in management. It's simply awful. No use of being in the fix they are — or at least that is what is said by people in position to know what they are talking about.
>
> I have never felt quite as "dumpy" about the outlook here as I do at present. [13]

High Road to Chisana

Cordova's economic doldrums were dramatically relieved in the summer of 1913 by reports of a gold strike on the headwater of the Tanana River that the Indians called "Shushanna," but that the new Boundary Commission maps designated as "Chisana." On July 18, Jim Morris and Dan Stacey, who had been to the field, confirmed the discovery, reporting to the *Cordova Daily Alaskan* that "pay had been found on Bonanza, Eldorado, and other tributaries of the Sushanna with pans ranging from 75 cents up common."

Two days later George Hazelet made the following entry in his diary:

> Left Cordova for Kennecott at 8:30 a.m. having made up my mind to go into the Chesthana, or "Susanna" as some term it, instead of the Johnson or Robertson on a hunting trip as I had planned to do with my two boys, Calvin and Craig. To be exact, there is a gold rush on and the boys were anxious to witness it and I cannot say but that I had a leaning that way myself.

Every year since the Klondike strike of 1898, a few prospectors had gone into this remote area, 400 miles from Fairbanks and 250 miles from Dawson, but the expense of sending in large outfits prevented any extensive search for gold. Completion of the Copper River and Northwestern Railway to the Kennecott copper mine in 1911 brought the Chisana country closer to prospectors who followed the Nizina River from McCarthy and then continued on up the treacherous "goat trail" along the Chitistone River and through Skolai Pass.

Although Hazelet's primary reason for joining the crowd heading for Chisana was to show the boys what a real gold rush was like, the Cordova Chamber of Commerce was undoubtedly relying on him for a realistic appraisal of the Chisana gold strike and its impact on the economy of the fledgling city.

Hazelet and his two sons packed an outfit for six weeks, including rifles, picks and shovels, to combine hunting and prospecting. When they reached Kennicott, they found that the stampede was draining men from nearby districts. Miners all along the Nizina River had left diggings at Dan and Chititu creeks to look over the new country. Only 10 miners were still working at Kennecott and everyone but the superintendent had left the Mother Lode copper mine on the other side of the mountains from McCarthy. [1]

Hazelet reached the Nizina River crossing on July 22 and found the river higher than he had seen it in 10 years. Since he was unsure about how the two horses that he had purchased for the trip in Chitina would perform in the water, Hazelet arranged to have the boys cross with a pack train from the Kennecott mine. After a good night sleep Hazelet awoke feeling "like a game cock," and crossed with the horses in the morning slack water without difficulty.

During the next two days they encountered more difficult river crossings, observing a dead horse and the grave of a Fairbanks man who drowned crossing Glacier Creek several days before. Experienced men like Hazelet helped many of the less seasoned stampeders who were marooned on sand bars, while young Calvin Hazelet hunted, unsuccessfully, for mountain sheep. Hazelet described the trail through the Chistilana Canyon: "This canyon is an extemely dangerous place for horses, the trail simply being a sheep trail widened to about two feet. The drop to the bottom is as much as 2,000 feet in many places and should horse or man lose his footing he could not stop till he reached the bottom. It is from one and a half to two miles through. After examining it carefully and doing a little work in the worst places we got through without accident." But it was clear to Hazelet that another route would have to be found for travel in the winter.

Weather was closing in as the Hazelet group reached Russell Glacier so they decided to wait a day until the snow stopped before attempting to cross the glacier. They feasted on ptarmigan that night and attacked the glacier the follow-ing day, working with pick and shovel to prepare the ice for the horses. After four hours on the glacier, they came out on the south bank of the White River with a "splendid view of the beautiful valley of the White reaching at least 30 miles out towards the east and almost to the boundary line of Canada and Alaska."

The Hazelet party reached Bonanza Creek, the heart of the Chisana field, at 8 p.m. on July 30 and "found 150 to 200 men in camp, most all short of supplies and some with none." The next day, Hazelet looked the area over and discovered that "stakes are everywhere, not only in the creek but high up the mountainside." The commissioner for the area informed him that 125 claims had already been registered and many more were staked. [2]

William James, a Dawson prospector, his wife Matilda Wales, and N.P. Nelson had discovered gold near the mouth of Bonanza Creek, a tributary of the Chathenda (Johnson) branch of the Chisana River, early in the summer of 1913. These prospectors came into the area from Canada, following up on some information that had been given to James the previous summer by a Native known as Indian Joe. Nelson and Andrew Taylor, another prospector who was in the area at the time, carried the news to Dawson when they returned for supplies. [3]

Carl Whitham, an American who staked one of the early claims, was getting ready to sluice on Little Eldorado Creek No.2 when the Hazelet party arrived. This claim impressed Hazelet as being better than James' because it had "more wash." Other early arrivals included Fletcher Hamshaw and a crew of men who had been looking for copper on the White River about 20 miles below Russell Glacier. When he heard of the strike, Hamshaw paid off his men and told them to stake claims, which he purchased later. [4] Hazelet noted that Hamshaw already had "a party crosscutting Eldorado and says he will crosscut Glacier and the others yet this fall — should he find pay on these creeks and on Wilson, this will make a camp — otherwise not." [5]

When Hazelet returned to his camp, he found that his son Calvin had met a college friend and heard about three claims that might still be staked that night. The Hazelets set out at 8 p.m. and returned at 2 a.m. after staking two claims on Chicken Creek, a tributary of Glacier Creek, and one on Clay Creek, also a tributary of Glacier.

After a productive caribou hunt and a good rest, Hazelet and his sons started their assessment work. They were better prepared than many of the stampeders, who had to return to McCarthy to get picks and shovels. On August 10, the Hazelets completed a ditch 45 feet long, 4 feet deep and 3½ feet wide on Chicken No.4, which they had located by power of attorney for their friend John Y. Ostrander. Two days later, they completed a similar ditch on Chicken No.3.

While the boys completed assessment work on the Clay Gulch claim, Hazelet, always alert to future commercial development, made a trip down Wilson Creek to look for an appropriate location for a townsite. He concluded that "just below Johnson, east of Chisana and south of Wilson about 3 to 4 miles was best," and two days later surveyed the land and located corners for two 160 acre tracts. [6]

While the Hazelets were spending the final days of their vacation hunting and prospecting, stampeders were descending upon the Chisana gold field from all directions. R.S. Reid, a special representative for the *Cordova Daily Alaskan*, described the new arrivals in the following report to his editor on August 20:

"The vanguard of the big bunch from Dawson and Fairbanks has arrived and are swarming over the diggings like bees. Some have been lost between White river and Tanana. A few came by way of Gulkana, others up the Tanana in river boats, some from the mouth of the White River and some from the Donjek and Snag rivers, both tributaries of the White River. Already there have been many glad reunions between the Copper river boys and their old time friends from Fairbanks and Dawson."

Sushanna stampeders arriving on SS MARIPOSA, Cordova, Alaska, August 7, 1913.
ANCHORAGE MUSUEM OF HISTORY & ART

When news of the Chisana strike reached cities in Alaska and the Yukon, their newspapers promoted routes to the gold field that would bring business to their respective areas. In Seattle, *The Post-Intelligencer* ran encouraging stories and the Associated Press spread news of the strike throughout the country. The Alaska Steamship Company and the Copper River and Northwestern Railway, both owned by the Alaska Syndicate, sold tickets from Seattle all the way through to McCarthy. The White Pass and Yukon Route, running from Skagway to Whitehorse, was also eager to promote business, and a Skagway paper advertised three routes from Whitehorse — by trail via Kluane Lake, by boat down the Yukon to the Coffee Creek trail, and up the White and Donjek rivers — as safer than trails from McCarthy. In Dawson and Fairbanks, riverboat companies prepared shallow-draft steam vessels for travel on the Yukon and Tanana rivers. Boats leaving Dawson ascended the White River to the mouth of the Donjek River or to Snag Creek where prospectors could proceed to Chisana by poling boats or hiking trails. Proponents of the Tanana River route from Fairbanks claimed that stampeders could pole boats to within 12 miles of the diggings, while they would have to pack a much longer distance after running out of water on the Canadian side. (7)

Many of the stampeders arranged other means of transportation. Horses and wagons regularly traveled the government wagon road from Valdez to Fairbanks, and in early August Robert Sheldon made the first trip from Fairbanks to Valdez in an automobile. Some prospectors from Valdez and Fairbanks used horses, bicycles, and the few available automobiles to get to the railroad at Chitina by way of a new government wagon road. Other Valdez sourdoughs took the wagon road as far as Gulkana and continued by trail to the Nabesna River, considering this route safer than the trail from McCarthy even though it was more than twice as long. Valdez residents openly criticised the promotion emanating from Cordova. When two young boys headed up Thompson Pass for the gold fields with only candy bars and a folder of matches, Valdezians barred the *Cordova Daily Alaskan* from "all homes in Valdez that have boys over two years and under 70, or at least until that paper quits booming the Shushanna." (8)

In response to requests from the White River prospectors for improvements on the Skolai Pass trail, the Cordova Chamber of Commerce sent Malcolm Brock to Seattle to talk with the vice president of the Copper River and Northwestern Railway and presented Colonel Richardson of the Alaska Road Commission with a petition requesting a better road to the White River country. In the meantime, local entrepreneurs were doing their best to meet the needs of stampeders and capitalize on the demand for services. Oscar Breedman, owner of hotels in Cordova and Chitina, established a roadhouse and ferry at the Nizina River crossing. (9) Crews from Copper River and Northwestern Railway constructed a corduroy road from McCarthy to the Nizina by placing logs over swampy areas, and also built a foot bridge over the treacherous Chitistone River. (10) Breedman and others sent pack trains over this trail with food, tobacco and ammunition for the stampeders, many of whom had rushed to the diggings with minimal supplies.

At the end of summer, prospectors with promising claims hurried back to Whitehorse, Dawson, Skagway, McCarthy, Chitina, Cordova, Valdez, Fairbanks or Seattle to purchase supplies for winter work and plan how to get them back to the diggings. Each city that envisioned itself as a potential supply center for the new camp boosted its own access route. Cordova businesses were thriving as a result of the summer stampede and were anxious to capitalize on the winter trade as well. A rival from Whitehorse commented that the Cordovans had "a taste of what stampede money is like, and it savors very much of milk and honey, and they want some more." (11)

In early August, George Hazelet apprised his friends in Cordova of the need to meet competition from other towns by establishing a new winter trail to Chisana because Dawson and Whitehorse were both "reaching out for the trade." [12] The battle of the winter trails was about to begin.

The *Dawson Daily News* announced some of the Canadian preparations on August 13. Yukon Territory Commissioner George Black was negotiating to allow Canadian material to enter the Chisana district without paying customs duty. The commissioner also sent out a crew to cut a winter sled road from the mouth of the Donjek to the Alaska border, and the Royal Canadian Mounted Police were sending 10 officers to patrol the trail.

Dawson entrepreneurs were also preparing. Charles D. Mack, a West Dawson farmer, announced that he was sending 30 dogs and 10 tons of dog salmon to the White River, and was making plans "to get a reindeer herd from the lower Yukon and have them herded in the moss-covered hills of the White river country by Eskimos, who will be engaged to come with the animals." [13] The Dawson paper touted its city as the best source of supplies for the Chisana miners and castigated a Seattle Chamber of Commerce petition to assign a customs collector at the border. The editor called the Americans "commercial war lords" who wanted to cut the struggling prospectors of the Chisana district off from what the Canadians claimed was their natural base of supply, and likened the suggestion of collecting customs at the border to a "deep-laid plot" of commercial manipulators who would have their nation's young men slaughtered on the battlefield to gain an empire for trade. [14]

In Whitehorse and Skagway, the White Pass and Yukon Route was also planning to assure winter access through the Yukon Territory. William Brooks Close, the president of the London banking firm that had financed that railway, was spending a month in Skagway as a guest of the railway president. His nephew, James Brooks Close, had joined the stampede and by mid September had located good building sites along the trail from the White River for roadhouses on a winter stage line. In the meantime, the railway announced plans to distribute hay along the White River for winter horse feed. [15]

Fairbanks no longer competed for travel to Chisana. Most of the stampeders returning by the Tanana River route had depressing tales to tell about the hardships of the trail and the poverty of the field. [16] Prospectors from the Valdez area were now stampeding to a new strike in the Nelchina area.

Hazelet returned to Cordova on August 28 and led the town's effort to capture the Chisana trade. He called for the federal government to place a customs officer on the border to help strangle traffic through Canada. Moreover, he urged Cordovans to act quickly: "Now is Cordova's time to get in and secure this trade. If not secured this winter it never will be."

The Canadian route's strength, Hazelet pointed out, was that water transport could bring supplies to points on the White and Donjek rivers, approximately 120 miles from the gold field. Even though the White Pass group was attempting to transport supplies on the river before freeze-up, they would still not be able to get enough placed along the route, in Hazelet's opinion, to "seriously affect the trade for next year." In order to get more supplies to the Chisana district after freeze-up, the Canadians would have to wait until the rivers were solidly frozen and then they would have to move the additional freight 350 to 400 miles from Whitehorse or Dawson.

In contrast, Hazelet reported that during the winter a route utilizing the Copper River and Northwestern Railway from Cordova to McCarthy would have a distinct advantage. "It is my belief that a route can be found from McCarthy up the Nizina Glacier to the Chisana Glacier that will cut the distance to 80 miles from McCarthy to the diggings, and over which a trip can be made every four days. This is a route which should be thoroughly investigated by the railway company and businessmen interested." [17] Hazelet had indirect knowledge of the route over Nizina and Chisana glaciers because his previous mining partner, Arthur H. McNeer, had accompanied the government cartographer, Oscar Rohn, over that route in 1899. [18]

The Cordova Chamber of Commerce, to whom Hazelet presented his plan, decided to send out an expedition on the next train to McCarthy. Hazelet volunteered to lead the expedition free of charge and requested authorization to hire six men to accompany him with funds supplied by the businessmen in Cordova, Chitina and McCarthy. Colonel Richardson of the Alaska Road Commission agreed to place two of these men on the Commission's payroll. [19]

Hazelet and his crew left Cordova September 3 on a special train to McCarthy, along with 50 stampeders from Seattle. The next special train carried an old-time prospector with a piece of unique new equipment on which he hoped to travel to Chisana. The *Cordova Daily Alaskan* gave the following description of this car belonging to T.G. Jones of Seattle, who had cleaned up $150,000 in the Klondike: "He had a specially constructed automobile, of narrow width, built for him in Seattle. It has ample power to run up hill and carry about a ton of supplies. ... Mr. Jones believes that from what he has heard of the newly built road from McCarthy that he will have but little difficulty in getting to the Nizina Glacier with his automobile. From there he expects to follow the Hazelet party over the new road they are marking."

Hazelet made no mention of the automobile in a September 10 letter to the president of the Chamber of Commerce. By then he had reached the Nizina

Glacier and procured four double-end sleds left by a government survey team, and was busy cutting stakes for the glacier trail. [20]

As Hazelet had predicted, prospectors using the Canadian trails were encountering difficulty due to low water on the rivers. Sid Barrington ran his shallow-draft steamer VIDETTE aground on a sandbar on the White River. Marooned miners had to content themselves with Mrs. Barrington's sweet singing and guitar playing and a goodly supply of "angelic candy" while waiting to join other prospectors camped along the White River until freeze-up when their supplies could be sent from Whitehorse or Dawson on the frozen Yukon. [21]

While prospectors on the Canadian side waited for ice to form, Hazelet's crew was making progress. Staking of the trail was a slow process complicated by the weather. On September 12, Hazelet described a typical day in his diary:

> Took two sled loads of stakes with Gwin's large horses, 100 to the load, and got over the moraine and ready to stake at 8:30 a.m. Fog over entire glacier — could not see ahead 150 feet. I led the way and denoted where stakes were to be set. Set 3 stakes in form of tripod — stakes 10 to 12 feet long and from 4 ft. to 5 ft. from where sleds were run. Set all tripods on right hand side going north, and where any crevasses were found, placed two tripods about 16 ft. apart —trail to run between them. Slow work all forenoon owing to fog. About 11 a.m. fog lifted and I found we were just on edge of Regal Glacier — a glacier putting in to Nizina Glacier from northwest. During afternoon made good progress. Found fine ice, very few crevasses and gradual grade — could pull 4 horse teams over every foot. Placed the entire 200 poles, some as close as 75 ft. where turns had to be made, and some as far as ½ mile apart. Will place tripods 100ft. apart if we succeed in getting over. We figure we have staked today at least 8 miles. ... Will stake tomorrow to foot of summit, at least, and will move camp about Monday to that point. Weather fair tonight.

Ross Kinney, a representative of the Alaska Road Commission, reported on September 25 that a passable trail over the Nizina Glacier was marked and the crew was working on the Chisana Glacier, three miles from the summit. Pack trains were already starting from McCarthy with contracts to haul supplies to Chisana for 25 cents a pound.

When Kinney joined the staking crew on September 29, Hazelet commented in the diary: "If he had dogs or horse feed would be glad to see him, but he has neither." Hazelet could not continue using the horses without more feed so he sent Kinney to get dog teams and left the glaciers with the horses to look for more feed. On October 4, he reached some homesteads where hay and oats was available. The following day, Hazelet sent the horses back to finish the staking and prepared to leave for McCarthy, commenting in the diary that he had "been away from home and business too long."

Upon arriving in McCarthy, Hazelet found that the train had departed for Chitina two hours before. He left the McCarthy depot on a hand speeder at 4:10 p.m. and stopped at 10:30 after covering 33 miles. On October 7, Hazelet wrote in his diary: "Got up at 4 a.m. and lit out. Ice on rails and very hard work — made mile 146, or Dwyers, for breakfast. Left Dwyers at 7 and have to make it to Chitina by 8 or get left again. Made it by 8:10 and found train waiting for me. Had been instructed to wait from Cordova. Now home and found Power Company had fired me. So endeth the first chapter." In Hazelet's absence, a rival group had gained control the Cordova's power supply, thus depriving him of the salary he counted on to support his family.

Hazelet reported to the Cordova Chamber of Commerce that roadhouses and relief stations were already established at convenient locations. He then went back to the trail with another crew of volunteers to complete some additional staking requested by the Alaska Road Commission. (22)

On November 5, Kinney, the road commission representative, arrived in McCarthy with a report that the glacier trail was complete with at least six roadhouses along the route, and relief stations on either side of the summit. He made an estimate that "a horse will have no difficulty in drawing double-enders containing from 500 to 1,000 pounds over any part of the glacier road, with the possible exception of the few steep places near the summit, where it may be necessary to relay." Kinney stated that he believed 90 per cent of the travel in the 1913-14 winter would go over the glacier trail. Mail carriers already were using that route.

By November 25, Hazelet was able to claim that "at least 15 outfits, ranging in extent from 400 pounds to 6 or 8 tons have passed over the glacier to the diggings or are now on their way — all since November 1st," and that Oscar Breedman would start with an eight-ton outfit in three days. The newly appointed commissioner for the Chisana district, Anthony Dimond, who would in later years be Alaska's delegate to Congress, was one of the earliest travelers on Hazelet's glacier trail.

In a letter to Dimond, who was in Valdez recovering from a severe leg injury, Hazelet wrote the following advice:

> ... You could ride all the way over the glacier on a sled if Gwin takes you. Your hardest trip would be from McCarthy to Nizina River. Trail bad but if cold weather keeps up you could ride a horse over it. ... You would have to decide for yourself whether your condition as regards your leg will permit such a trip. You could hardly go either by Skolai Creek or the Chittistone this time of year and if you went by Gulkana you would have to pack horse feed at least 150 miles.

Going our way you will have road houses to stop at till you get 5 miles up the glacier and there is another being established at the foot of summit. (23)

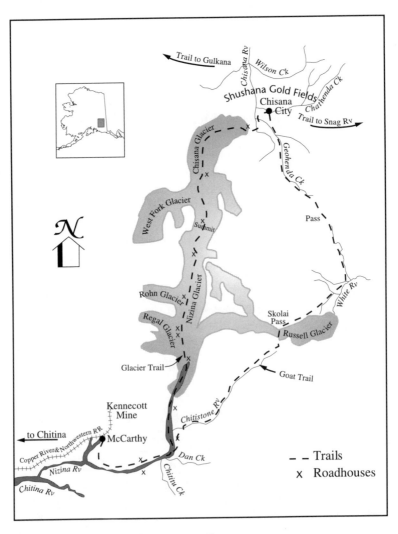

Routes to Chisana.
ADAPTED FROM BROCHURE PRINTED BY CORDOVA CHAMBER OF COMMERCE IN 1914

Some prospectors were hauling supplies with horses, others with dogs, while a few still did their own packing. Two men were even packing 1,000 pounds of window glass with one horse. (24)

Canadian business men were also working hard to lure the Chisana trade. Roadhouses were springing up along the Canadian route so that traveling to the diggings was "attended with practically no danger, with little hardship, and with few privations." The White Pass and Yukon Route announced plans to run winter stages all the way to Chisana.

Cordovans still had to contend with negative publicity, primarily from Dr. Leonard Sugden of Whitehorse who reported at length on his trip over the Kluane trail and experiences at Chisana, and gave the erroneous report that he had met the Hazelet party and that they had failed to get through on the proposed route over the Nizina and Chisana glaciers. He claimed that the Cordovans had subscribed $5,000 in 12 hours to support Hazelet efforts, but concluded: "There are no McCarthy trails in winter; three death traps, that's all they have." [25]

The *Cordova Daily Alaskan* immediately responded that Sugden was merely trying to induce people in Whitehorse and Skagway to subsidize his trips "outside" to misrepresent the routes from McCarthy. The paper recounted that Sugden had indeed met the Hazelet crew at Nizina in early September and asked to take some moving pictures. Hazelet cooperated and later recalled that Sugden had explained to him some techniques for taking "fake" pictures to exaggerate hazards on the trail. [26]

After assuring himself that the glacier trail was operational, Hazelet decided to concentrate his efforts on promoting use of the winter trail. In January 1914, he completed a folder advertising the advantages of Cordova as the gateway to the Nelchina and Chisana mining camps. The rivalry between the Cordovans and adherents of the White Pass and Yukon route even spread to Seattle, as described by Jack Underwood in the Cordova paper on January 21:

> Hundreds of copies of the Skagway papers, in which tales of death and desolation on the trail — on the Cordova trail of course — were printed and circulated in Seattle hotels where Alaskans congregate. The Cordovans, however, countered by buying up a number of these and throwing them in the bay.
>
> Sam Blum, a Cordova banker, George Hazlett [sic], one of the owners of the Cordova townsite, and Will A. Steel, editor of the Cordova newspaper, are now in Seattle, and heated arguments between this delegation and adherents of the Skagway route are the order of business whenever they meet. There are also a few from Valdez and Seward, who stand aside and cut in with a few remarks to the general effect that the Shushanna strike doesn't amount to much anyway, and that the only wise thing for a stampeder to do is to go to the Nelchina diggings, which can by reached advantageously from either Seward or Valdez, where riches await the arrival of the immigrant. ... Those who are planning to take outfits and boilers

into the Shushanna are standing on the sidelines and egging on the combatants in the hope that a rate war will be declared.

The men from Valdez and Seward were correct in their assessment of the value of the Chisana gold fields. About 200 prospectors stayed in the Chisana area during the winter of 1913-14 and built the "largest log cabin city in Alaska." Some called it the "good luck camp" because no shootings occurred, no one died, and no babies were born. Not much else happened — social life was restricted because few women remained during the winter. The only claims that produced much gold were those close to the initial locations. Hundreds of claims of no value were staked and then abandoned when the limits of the gold-bearing gravel were learned. Travel over the glacier trail continued until spring. There were no reported deaths on the trail but one of Oscar Breedman's horses fell into a crevasse. [27]

On May 17, 1914, *The Alaska Times* in Cordova reported that the Chisana area was in danger of "a terrible dry spell." According to advice received by letter in Fairbanks from Frank Miller, proprietor of the only saloon in Johnson City of the Chisana district, the miners would soon be deprived of the opportunity to buy a drink. Business had been so poor that Miller was planning to start for Fairbanks as soon as he disposed of his present stock of goods without waiting until his license expired.

Mining operators sent releases to papers throughout Alaska and the Pacific Northwest cautioning men not to go to Chisana looking for work because too many were already there for the jobs available. [28] The first year of mining in the Chisana field was probably the most profitable one, although a few miners continued to work the most productive claims for years.

The Chisana gold rush proved to be only a minor one compared to other Alaska strikes, but it provided Alaska and Yukon sourdoughs, like 50-year-old George Hazelet, with one last stampede while they were still young enough to show their sons what it was like in '98. Calvin Hazelet never actually mined gold from his Chisana claims [29], but Cordova and Chitina businessmen succeeded in mining the Chisana stampeders, thanks mainly to the efforts of George Hazelet. Although much of the early supplies for the miners came from Canada, most of the gold went out across the mountains from the White River to the Copper River drainage and down the railroad to the Alaska coastal towns. [30] The Canadian routes were abandoned after the initial rush and, according to a retrospective look at the rush by the U.S. Geological Survey, the trails from McCarthy on the Copper River and Northwestern Railway became the established routes to the Chisana gold field. [31]

Terminal for a Government Railroad

Even though the Chisana gold fields did not live up to expectations, George Hazelet soon had another reason for optimism about the future of Cordova. In the spring of 1914, passage of federal legislation to support building government railroads in Alaska raised Cordova's hopes that the Copper River and Northwestern Railway would soon be extended to Alaska's interior with a spur connecting Cordova to the Bering River coal fields. The *Ketchikan Morning Mail* commented on the Cordova's new wave of enthusiasm:

> The Alaska railroad project is already bearing fruit in the way of stuffing the optimistic cheer into Alaskans. Up in Cordova, before the Senate passed the bill, the only music one could hear was the sharp notes of an occasional school girl whistling "Everybody Works But Father" and "The Trail of the Lonesome Pine" but the news of the passage of the bill was like an electric shock. All of the sourdoughs in the city of the big bite who could tell the sweetest of angelic music from a stud cat's nightly squalls, met in musical convention and organized a cornet band. And this only the cracking of the ice. The breakup is coming later. [1]

Cordova celebrated at a town meeting chaired by Hazelet, now the Chamber of Commerce president, and praised President Wilson and Delegate Wickersham. Cordova's new newspaper, *The Alaska Times*, however, cautioned: "Our delegate and others have raised the Guggenheim issue so strongly in Congress that many shrewd political advisers are inclined to believe that President Wilson is too smart a politician to lay himself open to the imputation of favoring the Morgan-Guggenheim interests by selecting Cordova as the terminus for a trunk line railroad to the interior." [2]

One reason for the federal government to consider building railroads in Alaska was to provide access to coal fields that could supply battleships that still burned coal. Two Alaska coal deposits, the Matanuska coal field, located less than 50 miles from Cook Inlet in Southcentral Alaska, and the Bering River coal field, were reasonably close to tidewater. Before making a commitment on a railroad route, the Navy arranged to test coal from each of the fields to see if it was suitable for use in ships. The government hired Jack Dalton, the noted Alaska trailblazer who had contended in the courts with Hazelet's townsite company over a dock area in Cordova, to lay out a trail and bring coal from the Matanuska coal field to tidewater in Cook Inlet. Although the Bering River coal was closer to tidewater, the mining and delivery of coal there were poorly handled, giving rise to rumors that a deliberate attempt was being made to discredit Bering River coal. [3] Final reports of the tests were purported to show that the Bering River coal was not appropriate for naval use and that Matanuska coal was superior. [4]

Two potential routes to the Matanuska field were under consideration: the Kenai Peninsula-Susitna Valley route utilizing the Alaska Northern Railway from Seward to Kern Creek on Turnagain Arm and a spur line up the Matanuska River; and the Copper River route utilizing the Copper River and Northwestern Railway from Cordova to Chitina and a new spur line through Chickaloon Pass above the coal field. Government representatives met with J.P. Morgan and with the owners of the Alaska Northern regarding possible purchase of the existing railroads. The government also planned to extend a railroad to Fairbanks.

The newly-appointed Alaska Railroad Commission visited Cordova briefly on June 13, 1914, enroute to headquarters at Knik and Seward. Lt. Frederick A. Mears, one of the commissioners, met with Mayor Boyle, railroad superintendent Caleb Corser, and George Hazelet and H.G. Steele, representing the Chamber of Commerce. Mears also conferred with railroad engineer Henry Deyo regarding work on a possible Chitina-Matanuska route. [5] The Copper River route had the advantage of passing through a richly mineralized area that would produce more tonnage for a railroad than the Susitna route, which would pass through undeveloped agricultural land. The Cordova Chamber of Commerce, wishing to make the most of this advantage in promoting Cordova for the terminal of the government railroad, assigned Hazelet the job of collecting statistics on the potential tonnage that could be anticipated for a government railroad. [6]

Although Hazelet no longer managed the light and water utilities, he still acted as agent for the townsite company and joined Sam Blum and M. Brock in incorporating the First Bank of Cordova. He also continued to be deeply involved in state and local politics. Shortly before the 1914 election, Thomas J. Donohoe, who was active in the Valdez Democratic party, made the following appeal to Hazelet while urging Cordova Republicans to support Charles Bunnell, the Democratic candidate for delegate, rather than Wickersham: "The Democrats have been so long out of power that their organization is still rudimentary, while the Republican organization has always been noted for its cohesiveness and general working power. I trust that all its power will be used for us in this campaign. No one except Wick has anything to hope for from his candidacy." [7]

The Democrats failed to unseat the delegate and, as soon as a Wickersham victory appeared certain, the Cordova Chamber of Commerce wired congratulations, prompting *The Chitina Leader* to comment: "As this has heretofore been one of the towns strongly opposed to Delegate Wickersham the action of the Chamber is taken to mean that Cordova has buried the hatchet and will hereafter be found supporting the course of the Delegate." [8] The Cordovans welcomed Wickersham in late November with a banquet at which Chamber President Hazelet presided. Wickersham made special mention of the splendid work the Chamber was doing toward supplying him with information while he was in Washington, stating that he had received more benefit from the Cordova Chamber of Commerce than from any other commercial organization in the territory. [9]

While peace reigned, temporarily at least, among Cordova's Republicans, a storm was brewing in local politics. Hazelet was elected to the city council again in April 1914, but for the first time he found himself aligned with the minority rather than the majority of the seven council members. The council was hopelessly divided on a number of issues, including terms for granting the electrical franchise, tenure of the police chief, use of the fire hall, and even where to advertise actions of the council.

In a July 25, 1914, editorial, *The Alaska Times* suggested that, since the council was so divided that it could do no business, all the members should resign and call another election. The new paper supported Hazelet, describing him as "one of our first citizens, looking always toward a greater Cordova, polished, magnetic, genial, sound in judgment, concise in argument, a man who understands Cordova as well as anyone here, trail builder, tactful and wise." [10] The *Cordova Daily Alaskan*, which had always supported Hazelet in the past, however, began attacking him on the editorial page prior to the 1915 local election.

The Alaska Times began publication as a Sunday weekly on May 4, 1913, stating that it planned to foster harmony. The major stockholder in the new enterprise was U.S. Commissioner A.J. Adams, who had been one of the original locators and the surveyor of the Cordova townsite. In May 1914, the Times Publishing Company was leased to C.H. Scheffler and C.H. Wilcox, who had previously edited the *Valdez Prospector*. The rivalry between the newspapers intensified after October 23, 1914, when Will A. Steel, one of the editors of the *Cordova Daily Alaskan*, published an editorial that implied criticism of Commissioner Adams for the way in which he established election districts and advertised elections. Several days later Adams demanded an explanation and ended up pulling Steel's nose when the editor refused to fight. [11] Steel then accused Adams of assault. The matter was prosecuted by the city attorney before a packed courtroom and the jury found Adams guilty of assault and fined him $10 and costs. Hazelet, who was present when the assault occurred, testified at the trial that no actual blows had been stuck.

While the case against Adams was being prosecuted, *The Alaska Times* announced its intention to publish daily, utilizing the Associated Press wire service, which had recently become available in Alaska. On December 2, 1914, the first issue of *The Cordova Daily Times* listed H.G. Steel, who had severed his partnership with brother Will in publishing of the *Cordova Daily Alaskan* and *The Chitina Leader*, as publisher, editor and manager.

George Hazelet was not in Cordova in January 1915, when Will Steel began attacking him on the editorial page of the *Cordova Daily Alaskan*. In early December he had left town to spend the holidays with his sons in Seattle. At the request of the Copper River and Northwestern Railway management, he went on to Washington, D.C., to represent the railway and the Copper River district during negotiations over railroad routes. On December 19, the executive committee of the Chamber of Commerce passed a resolution "authorizing Hazelet to represent Cordova in all matters of interest to this section that come up for consideration at Washington during the session of Congress, and particularly in reference to the selection of a coast terminal for the new government trunk line." [12] While *The Cordova Daily Times* commented on how fortunate Cordova was in having one of its representative citizens in the national capital, the *Cordova Daily Alaskan* accused Hazelet of "lingering in Washington in hope of landing a job in connection with the government building of railroads in Alaska." [13]

Hazelet had dinner at least once with Wickersham while he was in the nation's capitol, and apparently had a good relationship with the delegate. [14] In recounting the railroad situation in Washington, the correspondent for the *Seattle Post-Intelligencer* quoted from Hazelet's report to the Alaska Railway Commission:

> Tonnage is the one essential of every railway enterprise. Without tonnage it
> must prove a failure. ... We assert, without fear of contradiction, that the Copper
> river route is the only route which promises any return upon the investment, or

even operating expenses, for years to come, because it is the only route that possesses tonnage. In making this assertion, we do not wish to discredit or disparage the agricultural resources of any section of the territory, but we do maintain that agriculture in Alaska must be developed in connection with the mineral industry and its success must depend upon that industry. ...

It therefore follows that the practical way to open up this country for permanent settlement is through the development of the mines and fisheries following up with agriculture as fast as conditions require. If this method is adopted, Alaska will have a population equal to that of Norway or Sweden within the next twenty-five years. ...

If it is argued that this section is already supplied with transportation we answer this is but partially true. A railroad passes through the extreme southern portion of this vast tonnage-producing section to a mine owned by the same corporation that controls the railway. No branches or feeders have been built to other properties, nor are they likely to be built, now that the government has entered the railroad field. Even though this corporation should decide to extend the road to other properties in order to increase its tonnage, the freight rates must of necessity be too high to permit the development of many properties because of interest charges. No corporation expects to earn less than 6 per cent on its investment, whereas the government can well afford to take 3 per cent, or even operate a few years at a loss in order to develop its territory.

A low freight rate is the key to the development of Alaska, and the government is the only institution that can give that rate. [15]

Hazelet also lobbied for the long-desired Cordova federal building and a new Navy radio station, and protested the inclusion of of 7,250,000 acres of non-forested land in the federally controlled Chugach National Forest. [16] D.C. Sargent, a Nabesna and Chisana mine owner who had spent the winter in Washington, returned to Cordova in March with praise for Hazelet's efforts on behalf of the Copper River region: "He has been a persistent and effective booster for Cordova and I know that through his efforts some results have been obtained. He is not only devoting his time to the railroad but also other matters that are of interest to your people, including the federal building, radio station and a reduction in the cable rate. ... Mr. Hazelet has personally prepared most of the data that sets forth your advantages, and you can take if from me that this information has had its effect upon Secretary Lane." [17]

While Hazelet was still out of town, his name was included on the People's Ticket slate for city council. The *Cordova Daily Alaskan* immediately started an editorial war on "King George" and "Hazeletism." Will Steel accused Hazelet of dominating local politics and attempting to block the granting of an electric power franchise to a company in which Steel and several council members had financial interests. He also implied that Hazelet had charged the city $600 for the crossing and planking of B Avenue without proper authority back in 1911. [18]

The Cordova Daily Times countered with an editorial stating:

> Practically the entire fight in the municipal election is being directed against Mr. Hazelet, and why? Because he is a man of force and intellect and the *Alaskan* cannot use him as it does the present majority in the city council. Advantage is being taken of his absence to publish trumped-up accusations and an attempt made to create sentiment against one of our most respected and loyal residents, whose integrity cannot be questioned. These character assassins have stopped at nothing, but their attacks do not reflect this community's spirit in the slightest respect, and is resented by all fair-minded people. [19]

The editorials in the *Cordova Daily Alaskan* apparently influenced the April 6 election in which Hazelet lost his council seat by two votes. The other members of his People's Ticket, however, were elected and the four men who had opposed Hazelet on the previous council were all defeated.

Hazelet left Washington on March 24, confident that his report had made a profound impression on the administration and that the government would adopt the Copper River route for the railroad. Upon arrival in San Francisco, however, he was surprised to hear that President Wilson had decided to purchase the Alaska Northern Railway for $1,150,000 and spend $27,000,000 developing the Susitna route. [20]

Wickersham, who also left Washington for Alaska in March, stopped briefly in Seattle. His diary entry on March 20 indicates that he dined with the Seattle Commercial Club and spoke on Alaska fishing. He commented that "this club is fighting the Fish Trust and hence is very friendly to me." Two days later, newspapers carried the story that the Seattle Commercial Club was protesting the purchase of the Copper River and Northwestern Railway as an "unwarranted diversion of public money." In a letter to Secretary of the Interior Franklin K. Lane, the Commercial Club further stated: "We are informed and believe that the present route runs in part over glaciers that are constantly moving and that the expense of operating a railroad and of shifting and changing the track will be enormous." [21] Wickersham, who had just spoken to the group, was undoubtedly the informant.

In his report to the Cordova Chamber of Commerce on April 30, Hazelet expressed his perplexity about President Wilson's failure to choose Copper River route. He indicated that a plan, presented by Fairbanks railroad builder Falcon Joslin, to extend the Copper River and Northwestern Railway to Fairbanks and build a spur to the Bering River coal fields within three years under a contractual arrangement had also been rejected by the government. [22] Joslin and D.A. McKenzie, the developer of the Nelson townsite on Orca Bay, had also spent the winter in Washington, D.C., while railroad negotiations were going on. In a letter to a Cordova friend McKenzie reflected on their activities in Washington:

> I have never seen men work more earnestly for a locality than George Hazelet and Falcon Joslin worked for the Copper River country. Your newspapers could be a great help if they were upholding the efforts of your citizens that were here. But instead of a help they were the other thing. I did not dare show a copy of our town papers to Congressmen, Senators, or officials. ...
>
> It certainly was an inopportune time to attack Hazelet. The Seward crowd took advantage of the situation and circulated Cordova papers to kill Hazelet's influence. I can't for the life of me understand how an intelligent community could act in this crazy manner, and over nothing at that.
>
> The fact that we did not get the Copper River route selected was not the fault of the Cordova delegation in Washington. There were two factors that worked against us. First, the Morgan-Guggenheim people asked a higher price than Secretary Lane was willing to pay. The other principal reason was that many Democratic Senators and Congressmen were afraid of the effect it would have on the Democratic party if the Guggenheim road were purchased by the President. I understand that many called on the President and protested, and this must have influenced the President's final determination. I am satisfied that Secretary Lane fully appreciates the great resources of the Copper River country and if the matter had been left entirely to him to decide I believe he would have taken the Copper River road. [23]

After *The Cordova Daily Times* published the McKenzie letter, Will Steel wrote a final vindictive editorial in the *Cordova Daily Alaskan* on May 22. On May 31, he announced that he had business to attend to that would force him to leave Alaska for several months and suspend publication because he was unable to "secure the right kind of man to conduct our newspaper business during our absence." *The Chitina Leader* also suspended publication shortly thereafter. When the Chitina paper again appeared six months later it was edited by Harry Steel who also continued to edit *The Cordova Daily Times* for many years.

Will Steel's failure to win support in his newspaper vendetta proved that Cordovans still respected and supported Hazelet in spite of his failure to convince the federal government to make Cordova the terminal for its railroad.

DISASTER ON LUSITANIA CLAIMS MANY VICTIMS

1,216 LIVES LOST AT SEA

COPPER IS ADVANCED TO 24 CENTS

Highest Figure Market Has Reached Since 1907 Copper Market Knows No Limit

The Alaska Time, Cordova   April 17, 1915

BIG PLACER DEAL CHISNA CREEK IS CLOSED

Craig P. Hazelet, who has been attending the University of Washington for the past school year, will return to cordova in the latter part of June. He is a senior and will graduate this year from the Department of Civil Engineering. Although uncertain as the future plans, he expects to join his brother Calvin, who is working with the Latouche Mining Company at Latouche. Craig won his numerals this year by playing on the senior basketball team. He is a member of the Phi Gamma Delta fraternity.

A mining deal which involves several thousand dollars and a large area of gold placer ground in interior Alaska has been consummated by John A. Hazelet, who just returned from the East, and left this morning on the train for Slate Creek.

Anchorage Daily Times   January 12, 1918

Birch Elected to Succeed Eccles

Mining Engineer Heads Alaska Steamship and Copper River Railroad

The Cordova Daily Times   June 21, 1918

NATURAL GAS FOR CORDOVA A POSSIBILITY

The Cordova Daily Times   June 17, 1918

BERING RIVER COAL FIELDS TO BE DEVELOPED

WORK OF PROSPECTING FIELD TO START AT ONCE

CIVIL WAR RAGES IN RUSSIA

BRAVERY OF ALASKAN MOSQUITO UNRIVALED

ANCHORAGE IS BOOTLEGGERS MECCA

Kennecott Corporation

While George Hazelet and his fellow Cordovans were protesting closure of the
Bering River coal fields and promoting their town as the terminal for the government railroad, Stephen Birch continued to push development of the Kennecott
copper mines. Even before the completion of the Copper River and Northwestern
Railway he had succeeded in constructing a 15,000 foot aerial tramway to the
Bonanza mine, 4,500 feet above the railroad terminal. All materials for this
tramway, in addition to cars, rails, and provisions for both people and horses, were
dragged 225 miles from Valdez on sleds during the winter under the capable
direction of R.H. McClellan. [1]

Unloading building materials for the Kennecott Mine.
PHOTO COURTESY OF WASHINGTON HISTORICAL SOCIETY, TACOMA, WA.

McClellan, one of the initial locators, also supervised the logging and sawmill operation. Soon after completion of the railroad, Birch started construction of a concentrating mill. Crude ore shipped to the Tacoma smelter before the mill was completed showed 72 percent copper and 18 oz. of silver per ton, justifying further investment, even though the New York financiers had already spent 30 million dollars on the mining property, steamship line and railroad without any return.

Kennecott Mine buildings about 1916.
ANCHORAGE MUSEUM OF HISTORY & ART. B72.32.1

Birch expressed frustration with the coal situation to a reporter from the *Seattle Times* in June 1911, while enroute to Alaska to supervise the installation of the large crushing mill and concentrating plant at the Bonanza mine:

> We have hoped against hope that the Alaska coal fields would be opened so that we could be saved the cost of transporting fuel a distance of nearly 1500 miles, but this has seemed impossible of accomplishment, and the Alaska coal situation has ceased to be of interest to the Alaska Syndicate.
>
> Under the belief that the government could not keep the coal lands tied up, the syndicate expended a good many millions of dollars in opening up the Bonanza copper mines and in building a railroad to open up the Copper River valley and the ore bodies contiguous thereto. There is not a railroad in the United States that could make a profit if paying $10 a ton for coal.
>
> The proposition figures out that we can get the equivalent of one ton of coal in crude oil at a cost of $3.50. Alaskan coal would be even cheaper. But the saving

effected as between coal and oil is sufficient to cut quite a considerable figure in the cost of production of copper.

With shipments of ore from the Bonanza mine leaving Kennecott twice weekly, Birch began to develop the Jumbo claim, two miles northwest of Bonanza, with a second complete tramway to the mill. The Jumbo tramway was completed in 1913 and the capacity of the mill increased to 500 tons per day. H. DeWitt Smith, who became foreman of the Bonanza mine in February 1914, described the status of the mine when he first arrived at Kennecott:

> Copper production of ten to twelve million pounds per annum was maintained from the Bonanza and Jumbo mines by milling 700 tons per day, with the mill shut down in the winter months due to water shortage. Mine operations had reached a depth of only 600 feet below the adit levels, and ore tonnage was maintained by hauling one-ton ships up 30-degree incline shafts, with 50 to 75 HP electric single-drum hoists. Ore was transported from each mine by aerial tramway to the mill, 4500 feet lower in elevation than the mines. Sorted high-grade ore and concentrates were sacked for rail and water shipment to Tacoma, with rail traffic to Cordova interrupted for four to six weeks during spring breakup with the yearly washing out of the wooden bridge over the Chitina River. The expenditure for bridge reconstruction represented a much lower cash outlay than the interest on the cost of a permanent steel structure. This was a nice little mine operation, which could not possibly repay the amounts expended by the Alaska Syndicate. [2]

Prospects for cash return from the mines began to look brighter in the summer of 1914 when another rich chalcocite body, which yielded up to 70 percent copper ore without sorting or concentration, was encountered on the Jumbo claim at the 500-foot level. The following year, the Alaska Syndicate decided to offer stock in the Alaska mines to the public. On April 29, 1915, the Kennecott Company was incorporated, retaining the misspelling of the name of the nearby Kennicott Glacier, named after the explorer Robert Kennicott.

In regard to this spelling, Lewis Levensaler commented: "Who changed the spelling to Kennecott, I don't know, perhaps Stephen Birch, who did not know any better." [3] Birch became president of the new corporation, which purchased the Kennecott Mines Company and Beatson Copper Company for 720,000 shares of stock, plus $10,000,000 in 6 percent bonds convertible into 400,000 more Kennecott Copper shares. William P. Hamilton, Silas Eccles, and John Steele, all former Alaska Syndicate officers, were listed among the directors of the new corporation, as was H.O. Havemeyer II. [4]

The following summer, Birch engaged Henry Krumb, a well-known consulting engineer from Salt Lake City, to examine and appraise the Alaska properties. Smith, who was present at the time, reported Krumb's advice to Birch:

> Mr. Krumb raised the point with Mr. Birch one day, while sitting on the Jumbo high-grade ore dump, of the uncertainty in length of life of the Kennecott properties, and that rather than pay total dividends of forty to fifty million dollars over the next several years and then drop down to a much lower rate, it would be preferable to initiate a modest dividend rate and use the balance of earnings to make a substantial investment in some property with ore reserves of such large tonnage as to give assurance of long life. (5)

Cottage built for Stephen Birch and bride at Kennecott Mine.
ANCHORAGE MUSEUM OF HISTORY & ART. B72.32.16

Birch followed through on this suggestion and found that several large, low-grade copper properties were desperately in need of capital for development. By December 1915, he had worked out an amazingly successful program. The Guggenheim Exploration Company was planning to disband and agreed to exchange their Utah Copper shares, representing a 25 percent interest, for 607,000 Kennecott shares, and 96.5 percent ownership of Braden Copper Mines in Chile for 770,000 Kennecott shares. An additional 200,000 shares bought a controlling interest in the Alaska Steamship Company from the Alaska Syndicate, which then dissolved. Birch's new corporation gained, in addition to the Alaska copper properties, railroad and steamship line, ownership of Braden, the largest underground copper mine in the world, and a quarter interest in Utah Copper, the world's most valuable copper mine, without substantial cash outlay. Following the merger, Edmund A. and Harry F. Guggenheim were listed as additional directors of the Kennecott Copper Corporation. [6]

At the time of its transfer from Guggenheim to Kennecott control, Braden, which had ore reserves estimated at 220 million tons containing 2.2 percent copper, urgently needed cash to build a plant to develop these great reserves. The Kennecott Corporation supplied the necessary cash over the next several years from the earnings of the Alaska mines. Utah Copper, in 1915, had ore reserves of 340 million tons containing 1.45 percent copper, and also owned 50 percent of Nevada Consolidated Copper shares. In 1916 and 1917, Birch borrowed $16,000,000 in short term notes in order to buy additional Utah Copper stock and increase Kennecott's holdings to 38 percent. [7]

Kennecott tramways.
ANCHORAGE MUSUEM OF HISTORY & ART. B72.32.223

Along with the Braden mines, Kennecott acquired the services of Earl Tappan Stannard, a brilliant metallurgist, who developed an ammonia leaching process to recover additional copper from Bonanza and Jumbo tailings. With Stannard in charge of Alaska mine operations, Birch was able to spend most of his time in New York City managing his far-flung financial empire.

On June 24, 1916, Birch married Mary Rand, daughter of Rufus R. Rand, president of Minneapolis Gas Light Company. The wedding party included H.O.

Havemeyer II as best man and Percy Rockefeller as an usher. The new Mrs. Birch was accustomed to all of the advantages consistent with her family's prominence in Minneapolis. Birch's elaborate preparations for their honeymoon were described in the July 15, 1916, issue of the *Cordova Times*:

> The private car KENNECOTT has been provisioned and will be at the disposal of Birch and his wife during the time they remain here.
>
> For the accommodation of the bridal couple, the steamship MARIPOSA was remodelled. Several large staterooms were thrown together, forming an attractive suite, equal in every way to the accommodations usually found in the best hotels on the coast.
>
> The fact that Birch comes north now with his bride in rooms as comfortable as those of an Atlantic liner, and is met at the dock by a private car as finely equipped as any in the world, emphasizes the contrast of conditions as they existed when he first came to Alaska.

Apparently these comforts were not sufficient to impress Mary Birch with the glories of Alaska. According to the Cordova paper the following week, the couple reduced their stay to "a flying visit." There is no record that Mrs. Birch ever returned to Alaska although a special cottage was built at the Kennecott mines for Birch and his bride in 1916.

The newlyweds settled in New York City and soon had two children, Stephen and Mary. According to family sources, the marriage was a difficult one. Stephen, now 44 years old, was considerably older than his wife, committed to his business obligations, and seldom at home. In 1917, he purchased the 730-acre Theodore Havemeyer estate in Mahwah, New Jersey, near where he had lived as a boy. He introduced game birds for shooting, and utilized the greenhouse for the cultivation of orchids. [8]

The Kennecott Copper Company prospered and acquired more property, including the Mother Lode mine on the other side of the ridge from Bonanza. Jack Smith and Clarence Warner, the original Bonanza locators, staked the Mother Lode in 1906 and attempted to develop it themselves, but did not have adequate capital. When snowslides during the winter of 1919 wiped out their frail tramway, they sold 51 percent of the stock to Birch. A 1,200-foot tunnel, connecting the Mother Lode mine to the Bonanza workings, extended the life of the Bonanza mine by enabling Kennecott to process the Mother Lode ore in their own mill, using the Bonanza tramway.

Katalla Oil Wells

As soon as President Wilson announced the route for the new government railroad, some of the Cordova businessmen took advantage of the opportunity to establish themselves in the railroad construction camp at Ship Creek, soon to be named Anchorage. Austen E. "Cap" Lathrop, who had served with Hazelet on the Cordova city council, immediately started construction on the first office building and moving picture theater in the new town. Lathrop, however, hedged his bets by continuing to manage identical operations in Cordova. Hazelet took a trip to Anchorage in the summer of 1915 "to size up the business first hand." He recorded his impressions in the June 29 issue of *The Cordova Daily Times*:

> Agents of the government are advertising that Anchorage is to be the ocean terminus, that coal bunkers will be erected, and a naval base established. It is evident it is their intention to make it an open port the year around if possible. However, this is not believed to be possible by men that are familiar with conditions. ... They explain that immense ice gorges pile up clear across the inlet in any ordinary winter, and move back and forth with the tide, sometimes for a distance of 60 miles. ...
>
> Here is a mass of 2,000 people squatted on the government terminals, from which they must soon move, many of them with just enough money to build a small building and start their business, forced to bid against some fellow from the states who has plenty of money and desires to speculate. This is un-American, and directly opposed to the avowed policy of the administration. ...
>
> The conclusion I arrived at after a week's examination of the town situation was that, during the construction period of the railway, Anchorage will do a fairly good business in a small way; that after the road is completed Anchorage will be the ocean terminus for governmental operations seven or eight months of each year, and that the balance of the year there will be but little business. ...

The amount of tonnage to be shipped from the port must necessarily depend on future development, for at the present time there is absolutely none in sight save a possible 125,000 tons of coal annually for use on the Pacific, and this amount is gradually being reduced each year by the replacement of coal by oil as a fuel. To my mind this condition will create a serious problem for the operating engineer of the government railway, and that problem will be how to make the railway pay even operating expenses when it is completed.

The business future of Anchorage did not impress Hazelet and he soon found a promising enterprise closer to Cordova. Oil had been discovered at Katalla, 50 miles southeast of Cordova, before 1900. One tract had been patented before Alaska oil lands were closed to entry in 1910. Several wells were already in production but closure of the oil fields in Alaska prevented cost-effective development. On May 8, 1915, an article in *The Alaska Times* announced that the Alaska Oil and Refining company at Katalla had been adjudicated a bankrupt in the district court at Valdez.

Falcon Joslin, the Fairbanks railroad builder who had worked with Hazelet in Washington during the railroad negotiations, expressed an interest in the Katalla area and accompanied Hazelet on an trip to examine of its natural resources in October 1915. Upon return to Cordova, Joslin mentioned the coal field and speculated about possible routes to connect it to the Copper River and Northwestern Railway or to a port at Controller Bay, but indicated that the oil there might actually be more valuable than the coal. He described the existing oil development:

> The oil field as proved by seepages extends from the Copper River delta on the west to Yakataga on the east, a distance of more than a hundred miles. It is not a small field as I had supposed, but a very large field. We found gas bubbling up in many places in Bering Lake and found we could with match light the bubbles as they came through the water.
>
> There are three or four producing wells near Katalla and a small refinery. There is about 45,000 gallons of crude oil produced monthly from which about 15,000 gallons of gasoline is produced. The rest is wasted. It is a pity to see the fine parafine base oil thrown away from the lack of means to refine and market it.
>
> In spite of these wonderfully fine resources the whole district is dead commercially. It is a sad example of the conservation policy of the government. Now a revival seems in prospect. Whether these resources are to be opened by private enterprise or under government ownership will probably be decided within the next few months. [1]

Although optimistic Cordovans initially thought that the Alaska Syndicate might still commit private capital to extend the Copper River and Northwestern to the Tanana valley and build a spur to the Bering coal fields, Stephen Birch dashed these hopes during a visit to Cordova in July 1915, by stating: "It was our original plan to build a spur to the coal fields with the possible extension of the railroad to the interior but the government, in its wisdom, saw fit to stop development of the Copper River valley and discourage capital from further railroad building. Now it is up to the government to open up and develop whatever section of the territory it sees fit. We will continue to operate our own mines and provide whatever railroad service is necessary to handle the tonnage." [2] Birch, as president of the Kennecott Copper Company, acquired control of the railroad when the Alaska Syndicate ceased to exist after selling the Copper River and Northwestern to the Kennecott Copper Company for $10,000,000 in Kennecott stock. [3]

Since Birch showed little interest in using private capital to extend the railroad, Hazelet realized that Cordova would need to rely on government cooperation and Wickersham's support to open up the Copper River country. Hazelet was not an enthusiastic Wickersham supporter but he realized that the delegate would undoubtedly run for re-election even if he did not get the regular Republican endorsement and he also knew that Wickersham would not get the Republican nomination unless he agreed to let National Committeeman Shackleford control patronage in federal appointments. In an effort to heal the rift in the Republican party, Hazelet decided to help Wickersham end Shackleford's control.

Wickersham visited Hazelet in Cordova in November 1915, and commented in his diary: "Dinner tonight with George Hazelet — just us two — in his fine dining room. He seems never to have recovered from the loss of his wife." [4] Later in the month, Wickersham returned to Cordova to discuss reorganization of the Republican party with Hazelet and other Cordova Republicans and urge them to attend the territorial convention. [5]

When the Republican convention was held in Seward in April 1916, Hazelet and the Copper River Republicans were unable to counteract the influence of Shackleford. Wickersham, as predicted, was unwilling to allow Shackleford to continue controlling federal appointments and, therefore, did not receive the Republican endorsement. The Republican convention adjourned without naming a candidate for delegate, and Wickersham was free to hold his own convention and run for re-election as an Independent without a Republican opponent.

Hazelet gave the following explanation in a letter to Edward C. Russell, the editor of the *Juneau Dispatch*:

> Now, Ed, you know, and every thoughtful man in the territory knows, who has watched the trend of events, that the fight which has been waged in Alaska

between what is known as the Wickersham faction and the Shackleford faction over political matters is the greatest menace the territory has had.

It is the direct cause of tying up the resources of the country. It caused the withdrawal of the coal and oil lands from entry. It was responsible for the formation of the forest reserve. The withdrawal of the coal and oil stopped railway building and new enterprise of all kinds, and brought about general stagnation in the territory. It was the primary cause of the Ballinger-Pinchot controversy, which almost wrecked the Taft administration. Taken in its entirety it has injured the territory to an extent that cannot be repaired in the next ten years.

Judge Wickersham and I discussed every phase of this question when he dined with me at my home last year, and he practically agreed with all I said. He expressed a very strong desire to end this fight, and for all factions to work together for the good of the territory. He even went so far as to say he would step down and out if this would bring peace. [6]

The 1916 election between Charles Sulzer, the Democratic candidate, and Wickersham was very close and not decided in favor of Sulzer for months. Because of confusion in the distribution and use of the newly adopted secret Australian ballot, legal contests over which votes should be counted persisted throughout the two-year term. Wickersham and Sulzer were both seated and paid salaries pending a resolution of the contested election.

Alaskans realized that the next two years would be crucial in mapping the development of Alaska. Although the Alaska Railroad Act authorized up to 1,000 miles of railroad construction, only 504 miles had been designated to provide access to the Matanuska and Nenana coal fields. Cordovans still hoped that the federal government would at least authorize funds to build 50 miles of railroad that would link the Bering coal field and the Katalla oil wells to Copper River and Northwestern tracks in the Copper River delta. The Cordova Chamber of Commerce drafted a petition to the President and the Congress on the request of Senator Wesley Jones of Washington. The petition pointed out that it was now imperative for the government to take the initiative in building railroads to provide access to the coal fields because proposed leasing legislation would not permit railroads to mine coal or coal mines to own railroads. [7]

Interior Secretary Lane's favorable reaction to this petition again raised hopes in Cordova that the coal and oil fields might soon be opened for development. [8] Falcon Joslin, responding to this renewed optimism, purchased the property of the Katalla Oil Company for $16,927 when it was sold in bankruptcy court in Valdez on June 14, 1916. Joslin, as president of the St. Elias Oil Company, accompanied Hazelet and Cordova banker Sam Blum to Katalla shortly after the purchase. On return to Cordova, he announced his intention to begin immediately pumping oil from four wells that were standing idle and to seek to obtain title to a number of additional claims that had been withdrawn. [9] Hazelet promptly returned to Katalla, this time accompanied by Edward Medley, a Cordova attorney, and E.T. Stannard, who was associated with Stephen Birch in managing the Kennecott Copper Company's copper mine at Latouche.

Hazelet made several additional trips to Katalla during the summer and fall of 1916 and assumed management of the oil wells. In November, Joslin returned to Cordova and wrote his wife that the oil company was earning over $2,000 per month and was capable of doing more. Joslin admitted that he had been neglecting the oil field while working on the development of a quartz mine near Fairbanks with Stephen Birch. [10]

Katalla was reached by launch from Cordova and winter storms made the passage difficult at times, but Hazelet continued trips between Cordova and Katalla throughout the winter of 1917, sometimes staying at the oil field for a month at a time. Calvin Hazelet had married during the summer, and he and his wife, Nan, now lived in Cordova and took care of the Hazelet home for his father. An article in the April 25 issue of *The Cordova Daily Times* reported that the St. Elias Company's new sawmill at Katalla was running full time making rig timbers for new derricks and that the drillers were about to start on a new well. Other activity in Katalla was also picking up. The Alaska Coal and Oil Company was already drilling a new well and a crew had arrived to begin building the Alaska Anthracite railroad between the coal fields and Controller Bay.

The two new wells, drilled during 1917, were not productive, but overall oil production was almost twice that of 1916. While Hazelet was in charge of local management, Joslin was busy acquiring capital for more development. On May 20, 1918, *The Cordova Daily Times* announced that the St. Elias Oil Company had leased all its holdings to the Chilkat Oil Company, a new corporation recently organized under the laws of Delaware. The new company took over management on May 1 with plans to develop the property on a larger scale. This new organization was said to be necessary in order to secure additional capital and meet peculiar requirements of the anticipated oil-leasing bill, but the same officers were expected to control the affairs of the new company. Subsequent correspondence between Joslin and his wife indicated that Stephen Birch had a financial interest in both Katalla coal and oil fields.

In mid-June Hazelet confirmed that Joslin had succeeded in securing a 2,560 acre coal lease in the Bering River field and that a party of miners was leaving Seattle at the end of the month to do development work to ascertain whether a mine there would have commercial value. When asked about possible railroad construction, Hazelet indicated that it would depend on the value of the coal. [11]

The Chilkat Oil Company was pumping oil from several wells, refining the oil on the ground and drilling new wells as fast as possible. Natural gas was escaping from one new well in such a volume that all fires in the area had to be extinguished for fear of explosions. Cordovans speculated about the possibility of a pipeline to their city that would provide natural gas for local consumption. [12]

George Hazelet (left) and Dr. Council examining trophies.
PHOTO COURTESY OF HAZELET GRANDCHILDREN

The usual autumn storms hit Katalla in September, blowing down two derricks, destroying phone lines, damaging buildings and uprooting trees, but Hazelet continued his regular trips throughout the winter, accompanied by F.R. VanCampen, the superintendent of the Bering River Coal Company. Hazelet took advantage of these trips to hunt bear with his Cordova friends. When Joslin joined the coal mining crew at Carbon Camp in May 1919, he wrote his wife that Hazelet had phoned to report that Dr. Council had killed three bears and "another man got one which he thought was the biggest bear in the world." [13] Joslin, who was joshed in the Cordova paper for having retreated at the sight of bear tracks, responded: "Of course I know there are some mighty good hunters like the great Roosevelt and George Hazelet who are said to be able to kill a bear with their teeth, but I've never tried it. I am sure I'd feel more confidence in myself in meeting a bear if I had a rifle." [14]

Joslin was enthusiastic about the prosects for a coal mine, reporting to his wife: "If these veins are as thick in the tunnel as they are on the surface we have one of the greatest coal mines in America. As soon as I know about vein eleven I will start for Seattle and New York and hope to get the money to start the railroad work this summer. ... Honey, this coal mine is one of the biggest things in the history of Alaska and the whole Pacific coast. It will make it possible to start a steel plant at Seattle for it will make the finest smelting fuel in the world. It will give Alaska a fuel supply so long needed and eventually bring smelters. I wish I had as big an interest in it as I have in the oil. I will try to get a better interest when I go east. But I am afraid I lost the golden opportunity when the Company was first formed." [15]

While Joslin was supervising the coal mining operation, Hazelet was at Katalla preparing to sink four more shallow oil wells on the 160-acre tract. Casing for a deep well had already arrived, but work on that well could not start until an oil leasing bill was passed and more land obtained. [16] In November, the drilling was suspended until spring. On a visit to Juneau, Hazelet reported that the Bering River Coal Company had 40 men working on developing the property and that indications were encouraging. He further stated that the Chilkat Oil Company had a dozen wells producing from two to 20 barrels a day of the finest parafine oil, which they were selling for local consumption. [17]

Falcon Joslin — Gold Rush Developer

Falcon Joslin did not actually prospect for gold, but he followed gold rushes, developing and providing facilities and services for the miners. A native of Tennessee, he moved west shortly after graduating from Vanderbilt Law School and opened a law office in Seattle. The 23-year-old Southerner was soon involved in the civic life of that community as a member of its Charter Commission.

Joslin was one of the first to leave for the Klondike in 1897 to open a law office in Dawson and handle real estate and mining claims. While in Dawson he also built a light plant, ran a coal mine, and built a narrow-gauge railroad. In spite of these enterprises, Joslin was ready to move on when he learned of the gold strike at Fairbanks. He realized that prospectors on the creeks would need a railroad connection to navigable water on the Chena River. Joslin had the dream and his friend, Martin Harrais, who had struck it rich in the Klondike, had money.

With additional financing from the English backers of the White Pass and Yukon Railway, Joslin and Harrais completed 26 miles of the Tanana Valley Railroad from Chena to Gilmore, with a 4.7 mile spur to Fairbanks, in September, 1905. The following year, they extended the railroad 20 more miles to Chatanika.

Joslin and Harrais had high hopes for the narrow-gauge railroad. They envisioned it as the first link in a vast network of railroads in Alaska — an extension to Circle City on the Yukon River, a 600-mile link to Nome, and another set of tracks up the Tanana Valley and across the Yukon boundary to Lynn Canal so that interior Alaska would have access to tidewater. Joslin wrote articles for the *Alaska Yukon Magazine* extolling the wealth of the Tanana country, not only in minerals, but also in potential farm land suitable for potatoes, timothy hay, and oats.

The Tanana Valley Railroad was barely completed when Joslin's dreams ended. By presidential edict, Theodore Roosevelt withdrew all Alaska coal, oil and timber lands to reserve them for future generations. During the earlier days of mining in the Fairbanks area, between 1906 and 1909, the railroad served the miners well and made money, but the fuel famine and high cost of doing business forced Fairbanks gold production to fall two-thirds in the next four years. The arrival of automobiles after 1912 sealed the fate of the little railroad. The Tanana Valley Railroad was in deplorable condition when bought by the Alaska Railroad Commission in 1917 for $300,000 to provide the first link from Fairbanks to Chena for the Alaska Railroad.

Joslin responded quickly when placer gold in paying quantities was discovered on Otter Creek in the Iditarod district of western Alaska. In 1910, he linked

Kaltag and Iditarod City with a wireless telegraph service that was eventually taken over by the federal government.

Between 1910 and 1914, Joslin spent most of his time in Washington, D.C., lobbying for the opening of the coal fields, for federal assistance to private railroads in Alaska, and for increased home rule for Alaska.

After selling the Tanana Valley Railroad and leaving Fairbanks, Joslin and George Hazelet bought the only patented tract of oil land at Katalla and founded the Chilkat Oil Company. They leased additional tracts when Alaska oil lands were opened again in 1916, and operated the only producing oil wells in Alaska at the time.

Joslin made a final, futile attempt to develop a coal mine in the Bering River coal field in 1919, but abandoned the effort when the coal proved unsuitable for naval use. After years of complaining to his wife in Seattle about his loneliness and discomfort while pursuing ill-fated development schemes in Alaska, Joslin was glad to join his family in western Washington. During his last 10 years, Joslin continued lecturing and writing about federal government mistreatment of its far-northern "colony."

GERMANY ACCEPTS TERMS
SURRENDER IS MADE UNCONDITIONAL

The Alaska Daily Empire, Juneau   April 24, 1920

HAZELET SUES HERRON FOR DEFAMATION

The Cordova Daily Times   May 31, 1919

AEROPLANE MAY HERD REINDEER OF ALASKA

The Cordova Daily Times   January 17, 1920

HAZELET ASKED TO HELP FRAME G.O.P. PLATFORM

Market Katalla Coal This Summer

Anchorage Daily Times   May 3, 1919

Chilkat Company to Sink Four Oil Wells at Once

COAL FROM BERING FIELD WILL BE PLACED UPON MARKET WHILE MINE IS BEING DEVELOPED

The Cordova Daily Times   January 17, 1920

REPUBLICANS RALLYING TO SUPPORT HAZELET

BIG COAL FIELDS CONTROLLED BY CORPORATIONS

Wickersham alleges that Guggenheim-Morgan Corporation controls Bering River Fields and Southern Pacific Railway Company has cinch on Matanuska field.

REPUBLICANS IN ALL PARTS OF TERRITORY UNANIMOUSLY IN SUPPORT OF HAZELET FOR GOVERNOR

The Cordova Daily Times   April 29, 1920

MᶜBRIDE WINS OVER HERRON IN PRIMARY
HAZELET DEFEATS VALENTINE FOR DELEGATE TO CONVENTION

VOTERS OF TERRITORY PLACE STAMP OF DISAPPROVAL ON VICIOUS CHARACTER DEFAMER

The Cordova Daily Times   December 2, 1920

PETITIONS BOOSTING WICKERSHAM ARE CIRCULATED AT KETCHIKAN
Former Alaska Delegate in Very Receptive Mood Concerning Governorship

Frontier Politics — 1920

As soon as oil well drilling was suspended for the winter, Hazelet left for a six-week trip to Seattle, New York and Detroit. Since passage of an oil leasing bill was anticipated, he needed to discuss future plans with Stephen Birch and other financial backers. They also had political matters to consider. Although Birch wished to avoid any recurrence of the abuse that the Alaska Syndicate had endured during the Pinchot-Ballinger controversy, he continued to work behind the scenes to promote the election of officials in Alaska who would not impede the development of the Kennecott mine and his other Alaskan interests. Earlier in 1919, Birch had attempted, unsuccessfully, to persuade Falcon Joslin to run for delegate on the Democratic ticket. [1]

With the war in Europe finally over, a Republican victory in 1920 was a distinct possibility. Since Hazelet had been influencial in overthrowing Shackleford's dominance in the Republican party, he emerged as a potential leader to counteract Wickersham. Birch continued to contact Wickersham indirectly through emissaries like Falcon Joslin to make sure that he did not ruffle the feathers of "James the Terrible." [2] Joslin was outwardly friendly to Wickersham, but privately wished that Birch would use his influence against the delegate.

The contested delegate election of 1916 was finally decided in favor of Wickersham, but not until after another close election between Wickersham and Charles Sulzer in 1918 had apparently been won by Sulzer. Sulzer died shortly after the election and the Democrats elected George Grigsby to replace Sulzer as delegate. Wickersham again contested the election. After this 1918 election, Joslin wrote Democratic National Committeeman Thomas Donohoe: "It seems to me that if the people of Cordova could be made to realize that Wick has been their worst enemy, he could not get a vote there. He undoubtedly prevented this Government Railway from being located from Chitina to Fairbanks and thereby hurt Cordova greatly and killed his own town (Fairbanks). Moreover, he once before prevented the opening of the coal and oil fields at Katalla by a railroad. And will probably do so again if he can." As a postscript he added: "Both Stannard and I wrote N.Y. about the matter but they decline to do anything." [3] E.T. Stannard was the current Alaska superintendent of the Kennecott Copper Company and Birch was undoubtedly the New York connection that they were asking to take a more active role in Alaskan politics.

While Wickersham was awaiting action on his protest about the 1918 election, he wrote an inflammatory letter to Interior Secretary Lane, accusing him of incompetence and political partisanship, and demanded his resignation. Wickersham asserted that Lane was allowing the Alaska Steamship Company to charge excessive freight rates and thereby impede development of the area served by the government railway, and that he was mismanaging the coal-leasing law so that the Alaska Syndicate would have a monopoly in the Bering River coal field. [4] These charges indicated that, although the Alaska Syndicate no longer existed, Wickersham was still prepared to do battle against the commercial enterprises that Hazelet, Joslin, and Birch were promoting.

Wickersham had already intimated that he would not run again for delegate, but would welcome an appointment as governor of Alaska in the event of a Republican victory in 1920. [5] In an effort to contest Wickersham's aspirations, Hazelet, who had previously held only local political positions, was persuaded to test his popularity by running for statewide office.

Hazelet returned to Cordova on Christmas day after conferring with Birch in New York and visiting his son Craig in Detroit. Craig, who had served in the Navy during the war, had finished his engineering education and was working on the construction of the Willow Run steel plant in Detroit for Henry Ford. In an interview with the *Cordova Daily Times*, Hazelet predicted that a Republican would be elected president and expressed his commitment to work for a united Republican party: "Ten years is a long time to be split up in all sorts of factions. It should be our aim to work for the election of a good Republican legislative ticket and insist upon the appointment of the best men to fill the territorial offices when a Republican president is elected." [6]

In early January 1920, Hazelet announced his intention to run for delegate to the Republican national convention. Within a week he received a letter from Will H. Hays, the chairman of the Republican national committee, requesting that he serve as a member of a group drafting the platform for the convention. Upon reading of Hazelet's appointment to this committee, Wickersham made the following entry in his diary:

Papers this morning announced that Hays, Chairman Republican National Committee, has just appointed 160 of so prominant Republicans in the U.S. to "assist and advise" etc., and he has appointed George C. Hazlett [sic] of Cordova, Alaska, to represent our territory. He is the Guggenheim manager in Alaska and it looks as though those of us who have tried to defend the territory from the Alaska Steamship Co. — the Kennecott Copper Corp. etc. are to take a back seat and the "Big Business" — the one big "Copper and Transportation" Trust will be given charge. It is discouraging — but will lead to more fighting. — However, it means that I will not have any standing politically with that crowd. [7]

In preparation for making platform recommendations for Alaska, Hazlet sent letters to Republicans and Republican clubs throughout the territory soliciting suggestions to be included in the Republican platform. "You will realize, as I do," he wrote, "that we are only a very small part of the United States, and that we can not hope to influence the declarations in the national platform to any great extent; but with this opportunity we should be able to secure a plank pledging a more liberal attitude toward the development of the resources of Alaska, and thus place our territory in a position to advance as against its present position of stagnation. All suggestions of whatever nature will be given careful consideration, and my only desire is to see something constructive worked out." [8] When Wickersham received the Hazelet letter, he wrote in his diary:

Geo. C. Hazelet sends me a printed circular letter inviting a suggestion as to important ideas for inclusion in the Republican national platform! I am answering saying the reduction of the present excessive transportation rates to and from and in Alaska, and sending him copy of a Resolution which I urge him to get adopted declaring the Party, if it secures control at the next election, will put on a line of steamships to run from San Francisco, Portland, and Seattle to terminals of Alaska Railroad at reasonable and just rates and will also control and reduce present rates so they will be reasonable and just, and asking him to secure its adoption and to announce his intention to do so before the April primaries! **He won't!** [9]

Several days later Wickersham indicated in his diary that he had sent out 50 copies of "my letter to Hazelet trying to force him to declare in favor of the U.S. putting on steamships from Alaska terminals of Government Railroad to Seattle, Portland and San Francisco." [10]

Wickersham, who was in Washington, D.C., at the time, also indicated that the President had signed the bill that would open oil and gas lands in Alaska for leasing. [11] Back in Cordova, Hazelet announced that the Chilkat Oil Company would push ahead to determine whether more oil would be found at deeper levels. Drilling by other companies was also anticipated now that they could take over additional claims. (12) Hazelet also revealed that Joslin had wired him from New York concerning other ambitious plans. The Bering River Coal Company was planning to build an auto-truck road from the mine to Canoe Landing on Bering Lake where tunnel boats would take coal across the lake to barges that would tow it to steamships at Cordova or Controller Bay. With the purchase of three 2,000-ton barges and the installation of a small washing plant, the coal company hoped to ship coal to market by July 1920. (13)

When Wickersham received the anticipated negative response from Hazelet to his demand for government-run steamships to serve the Seward railroad terminal, he started to stir up regional opposition to Hazelet's bid for election as delegate to the Republican national convention. Wickersham also opposed J.C. McBride, who was a candidate for Republican national committeeman, running against Charles Herron, the publisher of newspapers in Anchorage and Juneau. On April 7, Wickersham indicated that he had sent telegrams to the *Seward Gateway, Anchorage Times, Nenana Times*, and supporters in Fairbanks and Nome "urging all citizens to vote for Herron, National Committeeman, Valentine and Reid, Delegates Republican National Convention, and especially to oppose Hazelet for Delegate National Republican Convention because he represents Guggenheim transportation, coal, oil, etc. etc." (14)

The *Alaska Daily Capital*, Herron's Juneau publication, pointed out Hazelet's connection with the Bering River coal development plan, and the *Anchorage Daily Times* published a letter, implying that a Hazelet and McBride victory would threaten Anchorage area development:

The political battle soon became considerably more bitter. On April 13, 1920, *The Alaska Daily Capital* in Juneau ran an editorial accusing McBride of having made a deal with the Democrats. "As a matter of fact," the editorial explained, "he (McBride) did not present his candidacy until called upon by one George Hazelet of 'Keystone Canyon' fame, who, after a trip to New York and a conference with Steve Birch, seized upon McBride as the logical man to further certain interests in Alaska which could only be done through a Republican national committeeman who would take orders. All matters pertaining to the McBride campaign have emanated from one source and that source is Cordova. Is there any Alaskan who does not know what the word 'Cordova' means and what it stands for? It is the headquarters of Tom Donohoe and of the same corporation that staged the Keystone massacre."

The following day *The Alaska Daily Capital* resurrected the story of the Keystone Canyon shooting under a headline stating: "How George C. Hazelet Furnished Arms and Ammunition to Hasey Who Killed One Man and Wounded Several Others in the Employ of a Rival Company From the Guggenheim's

Interest — Black Page of Alaska History Is Reviewed." The editorial asked: "Are
Alaskan voters so forgetful that they will place in power these men, that they may
again place the territory at the mercy of these same ruthless destroyers of law and
order? By what right can a man of the type of George Hazelet, the man who by
the written record of the United States furnished the arms to kill innocent men,
claim recognition by the decent citizenry of Alaska?"

The *Anchorage Daily Times*, also published by Herron, made similar accusations
and emphasized the threat Hazelet posed to development of the Matanuska coal
fields, [16] while others came to the Hazelet's defense. E.E. Ritchie, the Valdez
lawyer who had represented John Phillips in the 1910 damage suit against the
Copper River and Northwestern Railway, sent Hazelet a letter which stated:
"I never considered you responsible for the shooting; in fact, I never considered
any one responsible for that except Ed Hasey himself. I do not believe that any
one connected with the railroad company ever dreamed that Hasey would act as
he did. I regret that a newspaper owned by Mr. Herron, whom I am supporting
for national committeeman, has seen fit to resurrect this ancient history and
attempt to place on you a responsibility of which you could never be justly
charged." [17]

Three days before the primary election, Hazelet brought a criminal libel suit
and a civil damage action for $50,000 against Herron and the editor of *The Alaska
Daily Capital* for defamation of character. Herron responded that the suit would
strengthen his candidacy because "no newspaper in the world ever became really
famous without being sued for libel." [18] The day before the election, *The Alaska
Daily Capital* published Wickersham's speech before the 63rd Congress in which
he again presented the Morrisey expense account as evidence that the Alaska
Syndicate had bribed witnesses during the Hasey trial.

In spite of this resort to muckraking, Hazelet and McBride were both elected in
the Republican primary, while Donohoe, who was unopposed, continued to serve
as Democratic national committeeman. The *Juneau Empire* commented: "The
election of George C. Hazelet for delegate to the Republican national convention
is gratifying to those who are opposed to mud-slinging politics. Mr. Hazelet is one
of the most substantial of Alaska's leading citizens and a worthy representative of
his party." [19]

On May 15, Herron pleaded guilty to charges of criminal libel during a hearing
before the United States commissioner in Cordova and was fined $100. Hazelet
dropped the civil charges after Herron published a retraction which stated:

> Whereas a full investigation of the facts surrounding the transaction discloses
> that at an exhaustive hearing before the then United States commissioner at
> Valdez, and that after a prolonged consideration by a federal grand jury of the

Third division, Mr. Hazelet was exonerated and absolved from liability. Further that Judge Cushman, of his own motion, at the trial of the civil case growing out of the trouble dismissed such action against Mr. Hazelet, thereby establishing conclusively that George C. Hazelet was not responsible for the death or injury of any person. All the competent evidence shows that the actions of Mr. Hazelet throughout were characterized by caution, and his repeated efforts to reconcile the contending interests showed an earnest desire to avoid trouble and disorder.

Therefore, in view of the wrong done to Mr. Hazelet through the untruthful statements published in the said *Juneau Capital* and said *Anchorage Times*, and as reparation for the wrong done to an honorable and respected citizen of Alaska, I hereby publicly retract said published statements and editorials. [20]

Immediately following the hearing Hazelet left on the night steamship to Seattle to confer with Joslin about summer plans for the coal and oil fields. He then proceeded to the Republican national convention, where he hoped to promote national legislation to create an Alaska-based board of control to consolidate all federal bureaus with programs in the territory. [21] The convention nominated Ohio Senator Warren G. Harding for President and Calvin Coolidge for Vice-President. Hazelet was pleased to have picked both winners, but did not succeed in getting an Alaska plank included in the party platform. [22]

Fight for the Governorship

Falcon Joslin was glad to see Hazelet return to Alaska after the Republican national convention. While Hazelet was away, Joslin was at Katalla overseeing the oil drilling, coal mining and road building and wishing that he was back in Seattle raising potatoes with his family. In a letter to his wife he lamented: "It would be like heaven to get back to Seattle. This is my very last season in Alaska. Never again for me! I am not sure whether it is my nerves or the unsatisfactory situation of things or both. But I have never in my life been more uncomfortable. I was foolish to allow myself to get into the actual management of this work. I never intended to do so and I am meditating ways of getting out." [1]

George Hazelet, circa 1920.
PHOTO COURTESY HAZELET GRANDCHILDREN

When Hazelet returned to Alaska in early July, Stephen Birch was in Cordova on an inspection trip with W.P. Hamilton, the son-in-law of J.P. Morgan, and E.T. Stannard, who had recently assumed the management of Birch's three big Alaska companies — the Kennecott mine, the Copper River and Northwestern Railway and the Alaska Steamship Company. The Birch party had already been over at Katalla with Joslin and were about to leave for Latouche and Kennecott. After completing the inspection trip, Birch reported his intention to build a railroad spur from the Bering River coal field to the Copper River and Northwestern Railway if the coal mine proved to be commercially productive. (2)

Hazelet conferred with the Birch party in Cordova and then took the boat to Katalla to assume management of the oil operations, which now included a new refinery. Joslin was optimistic about future prospects: "We have the derrick up for a new well which I am sure will get pay. I also feel certain we can drill a number of wells from now on and get pay every time. ... It has been fearfully unlucky that we should have taken four years to learn and drill so many deep and dry holes all around the good ground." (3)

Joslin returned to the coal mine and soon found himself mired down in the road-building project. "Have been working all day with grubbing hoe and axe," he wrote his wife. "This day and yesterday were sunny and beautiful but the day before yesterday it rained a deluge of 4.6 inches in 24 hours. I lay in my tent at night and listened to the rain coming in sheets and torrents and it was as if it was falling on my naked soul. I was out in it most of the day working with the men to keep their spirits up. ... I am one smart man to originate plans and then be invited to carry them out and supplied the money to do it with. Then to discover that I have under estimated it about 150 per cent in time and money and stick to it and try to get it through anyway. Such has always been the result of my infantile enthusiasm." (4)

When he went over to Katalla the following month, Joslin noted that Hazelet was getting along well with the drilling, but he couldn't get enthusiastic about the small wells that produced only five to 10 barrels a day. He was even less optimistic about the coal prospects: "I hope the truck road will be finished by the middle of September. But Mr. Jones says October first and perhaps he knows. If it is as late as that we shall get no coal out this year. We have been making some interesting washing tests on the coal which look as if we could turn out some very clean coal. But it will take years to make it a big mine and I have it in mind to tell Mr. Birch I don't care to spend so much more of my life in Alaska and ask him to put the work under someone else." (5)

Hazelet, on the other hand, had not lost his enthusiasm. In an interview for *The Rig and Reel* he expressed the same joy and faith in the north country that he felt years before after crossing Valdez Glacier:

The oil game in Alaska is a queer one — but I like it. From fighting seven feet of snow and blizzards in the winter, to fighting mosquitoes and bears in the summer, I like it. I've lived in the country twenty-four years. Alaska is my home, and I want no other, for I have faith in the country.

I know there is oil here because we are getting some. Time will work these things out. The Government will eventually realize its mistakes from the development point of view, and right them. They are sending in men of discernment now whose investigations are bound to result in good.

Alaska is not hopeless by any means. Before long we will have a country here equal to any country in Northern Europe — a country filled with happy homes and prosperous people.

Hazelet spent most of the next three months at Katalla and reported that the new wells were producing the expected five to 10 barrels daily. On October 8, the *Cordova Daily Times* reported that the Chilkat Oil Company's first oil tanker had arrived from Seattle. The MARGARET, with a cargo capacity of 12,000 gallons, was designed to deliver oil to ports around Prince William Sound and tow scows loaded with coal or drums of fuel oil. (6) The road to the coal mine was finally completed at the end of October. The mine, employing forty men, was planning to continue operation throughout the winter, but delivery of coal to Cordova would depend on the freezing of Bering Lake. (7)

The November election brought the expected Republican victory and Alaska Republicans started to anticipate appointments by President Harding in the next administration. Hoping for an appointment as governor of Alaska, Wickersham had stayed out of the delegate race and thrown his support to his protege, Dan Sutherland. Cordova Republicans also supported Sutherland in his victory over George Grigsby. The new delegate-elect sent the following letter to Hazelet on November 3: "Thank you and your fine organization for the splendid work done at Cordova and the Copper River valley. I sincerely appreciate the confidence placed in me by the electors and am fully aware of the responsibility that it carries with it." (8)

The Cordova Republicans immediately started to promote Hazelet for the governorship with the *Cordova Daily Times* presenting the following rational in a front page editorial:

The Republicans of this section of Alaska feel that they have the most available candidate for governor of Alaska in the person of George C. Hazelet of Cordova and insist that he allow the use of his name for the office, the duties of which he is so eminently qualified to discharge. Mr. Hazelet is one of the pioneer residents of Alaska, has blazed trails, helped to develop its resources, established new industries and is one of the substantial and successful business men of the north.

Mr. Hazelet has the confidence and respect of the people of Alaska, regardless of party affiliations, as was demonstrated at the primary election last April by the large vote he received when elected as a delegate to the Republican national convention in Chicago. His home town gave him its almost unanimous support, a compliment which any candidate may well feel proud of. ... Mr. Hazelet long has had a wide acquaintanceship with the leaders of both parties throughout the nation and in his attendance at the national convention he strengthened this position. [9]

Wickersham, who was still in Washington, D.C., preparing his contest to replace Grigsby as delegate in the waning days of the Congressional session, was furious when he learned of the developments in Alaska. "**Hell's to pay!**," he wrote in his diary. "Sutherland made an agreement with McBride that in return for his election he would pledge himself not to intermeddle in any way with the power of McBride, Hazelet, et. al. over Federal appointments in Alaska! ... Dan has done the most disastrous and fool thing and utterly betrayed all his old friends for a bunch of enemies — and a small bunch at that. The pitiful part of the mistake is that it was entirely unnecessary — for Dan could have been elected without it with ease — and will be anyway, but it leaves him powerless and an object of contempt even to his enemies. He will be no more in the political situation in the Territory than a white chip in a poker game. He has sacrificed himself, his friends and his standing. I am horribly chagrined at his conduct." [10]

Two days later Wickersham reiterated his displeasure: "Dan Sutherland went the limit in his speech last night and turned the Territory over to the McBride-Hazelet crowd of the representatives of the Big Interests. He declared very positively that he favored the 'organization' — meaning McBride, whom he openly named as his 'life long friend,' Beigle of Ketchikan, Hazelet of Cordova, Marquam of Fairbanks, and Lomen of Nome —the four latter having been appointed by McBride without any action by the Republicans of Alaska. Dan announced in a loud voice his intention of accepting the guidance of these men in all political appointments in Alaska — which will give the government over to the Gugg. and Trans. Co. **wholly! Selah!**" [11]

While the Hazelet candidacy for governor was receiving endorsements from Republican organizations throughout Alaska, Wickersham was plotting his campaign. He spent the next several days working with supporters in Juneau to compile charges against Hazelet and the "Guggs." [12] When interviewed about the possibility of receiving the governorship himself, Wickersham indicated that he would take it if offered, and declared emphatically his opposition to the candidacy of George Hazelet. [13] In the meantime, Sutherland met him in Washington and Wickersham commented: "Sutherland spent the morning in my office and he impresses me that he has made a bad promise to our enemies and can not get away from it — though he evidently intends to 'cut under' the fellows to whom he has made the mistaken promise. Am sorry for him." [14]

Support for Hazelet continued to mount in early January 1921, with the unqualified endorsement of Republican National Committeeman J.C. McBride, who stated: "I have a very high personal regard for Mr. Hazelet and feel that Alaska is very fortunate to have at this time a man of his caliber available for governor and I am glad indeed to give him my endorsement. I know that he is in every way qualified to discharge the duties of the high office of governor of Alaska and I will do everything in my power to aid him in securing the appointment." [15] After Hazelet added endorsements from Republican groups in Sitka and Ketchikan, Wickersham prepared to take a more active role in the contest.

The January 6 issue of the *Alaska Daily Empire* printed the following statement from Wickersham after interviewing him in Juneau:

> Mr. McBride's endorsement of Mr. Hazelet of Cordova for Governor was, of course, the only thing he could do. Hazelet and Donohoe elected McBride as National Committeeman at the primary election on April 27 last through big majorities in the Alaska Syndicate precincts at Cordova, Eyak, Latouche and at the Kennecott precincts. ...
>
> The issue is now squarely presented to President Harding: Shall the Alaska Syndicate, in addition to its present control of Alaska transportation rates, its control of Alaska copper and coal, and other great natural resources on the public domain in Alaska, also have control of the government of Alaska through the appointment of its agents and servants as Governor and Judges and other governing officials in the Territory? ...
>
> This situation presents to President Harding, even before he has taken his oath of office, the same problems that beset President Taft in 1910. The Alaska Syndicate's attempt to control the great natural resources of Alaska in 1910 destroyed the Taft Administration, severed the bonds of friendship between President Taft and Colonel Roosevelt, split the Republican Party into two great factions, which destroyed each other in 1912, elected President Wilson, and defeated Hughes for President in 1916.
>
> Will President Harding begin his administration where President Taft left off, and appoint the Cordova agent of the Alaska Syndicate, with his Keystone Canyon record, as Governor of Alaska, and turn the government of Alaska over to it bodily? Mr. McBride thinks that he will, but I think he will not.

> Mr. McBride declares in his endorsement of Mr. Hazelet, in yesterday's *Empire*, that he would do everything in his power to help Mr. Hazelet secure the appointment, and I now declare that I will do everything in my power to warn President Harding of the danger of the situation, and everything possible to defeat the appointment of Hazelet and every other man endorsed by the Alaska Syndicate combination. In that contest I ask the assistance of all Alaskans who want a square deal in Alaska, free from the domination of the Alaska Syndicate and its bipartisan political organization.

Wickersham, who had already supplied newspapers with his analysis of the Keystone Canyon shooting and the Hasey trial, also tried to associate Hazelet with prostitution in Alaska, citing a case in Cordova in 1911. [16] This case, Matilda A. Snyder vs. Edward Kelter and George C. Hazelet, trustee, involved a nuisance complaint about excessive noise from a boarding house that Mrs. Snyder claimed was a brothel. Hazelet's only contact with the case was that he had sold the lot to Kelter. Judge Cushman's instructions to the jury stated: "A non-suit has been ordered by the court as far as the defendant Hazelet is concerned, as there was no evidence that he had maintained or was in any way maintaining a bawdyhouse on said premises. You will therefore confine your attention to investigating the liability, if any, of the defendant Kelter for the acts of which complaint is made." The case was subsequently decided in favor of the defendant. [17] (Wickersham apparently was unaware of Hazelet's problems with the Populists back in O'Neill, Nebraska, in 1890 or he would certainly have attempted to resurrect that ancient history as well.)

Later in January, the fourth division Republican committee endorsed Hazelet over Wickersham by a vote of 54 to 2. [18] Wickersham, enroute back to Washington, D.C., reiterated to a reporter from *The Alaska Dispatch* that he was bent on wrecking the ambitions of George C. Hazelet and opposed to every man proposed by the Alaska Republican organization. [19]

Wickersham's bid for the governorship received a boost on February 12 when the House Elections Committee finally voted to oust Grigsby and seat Wickersham as delegate until the end of the Congressional session on March 4. The committee determined that Grigsby had no right to sit in the House because he was elected at a special election called to fill a vacancy when no vacancy existed, because the 1918 contested election between Sulzer and Wickersham should have been decided in favor of Wickersham. [20]

Three days before the Harding inauguration, headlines in the *Juneau Sunday Capital* announced: "Fighting Jim Wickersham Is Again Victor — Delegate Wickersham Is Given Seat in Congress By Vote 177-162." The *Capital*, which Hazelet had sued for libel, had been actively promoting Wickersham's candidacy for governor following a discussion the previous month between Wickersham and a member of the editorial staff about the future policy of the paper. Wickersham had pointed out that, since Juneau's other paper, the *Alaska Daily Empire*, which usually favored the Democratic party, was now supporting Hazelet and the Guggenheim interests, a Hazelet victory would put the *Empire* under control of Harry Steel and make it the Republican organization paper. The *Capital*, usually a Republican voice, would then suffer. [21]

Will Steel, who had waged the fight against Hazelet in Cordova back in 1915, took over the editorship of the *Alaska Daily Capital* and the editorial page of the *Capital* began to sound like the final issues of the *Cordova Daily Alaskan* with Hazelet regularly referred to as "King George." Steel suggested early in February that the fight might get so bitter that a third party, perhaps a non-Alaskan, would win the governorship. He prophetically mentioned the name of Scott Bone, former editor of Seattle's *Post-Intelligencer*, as a possible compromise candidate. [22] In another editorial, however, he refuted that suggestion: "Their cry that Wickersham seeks only to kill off Hazelet and is perfectly willing that a new man from outside be named is hardly to be given credence. Those who know Fighting Jim realize that first he wants the position for himself, and second that under no circumstances should Hazelet and the interests he represents be permitted to dominate the Territory, and third that a bona fide Alaskan should be named." [23]

While Will Steel was in Juneau writing editorials favoring Wickersham for the *Juneau Daily Capital*, his brother Harry was in Seattle with Hazelet, awaiting a call from McBride who was in Washington lobbying on his behalf. Upon his return to Alaska, Harry Steel exuded confidence in an interview with an *Alaska Daily Empire* reporter: "We have had nothing but encouraging news from Washington regarding Mr. Hazelet's candidacy, and it seems, everywhere I have been, to be a foregone conclusion that he will be appointed. ... Not only will Mr. Hazelet be appointed, but his confirmation by the Senate is practically sure." [24]

Predictions of a prompt appointment of Alaska's next governor were premature. Hazelet remained in Seattle until late March and then joined McBride in Washington. Delegate Sutherland adamantly refused to make any endorsement and Wickersham commented in his diary: "**He won't budge — he has refused to endorse me** or to go to the Secretary or the President in the matter — **and has just abdicated his duty to the people of Alaska and permits McBride, Herron, and 'any old thing' to prevail on the President if they can to give the Government of Alaska over to the Syndicate or to any one who wants it. He has lain down like a whipped dog.** [25]

President Harding was approached by various senators, by Alaskans and by other interested parties in an effort to influence the gubernatorial appointment.

Names of various compromise candidates were mentioned and eventually discarded. Karl Behr, a young New York financier and tennis champion, was boosted and then dismissed because he knew nothing about Alaska. General Richardson was considered an ideal candidate until he admitted to being a Texas Democrat. Colonel Charles Forbes from Spokane was said to have strong support but did not want to go to Alaska. Back in Alaska, the territorial legislature passed a resolution urging President Harding and Secretary Fall to appoint only a bona fide Alaskan to the governorship.

Colonel William Perkins, a former Alaskan living in Seattle, was considered a likely prospect at the end of April but the McBride forces considered him too closely allied with Wickersham.

Wickersham spoke frequently with Sutherland, who was still wavering. On April 30, Wickersham wrote in his diary: "Sutherland has been 'bunked' by Charles Herron and other Col. Perkins boosters into the belief that I am out of the race for Gov. and he now says he will support Hazelet etc.! It looks as if he wants credit, first, for endorsing me — then, second, endorsing Hazelet, so he can square himself for both and thus satisfy the friends of both — while as a matter of fact he has not supported either fairly or honestly. I tried to show him that if he now endorses Hazelet —**it might happen** — that with his and McBride's support, the President might appoint Hazelet — and then he shivers, for he does not want Hazelet appointed."

During May, more men who had been prominent in Alaskan history over the past 20 years attempted to express their opinions about the governorship to President Harding. Former Alaska Governor Walter Clark spoke for Hazelet while Gifford Pinchot promised to use his influence to support Wickersham. [26] Wickersham's diary entry on May 14 indicated that Stephen Birch was involved in the governorship controversy: "Sutherland talked to Secretary Fall today. He told Dan he intended to consult with Steve Birch about governorship of Alaska! and asked Dan to get a compromise with McBride and the Birch interests to agree on some Alaskan if possible for governor. They seem to be afraid to use their power and want to hedge! Probably want to appoint one of Birch's friends who is first approved by Dan and McBride — the Organization."

Although a group of Alaskans met in Washington, D.C., they were unable to agree on an Alaskan. On June 1, 1921, President Harding announced the appointment of Scott C. Bone, a former Seattle editor and personal friend of President Harding. Sutherland had failed to keep a promise that he would support Hazelet if given the ultimatum that the choice would be between Hazelet and an outsider. [27] Both Hazelet, who had remained aloof from the discussions in Washington, and Wickersham seemed relieved that the battle was over and that at least the other one had not been appointed. Both men pledged to support Governor Bone, whom they considered to be the personal representative of the President.

When Hazelet returned to Alaska on June 21, he indicated that he had had several interviews with President Harding, whom he found friendly to Alaska and prepared to aid in the development of the territory. [28] The *Anchorage Daily Times*, published by Charles E. Herron whom Hazelet sued for libel the year before, carried the following complimentary editorial on June 30, 1921:

TURNS DEFEAT INTO VICTORY

George C. Hazelet, defeated candidate for gubernatorial honors, has proven himself an Alaskan worthy of emulation. In his contest for the executive chair Mr. Hazelet did not enter into personalities, except in defense of his character: At all times he treated his opponents with the same courtesy and consideration he has ever shown friends and enemies alike.

Mr. Hazelet belongs to the enviable class of citizens who follow the teaching that "consideration is the height of politeness." Defeat invariably brings out the true character of men. In Mr. Hazelet's case defeat was really victory; his becoming conduct throughout the bitter political fight was typical of a man who writes his friends to "boost for Governor Bone in all things tending to benefit Alaska; support him as you would have supported me in a similar position; let's give Governor Bone our assistance to the end that Alaska will grow bigger and better in every way."

There is no sting in these words but on the other hand they express the true sentiment of a loyal man; a big man and one who can rise so far above personalities that what may seem to be defeat is turned into glorious victory.

Hazelet, who had rebounded from more than his share of setbacks over the years, was, at age 60, able to accept another defeat philosophically.

The Alaska Weekly, Seattle   March 20, 1923

GUGGENHEIM GHOST RAISED TO FRIGHTEN PRESIDENT AND PARTY

The Alaska Weekly, Seattle   March 23, 1923

ALASKANS STAMPEDE TO MEXICO

The Cordova Daily Times   July 30, 1923

PRESIDENT HARDING SICK MAN

Complications form Ptomaine
Poisoning bring Anxiety

The Cordova Daily Times   July 30, 1923

BERING RIVER COAL FAILS NAVY TESTS

Claimed is Mechanically
Unsuited for Steaming
Requirements

The Alaska Weekly, Seattle   March 16, 1923

KENNECOTT-UTAH MERGER PLAN AGREED ON

Basis of Exchange of Stocks Favorable to
Big Alaska Corporation

ALASKA COLLEGE DEDICATED WITH AUSPICIOUS EXERCISES

GOVERNOR SCOTT C. BONE DELIVERS ADDRESS

The Alaska Weekly, Seattle   March 16, 1923

HISTORY OF ALASKA SOON IN THE PRESS

JUDGE JAMES WICKERSHAM PUTTING FINISHING TOUCHES TO CROWNING ACHIEVEMENT OF LIFE

HAS BEEN GATHERING DATA DURING TWENTY YEARS IN NORTHLAND

The Cordova Daily Times   January 8, 1921

KATALLA OIL FIELD STEADY PRODUCER NOW

ELEVEN WELLS NOW PRODUCING

TWELVE HUNDRED BARREL A MONTH OIL OF FINEST QUALITY

REFINERY SAVES 24 BY-PRODUCTS, INCLUDING KEROSENE

TWELFTH HOLE NOW BEING SUNK BY CHILKAT COMPANY

OTHER COMPANIES PLAN

SLEEPING CAR SERVICE INAUGURATION ON ALASKA RAILROAD

FAST THROUGH SERVICE ESTABLISHED BETWEEN SEWARD AND NENANA

Chilkat Oil Company

Scott Bone had not sought the governorship of Alaska but, once appointed, he promptly began his orientation to the territory. Enroute to Juneau he met commercial groups in Seattle and stated: "I am taking up the work just as I would a business proposition. As a matter of fact that is just what Alaska is — a business proposition — with vast resources that are yet practically unscratched. There's no bigger business proposition in the world and I am convinced a new era is coming for the territory." [1]

George Hazelet hosted Bone at a private dinner when the new governor visited Cordova in early August. At a public reception during his Cordova visit, Bone mentioned the difficulty he was experiencing in convincing the nation at large that he was not going to live among polar bears and icebergs. Hazelet also spoke at the meeting, stressing that enormous amounts of capital would need to be expended before real development could occur in Alaska, and that the future of the territory would depend upon the abolition of bureaucratic rule from a distance and the relaxation of obnoxious conservation policies. [2] Although he continued to be president of the Cordova Chamber of Commerce, Hazelet was no longer active in local politics. During the balance of the summer he directed his energy toward preparing for extensive drilling in the Katalla oil field.

The passage of oil-leasing legislation was bringing increased interest in the Katalla oil field as well as an area on the Alaska Peninsula where claims had been filed prior to the 1910 withdrawals. Falcon Joslin and his associates were asking for patents on two claims containing 320 acres each and for leases on three claims, one surrounding the 160-acre patented claim on which the Chilkat Oil Company's producing wells were located. Joslin had decided to limit drilling to shallow wells since the attempt to drill a deep well had not been successful. [3]

The oil company suffered another setback in July 1921, when the tanker MARGARET exploded, injuring three men. The boat was destroyed and flames spread to the wharf and a warehouse, but the refinery and oil tanks were saved through heroic efforts of the men at the plant. After escorting the burned men to Cordova, Hazelet assumed responsibility for rebuilding the dock. [4]

Hazelet continued to supervise drilling of additional wells throughout the winter of 1921-1922, returning to Cordova periodically to attend meetings of the Chamber of Commerce, which was attempting to promote a statewide organization. In April, he reported that 11 wells were producing 1,200 barrels a month of high-grade parafine-base oil that was being used by canneries and other industries around Prince William Sound. In addition, 24 by-products were being saved, including kerosene of the best quality. Several other oil companies had received patents or leases and were planning to resume activity the following summer. [5]

Chilkat Oil Company near Katalla.
ANCHORAGE MUSUEM OF HISTORY & ART. B87.43.4

The Bering River Coal Company also looked forward to increased activity in the summer of 1922 since the Navy Department had let a contract for the delivery of 600 to 700 tons of coal for a naval steaming test. The mine resumed operations with a large force of men in anticipation of a battleship coming north to make the test before August 1. Several groups were also working on means of transporting coal to tidewater. The Alaska Anthracite Railway was building a line between the coal fields and Controller Bay, and the Cordova Chamber of Commerce was attempting to interest the Forest Service in building a road between Katalla and Mile 39 on the Copper River and Northwestern Railway. [6] The Forest Service upon further consideration, however, recommended an alternative plan that would connect Katalla and the Chilkat Oil Company to Softuk Bay, which would be a safer harbor than Katalla during heavy weather. [7]

The enthusiasm of 1922 was dampened in February 1923, by a report that Bering River coal had once again failed the Navy tests. W.E. Dunkle, a mining engineer connected with the Kennecott Corporation, reported that "the coal would not cake properly and when a layer was spread over a bed of live coals it blanketed the fire and shaking resulted in the coal going through the grates before it was consumed." Mr. Dunkle further reported that the Bering River Coal Company would close the mine and discontinue development for an indefinite period after having spent about $500,000 in constructing more than a mile of underground tunnels and building a four-mile tramway. Since the company had been unsuccessful in efforts to find unbroken coal veins, it would turn almost all the ground back to the government. [8] At this time tests on Matanuska coal were thought to have been more successful but the Navy soon abandoned efforts to develop the Chickaloon Naval Coal Reserve as well.

Local demands for Chilkat Oil Company products, on the other hand, were increasing. After spending most of the summer and fall of 1922 at Katalla, Hazelet left Cordova on February 2, 1923, for a six-week trip during which he planned to study refinery methods in small oil fields in California, Montana, and Oklahoma. He also hoped to visit his son Craig in Chicago. [9]

Hazelet kept a diary during the last month of this trip in which he has described his observations in detail. On February 28, he was at Santa Fe Springs in California, and then he went to Bakersfield, where he visited the Kern River and the Maricopia and Taft fields. He studied both compression and absorption techniques for increasing the gasoline yield. On March 6, he arrived in Bartlesville, Oklahoma, where he spent three days consulting with experts on methods of dewaxing oil and making lubricants.

Hazelet arrived in New York on March 19 and met briefly with Stephen Birch before leaving the next day for the Superior Oil Works in Warren, Pennsylvania, where he found very shallow wells that had been pumping for years. On Thursday, March 22, he went to Tidioute, Pennsylvania, to study a gasoline extraction plant that was selling all produce locally.

A consultation with Mr. George of the Bureau of Mines in San Francisco was next on the schedule. While there, Hazelet procured data on production and care of wells. From San Francisco he went to Washington, D.C., where he met cabinet officers and other officials concerned with Alaska affairs.

Hazelet finally returned to New York at Birch's request to meet President Tiegle of Standard Oil of New Jersey. On Tuesday, March 27, he lunched with Birch, Tiegle, Mr. Hurd, head of the production department, Mr. Bowman, the head geologist, and Mr. Cobona, manager of Imperial Oil of Canada. The Standard Oil executives decided that they would not get involved in Alaska exploration because it was too far from their other operations, but felt that Imperial Oil of Canada might be interested.

Although Hazelet had intended to leave for Alaska, he agreed to stay over the weekend in order to talk with President McKeon of Imperial Oil, who was arriving from South America on Sunday.

That meeting never took place because Hazelet was operated on for acute appendicitis on Sunday, April 1. At the time of the operation his condition was considered so serious that both Craig and Falcon Joslin rushed to his bedside. After a week in New York, Joslin wrote his wife that Hazelet was improving and would soon be discharged from the hospital. He commented that Stephen Birch had shown him "studied discourtesy," but then tempered his remark by saying that Birch was probably preoccupied with sick children. (10) By the end of May, Hazelet was back at work at Katalla, and in June he accompanied Joslin and a group of oil geologists to Yakataga Beach, where the Chilkat Oil Company had claims. (11)

Hazelet had other duties to perform the summer of 1923 during President Harding's trip to Alaska to celebrate completion of the Alaska Railroad. When Harding visited Cordova on July 20, Hazelet, as president of the Cordova Chamber of Commerce, presented him with a series of recommendations. These suggestions, which were being made at the President's request, included emphasis on the building of roads and trails, population-based representation in the territorial legislature, and an increased share in the revenues from federal lands. The Chamber also stated its opposition to "the embarkation of the government in the shipping business in Alaska." (12) In presenting these recommendations to the President, Hazelet stressed that Cordovans had no grievances, a statement which was in marked contrast to complaints heard in towns along the Alaska Railroad. Correspondents accompanying Harding remarked in a release to the Cordova paper: "Everyone from Seward to Fairbanks has his own theory of government and knows just what is wrong. The result thus far is a heavy deficit and more or less stagnation. Cordova, on the other hand, depends on the private enterprise of the copper mine owners, and the president of the Chamber of Commerce made the astonishing statement that the people of Cordova have no grievances to be redressed and had no new theories of government to propound. President Harding has seen no more prosperous and contented town in the North." (13)

Prior to coming to Alaska the Presidential party received the same old propaganda about Guggenheim control in Alaska from John Ballaine, a disgruntled Seward developer. Upon return from the trip, one member of the Congressional party observed that "what Alaska needs is more Guggenheims and Rockefellers."

Hazelet had great faith in Harding and was deeply shocked by the death of the President shortly after returning from the Alaska trip. In a letter to his son Craig he expressed this grief as well as his continued pain from the untimely death of his wife and his hopes for the future of Alaska:

> ... I sometimes doubt if it is best to look back to the past too much — and yet if it were not for that privilege, I hardly see what one of my age would do. As one's mind runs back over his past life, he sees so many things he would now do differently, so many little attentions, so many little kindnesses, that he did not do which he should have done — all this and a thousand and one other things left undone — and they come pouring in on him, till he is forced to cry out in dispair.
>
> Craig, your mother is very close to me yet, notwithstanding 11 years have gone since her passing. I feel at times I must stretch out my hands and touch her. Maybe some day I may, who knows! But I must not dwell too much on this. I have our boys and our grandchildren to live for and that is much. ...
>
> Yes! Harding's passing was a great shock to all the nation — but I think it peculiarly severe on Alaska. You see we are such a small community — even as a whole — and he had just visited each separate town and came in such close contact with the people. He was such a human man that the personal contact was very close indeed. All seemed to take to him at once, and really, for Alaskans, it seemed more like losing one of our own. That's the way our people felt, and still feel. We feel also it means a great material loss. Having seen conditions for himself he was much better able to deal intelligently with questions as they arose. To my mind, he had arrived at a right understanding.
>
> On our trip to the glacier, he asked me what the administration could do for Alaska. I said, give us plenty of roads and trails, liberalize some of our land laws, conserve our fish, with the greatest possible use compatible with the preservation of the industry, and allow us to work out our own salvation. He said, "That is exactly the conclusion I have arrived at, and I think I will say that in my Alaska speech." I see he did.
>
> Coolidge will make an ideal president for these times. We could not have a better man. Whether he can be nominated next time I do not know. The country seems to be going more and more to the extremists. Now is the time it stands all Americans to look out well as to what they do. ...

The oil game is very bad. Production is so large in the states that prices are cut almost to nothing. Prices have been cut here, more than 8 cents per gallon since last year. This eats up the big end of our profit and we will drill no more wells for the present or till there is a change. I'm cleaning out an old well, putting in my pumping power, and expect to get in a gasoline extraction plant to take the gasoline out of our casing head gas. If conditions keep on we may have to close down entirely.

Calvin is getting on fairly well with his fish business. Of course there is no money in it for him at the present time, but it gives him lots of experience and will put him in a position to command attention later on in the Territory — for our fishing industry will always remain our largest. Don't allow yourself to become discouraged if you don't secure contracts right along. They will come later, and things are bound to come your way sometime because you give the right attention to business. Please remember, if it should become hard sledding for you, I can always help you out. That is what a Dad is for, and don't forget it. [14]

George Hazelet with family.
Calvin and wife, Nan, (seated), Craig (standing)
PHOTO COURTESY OF HAZELET GRANDCHILDREN

In January 1924, Hazelet retired from the presidency of the Cordova Chamber of Commerce and was succeeded by his friend J.L. Galen. Donohoe, who had moved to Cordova from Valdez several years before, was listed as a new member of the executive board. Hazelet continued to be optimistic about the future for Cordova but stressed the potential of tourism and fisheries more than his oil prospects. John Hazelet, who had operated the Chisna gold mine for years, was now engaged in transporting tourists from Cordova to Fairbanks over the Copper River and Northwestern Railway and the Richardson highway. [15] The Great Circle Route, promoted by the Alaska Steamship Company, then routed passengers from Fairbanks back to Seward on the Alaska Railroad.

The sixth annual report of the Chilkat Oil Company, issued in April 1924, noted that the company would soon own outright 471 acres, the only patented oil lands in the territory of Alaska. With 16 producing shallow wells, the company enjoyed the distinction of having the first and only producing oil wells in the territory. New installations were designed to lessen production costs and assure a bright future. [16] Machinery for the gasoline absorption plant, costing $10,000, arrived in September 1924. After spending several months supervising its installation, Hazelet left Cordova in early December to spend the holidays with Craig in Chicago.

Drilling was resumed in May 1925, and modifications were made so that more gasoline could be produced to meet the growing demands in the area. The seventh annual report of the Chilkat Oil Company indicated that E.T. Stannard was now the president rather than Falcon Joslin. Although oil engineers continued to visit the Katalla field, Hazelet indicated that none of the other companies had done anything during the summer of 1925.

Hazelet's health began to fail during the winter of 1926 and he spent several months in Seattle receiving medical treatment. When he returned to Cordova on April 22 he reported that his health was greatly improved and that the Chilkat Oil Company would continue its usual operations. The *Cordova Daily Times* printed this description of the current status of the Katalla oil field on May 28, 1926:

> Just what the Katalla region will ultimately yield is an unknown quantity. Most of the wells there now are 1,000 to 1,500 feet deep. Eventually the test will be made to 5,000 feet, but that is an experiment involving a large investment. Perhaps then only will the true worth be known.
>
> To the uninitiated the Chilkat suggests a remarkably rich field. Seepages are visible over a large area. Crude oil drips out of the ground in sticky streams. Gas bubbles from the bottom of pools. In some areas the ground is an oily bog. For

centuries, perhaps, oil has been escaping from the earth and the wastage even now is fairly large. A small fortune is seeping away annually.

Yet, with the land like a petroleum soaked sponge, oozing its precious saturation, the wells themselves are scant producers possibly because they are not deep enough. They yield only a few barrels daily and a gusher is unknown. However, the product, what there is of it, is rich, having a parafine base. It comes from the ground at a gravity of 15 to 48 and after it is distilled the gasoline averages a gravity of 65 and distillate, 52. Kerosene manufactured from it is equal to any and the Diesol oil is of fine quality.

For miles around Katalla one may walk through the timber and come upon abandoned wells or drilling equipment. There are casings into which one may dip a bucket and bring up the rich crude oil. The Chilkat Company is pumping 16 out of 24 wells and a small refinery is in operation. Last year a gas reduction plant was installed, adding from 5,000 to 6,000 gallons to the monthly output. ... The total output each day is 30 barrels. At the present time the company can supply only one-tenth of the oil needed for consumption on Prince William Sound.

Gasoline is brought here in 100 gallon drums on the PIONEER, which at high tide can enter the slough on which the oil dock is situated, three miles out of Katalla. There are no storage facilities at the field, so the petroleum has to be moved steadily. ...

The gas reduction plant utilizes the casing head gas, originally used only for lights and heat at the company buildings. It is now compressed to about 30 pounds, passed through absorption oil, which the company makes itself, and when the liquid is thoroughly impregnated with gasoline, it is passed off through a still. The oil is used over again, making the process continuous. The gas available flows at the rate of 200,000 cubic feet daily and can be burned again locally after the gasoline is extracted.

One of the curious sights at the oil well colony is the big gas flame burning day and night. All heating and cooking is done by gas and the houses are snug in the coldest winter weather.

The only means of travel over the oil swamp is by following a small railroad built on timbers and planked, so that horses can drag flat cars on the rails. Each time a new well is put down, the track is extended, otherwise heavy equipment would be mired.

Hazelet's trips to Katalla were shorter and less frequent during the summer of 1926, and he took a pleasure trip to Fairbanks over the Richardson highway and the Alaska Railroad. On August 2, the *Cordova Daily Times* reported that Hazelet was critically ill in the Cordova hospital. Despite his illness, Hazelet had been attending to business and was among those greeting the Commissioner of Fisheries Henry O'Malley and a visiting Congressman several days before. Hazelet died on August 5 from complications of high blood pressure. After a funeral service at the Presbyterian church, his casket was escorted to the ocean dock by a procession of merchants and friends for burial at Seattle.

During the funeral service Rev. W.A. Couden summerized Hazelet's commitment to Alaska by stating: "This was a man who came here in the pioneer days and suffered hardships and privation because he believed in the country. Even when urged to remain in the States and prolong his life, he would not stay away, because he loved Alaska." (17)

The editor of the *Cordova Daily Times* summarized more completely Hazelet's contribution to Cordova:

> And thus death has come to Cordova, severing the vital cord of a true man. It came, as it must come to all men, to the one man in Cordova whom this community can least afford to lose, to George C. Hazelet. There is offered to few men in their lifetime the opportunity to write themselves so largely into the warp and woof of a community, as George C. Hazelet has done in the history and well-being of Cordova. Years ago this paper wrote of Mr. Hazelet that he was Cordova's First Citizen. He remained so to the end, admitted to be so by those who disagreed with him as much as by those who agreed with him. We in Cordova will be hard put to it to fill the place held by him in all aspects of our community life. His loss is still too recent for us to realize how much we will suffer by his taking away.
>
> With the death of Mr. Hazelet passes the last of the three men, Heney, Hawkins, and Hazelet who had most to do with the founding and building of Cordova. They were all pioneers and builders. Strong men in a rough country, fighting their way through and bringing civilization and comfort with them. To these three, the present inhabitants of Cordova are indebted for the heritage they enjoy in living in a community that is the most stable of any community in Alaska, well built, with wide streets, and all the essentials to decent living found in any town in the States. All of them, and not the least Mr. Hazelet, were men of vision.
>
> If this town has a personality, George C. Hazelet contributed most to make it what it is. Up to the end he gave himself without stint to any and every forward-looking movement which interested our people. A recital of his accomplishments is not necessary. We have but to look around us and see the results of his work. We can best mourn him by continuing in the paths that he has hewn and striving to imitate his impartial outlook on all matters of common importance. We, who knew him so well, who so often have benefitted by his kindly advice and wisdom, who share in furthering the work in which he played so great a part, join with his family

in mourning his passing. Our only consolation will be that his influence will remain with us and continue to work for the things for which he stood in life. [18]

By all measures, George Cheever Hazelet lived a rewarding life in spite of the doubts that he expressed in his journal when he came to Alaska in the 1898 gold rush. Although he was not as successful in acquiring wealth and nationwide power as Stephen Birch, he was loved and respected by the community to which he dedicated his life. Hazelet's greatest asset was his ability to rebound time and again from failure without letting it destroy his self confidence and faith in eventual success. When attacked, he fought back and prevailed.

Ghosts

Cordova was booming in 1926 when George Hazelet died. He could take just pride in the prosperous little town that he had worked so hard to develop. His latter years, following the death of his beloved wife in 1912, had been lonely ones, but his sons were well-educated and prospering. The Copper River and Northwestern Railway linked Cordova to the rest of Alaska and was beginning to attract tourists who continued on to Fairbanks over the Edgerton and Richardson highways and then returned to Seward on the Alaska Railroad.

Kennecott Mine.
ALASKA STATE LIBRARY. PCA210.1

Although the Kennecott Copper Company had expanded in Alaska by linking the Mother Lode mine on the other side of the mountain to its tunnel system, Stephen Birch looked toward the vast low-grade ore deposits in Utah and Chile for future expansion. Kennecott already owned 38 percent of the stock in Utah Copper, and Birch borrowed money in 1917 to buy additional Utah Copper stock. In 1923, Kennecott offered stockholders the option of exchanging one share of Utah stock for one-and-three-quarter share of Kennecott stock, thus increasing their dividends. At the end of that year Birch announced that Kennecott had acquired an additional 628,702 shares of Utah Copper and owned 76 percent of the stock in the company. [1] Daniel C. Jackling, who developed the process for extracting copper from Utah's large porphyry copper orebody, continued to run the Utah and Nevada mines as a division of the Kennecott Copper Company and became a director of the corporation.

Stephen Birch (fourth from right) with Kennecott staff.
HELEN VANCAMPAN ALBUM. UAF74.27.427

Cordova's prosperity, however, was limited. As the reserves of high-grade ore in Alaska diminished, the Kennecott Copper Company depended more on the larger mines in Utah, Nevada and Chile, and diversified into the manufacture of copper and brass products at Chase Brass plants in Cleveland, Ohio, and Waterbury, Connecticut. The Alaska mines closed temporarily in 1932 and permanently in 1938. The Copper River and Northwestern Railway ceased operation when the mines closed and Cordova lost its land connection to the rest of Alaska. Although the Kennecott Corporation gave the railroad right of way back to the federal government with the expectation that it would be used for a permanent road, depression, war and legal challenges by conservationists have prevented development of a road to Cordova. During the ensuing 57 years Cordova has changed from a bustling railroad town to a quiet fishing village.

The Chilkat Oil Company operated until 1936 when the refinery burned. The production in later years, however, never matched the yield under Hazelet's management. [2] The Alaska Steamship Company continued for an additional 20 years as the only remnant of the former Alaska Syndicate empire in Alaska.

Stephen Birch resigned as president of the Kennecott Copper Company in 1933 and was succeeded by E.T. Stannard. Birch continued to be chairman of the board of directors and executive committee of the company he founded until he died on December 29, 1940, at the age of 68, following abdominal surgery. In addition to his positions with Kennecott, Birch was president and director of the Alaska Steamship Company, chairman of the board of directors of the Braden Copper Company, and a director of the Alaska Development and Mineral Company, the Banker's Trust Company of New York, the Chicago, Burlington and Quincy Railroad Company, the Colorado and Southern Railway Company, and the Northern Pacific Railway Company. [3] *Who Was Who in America* provided the following summary of Birch's empire:

> In the year of Birch's death the company employed 28,872 and had sales of $177,250,036. At this time Kennecott also had mining developments in New Mexico, Arizona and South American countries. Under Birch's direction the Kennecott corporation became the largest copper producer in America and the second largest fabricator of copper. Its properties held an estimated 14 percent of the world's copper, and at capacity it was capable of producing 1,000,000,000 pounds of copper annually. [4]

The Kennecott Copper Company has continued to be a major copper producer for years following the death of its founder. In Alaska, however, the name Kennecott invokes visions of the state's largest and most spectacular ghost town, with deteriorating barn-red buildings set in breath-taking mountain scenery. The figure of Stephen Birch remains as ghostly as the town he created. During his lifetime Birch shunned publicity. Even in years when the Kennecott mines were Alaska's major industry *The Alaska Weekly* needed to remind readers who Birch was in the following March 23, 1923 article:

> A metropolitan newspaper the other day made casual mention of the fact that Stephen Birch had given $2,000 toward a fund for the purchase of a library of the Agricultural College and School of Mines at Fairbanks, Alaska.

And the casual reader will probably ask, "Who is Stephen Birch?"

Stephen Birch is the father of copper production in Alaska; he is the man who made one of the world's greatest copper mines out of a great prospect; the man primarily responsible for the building of the Copper River and Northwestern railroad; the man who put the prosperous town of Cordova on the map; the man who made possible the establishment of one of the big steamship lines now plying between this port (Seattle) and Alaskan ports. In short, he is one of the big constructive figures in the industrial life of Alaska.

Birch rarely gave interviews or had his picture taken. An article in the May 23, 1921, issue of *The Financial World* described him as "husky" and "red-headed." Edward Morgan, a purser for the Alaska Steamship Company, gives the following description of Birch in *God's Loaded Dice*:

Of all the many sourdoughs I have met in my thirty years in the North, Birch was the most romantic and inscrutable figure. Thirty-odd years ago a prospector warming his beans in a skillet over a fire on the Arctic trail, he became a millionaire many times over, a power only less potent in the political world than in the mining world, and the most outstanding personality in all Alaska. Yet in New York, where he worked eighteen hours a day when not traveling over the country inspecting his vast properties, his name meant less to the general public than that of a fairly prosperous broker in Wall Street. And that was as Stephen Birch would have it. Years ago Jack London and Rex Beach told me that, attracted by the glamor of his Alaskan exploits, they had asked Birch's permission to write his life. He refused them with so much finality that they did not insist.

I can well imagine the icy decisiveness of his tones as he refused, for there was something of the Arctic in the chill of his manner. That this was exterior I am convinced through my observations of him over the years, and in this opinion others, who knew him better than I, concur. George Esterly, who prospected with him in the early days, has often told me that Birch was the best fellow in the world as a companion when there were only the two of them, that he always towed his weight, cheerfully did his share of the cooking, dishwashing, and the rustling and cutting of firewood. It was different, however, whenever a third person joined them. Then he would shut up like a clam, withdraw within himself, and maintain a cold and silent attitude. (5)

Katherine Wilson gaves a similar description of Birch in *Copper Tints*, which she wrote in Cordova in 1924:

Reserved and taciturn, somewhat aloof except with his companions of the trail and his close associates in business, Stephen Birch is personally little known.

Today one of the financial powers of New York City, he shuns publicity and evades acclaim as a "captain of industry." Strict to the last penny in the observance of his own obligations, he expects the same of others. But to those that know him best he is a man of deep and broad humanity, inspired in all that he does by a keen sense of his responsibility to the national welfare. With his intimates he is a finely perceptive and generous friend, of an unshakable loyalty.

If the highest type of citizen is that man who, through his vision, his initiative, his constructive power and personal integrity, produces the means by which thousands of others are enabled to live and prosper and the nation is advanced in wealth and power, then Stephen Birch, born Anglo Saxon and self-made man, is an outstanding American. [6]

Birch mansion, Mahweh, New Jersey, now the administration building for Ramapo College.
PHOTO COURTESY OF WILLIAM COLLINS, GREAT-NEPHEW OF STEPHEN BIRCH

This reference to Birch as "Anglo Saxon," and other details of his private life, suggests that he may have envisioned himself more as an English country gentleman than as a captain of American industry. Rugged Alaskan sourdoughs may have had difficulty understanding an Anglophile who insisted on strong tea and objected to cigarette smoke, [7] but negative comments usually came from people like Herman Barring, who lost out to Birch in the lawsuit over the Bonanza claims. Barring referred to him as "an all-around schemer" when testifying before the House Committee on Territories in 1908.

Although the Kennecott Corporation has been criticized for not investing profits in further Alaska development, Birch can scarcely be faulted for reacting to the unfavorable political climate in Alaska after the Pinchot-Ballinger controversy and to Wickersham's attacks on the Alaska Syndicate. As Martin Harrais, a frustrated miner and railroad developer himself, wrote in his unpublished manuscript *Gold Lunatics*:

> There comes a point beyond which human nature cannot, or will not, stand abuse, either physical or mental. The unjust character assassination was hell throughout the entire time the Alaska Syndicate was constructing the railroad and Stephen Birch was developing the mine — spending millions of dollars in good faith. The reaction came. The road was not completed as per original plan. They were through with developing Alaska and gave up, no doubt, in disgust. The tradition still lives in the Copper River Valley that it was the avowed policy of the Corporation that they would never spend another dollar in the development of Alaska. This may be only tradition, but it conforms closely to history. They took their profits and bought Utah Copper Co. stock and others; they even took millions of Alaska-made money and invested it in Chile — a South American-revolution-infested country — and considered it safer than investing in Alaska. The irony of it! [8]

Review of sources provides ample evidence that the Alaska Syndicate initially did have aspirations that transcended profit from the copper mines. During the Pinchot-Ballinger controversy in 1910, before the wealth of the Kennecott mines was appreciated, John N. Steele, speaking for the Alaska Syndicate, told the House Committee on Territories:

> The idea in building this road to the Bonanza mines was to get that country developed. Where we have looked, and where we will look, for the ultimate profit on this road, if there is ever going to be any profit, is the development of Alaska up in the Chitina and Tanana Valleys, where they will be permanently settled, where people will go and raise families and devote themselves to agriculture, because those valleys are entirely suited for the raising of a great many crops. That is where we expect to get our permanent returns from the road if we ever get any. The tonnage of the Bonanza mine is comparatively small, although the ore is very high in copper. [9]

Investment in Utah and South America mines did not occur until after President Woodrow Wilson turned down J.P. Morgan's offer to sell the Copper River and Northwestern Railway to the federal government for less than the cost of construction. Delegate Wickersham and the muckraking press had been so successful in slandering the Alaska Syndicate that the President ignored Secretary of Interior Lane's advice to buy the railroad for fear that any negotiation with the notorious Morgans or Guggenheims would cause adverse public reaction.

Melody Webb Grauman attempted to compare the approach of the Kennecott Copper Corporation to that of the Alaska Syndicate when she wrote in her monograph *Big Business in Alaska*:

> The Alaska Syndicate, comparable to the early Rockefeller and Carnegie enterprises, typified the nineteenth century business organization and tactics. Kennecott Copper Corporation, on the other hand, applied the methods and philosophy of twentieth century business management. This interesting contrast becomes fascinating when it is recognized that essentially the same people directed and controlled both organizations — Stephen Birch and the Guggenheims.
>
> The basic goals of both organizations were to keep down production costs and raise copper prices. The Syndicate employed political means to achieve these business goals. As a result, threatened politicians lashed back crying "monopolism." Kennecott adroitly succeeded by controlling labor, acquiring competitive mines, and ensuring a ready market. [10]

Actually, the Kennecott Copper Corporation may have escaped the problems faced by the Alaska Syndicate as a result of an agreement between Birch and Delegate Wickersham reached during their meeting in April of 1910 — an agreement that may have led indirectly to the untimely death of Capt. David Jarvis. Wickersham and Gifford Pinchot created the "Guggenmorgan" monster to serve their own political ambitions and then Wickersham personified Jarvis as the mastermind behind the monster. There is little evidence that Jarvis or the Alaska Syndicate tried to control Alaska politics or oppose self-government in Alaska. John W. Corson, the candidate Birch and Jarvis supported in the 1908 delegate election, actually advocated "home rule" for Alaska before Wickersham decided to espouse that cause.

Although he mercilessly attacked Jarvis, Wickersham usually spoke well of Birch. In his book *Old Yukon, Tales, Trails and Trials* he referred to Birch as a "bright-eyed young man," and a letter, written by an aged Wickersham to Territorial Governor Ernest Gruening in 1938, contained the following analysis:

> One should not underestimate Mr. Birch's ability as a financier and high grade business man, even on Wall Street. While he organized the Morgan-Guggenheim

Alaska Syndicate, he was not a mere employee therein — he was the third member of the Syndicate and furnished the ideas and rules upon which its copper trust and business was based. He furnished these ideas and plans and carried them to success, while the New York partners merely furnished capital. [11]

Birch may also have had a vision of contributing to the development of Alaska in his early days before Wickersham started attacking the Alaska Syndicate. In 1910 he wrote an article, entitled "Pioneering Capital," for the *Alaska-Yukon Magazine* in which he spoke in glowing terms of the development potential of Alaska both in mineral exploration and agriculture. He argued that pioneering capital was still needed to finance lode mining and build railroads in Alaska as it had in the West a half century before. Although Birch foresaw greater governmental involvement in the future, he pointed out that the lack of progress in Alaska was a flagrant example of those things which the government had left undone. At the close of this article, Birch referred to the controversy that would haunt governmental policy in Alaska for the rest of the twentieth century:

> A public recognition of the fact that there are these two sides in the whole question of conservation and development, each of the utmost importance, will go far toward a more equitable solution than is promised in unthinking antagonism to all large industrial enterprise. [12]

George Hazelet, unlike Birch, never lost his vision and faith in the development potential of Alaska. During his lifetime, however, he did not realize where his major contribution to that development would be at the end of the 20th century. While spearheading programs for the Cordova Chamber of Commerce, Hazelet thought little about his "hay farm" on Mineral Creek near Valdez, but, many years later, nature revealed what Hazelet had known all along — that his Mineral Creek townsite was superior to the old Valdez location.

The great Alaska earthquake in 1964, registering 9.2 on the Richter scale, altered the future for the two small cities on Prince William Sound. Elevation of the ocean floor in the eastern part of the Sound altered the port at Cordova so that it could no longer accommodate large vessels, while recession of land on the western side caused flooding in the original townsite of Valdez. In order to help in the reconstruction of Valdez, the Hazelet and Meals descendants offered part of the "hay farm" for the relocation of Valdez, retaining the rest for future development.

When Valdez was selected as the terminal for the Trans-Alaska oil pipeline in the 1970s, the area boomed and the property retained by the Hazelet and Meals families became more valuable than any of Hazelet's other enterprises. Although thwarted in some of his development schemes, Hazelet accomplished his main goal in coming to Alaska in 1898 — he assured a more prosperous life for his family. Almost a century later his grandchildren own land and rental property in Valdez and his grandnephew still operates productive gold mines at Chisna.

Capt. David Jarvis also provided well for his family with Alaskan investments. Shortly before his death he invested with Henry Bratnober in the highly productive Chicagoff gold mine in Southeastern Alaska. His wife Ethel continued to be a director of the mine, which provided comfortable living and good educations for the three Jarvis children. David, the eldest son, became a lawyer and returned to Seattle, where he practiced in the same office as John P. Hartman, the lawyer who may have been an unwitting collaborator with Wickersham and Douglas in making the accusations that led to his father's suicide.

Although none of the Jarvis descendants have lived in Alaska, they continue to be fascinated by the far-northern state and are still haunted by the circumstances of the suicide. A large portrait of Jarvis in his Revenue Marine uniform occupies a prominent position in the home of his only granddaughter and his ceremonial sword hangs on the wall. Family members have flown over Mt. Jarvis in the Wrangell Mountains and donated memorabilia from Revenue Marine days to Alaska museums. This granddaughter has researched and written extensively about Jarvis' associates in the Revenue Marine, but has shied away from making an attempt to analyze her grandfather's life or death. A legally-trained great-grandson, however, is intrigued with the possibility that Jarvis might have been murdered although there is no evidence to support this conjecture.

Stephen Birch has no living direct descendants. When his daughter Mary died in 1981, the family possessions were sold at auction. The extensive Birch fortune is now administered by the husband of Mary Birch's former secretary, who has failed to respond to repeated attempts by Alaskans to contact him. Information about the Birch family has been provided by a great-nephew. Renewed Alaskan interest in the Kennecott mine and its contribution to mining technology has resulted in efforts to preserve the remaining Kennecott buildings. In September of 1993, Stephen Birch was belatedly recognized by the Miner's Hall of Fame.

Icebound Empire

ENDNOTES

I. North to Alaska

(1) *The Pathfinder*, March 1920, pg. 6.

(2) Carolyn Jean and Marlene Conger Holeski, *In Search of Gold*, Anchorage: The Alaska Geographic Society, 1983, pg. 17.

(3) *Ibid.*, pg. 23-4.

(4) *Ibid.*, pg. 43.

II. Down The Klutina

(1) Holeski, pg. 91.

(2) *Ibid.*, pg. 143.

III. Nebraska Republican

(1) *The Frontier*, O'Neill, Nebraska, August 12, 1888.

(2) Nellie Snyder Yost, *Before Today: A History of Holt County Nebraska, Centennial Edition*, Miles Publishing Co., O'Neill, 1976, pg. 240.

(3) *The Frontier*, January 12, 1887.

(4) *Ibid.*, January 2, 1890. — A section of O'Neill is still known as the Hazelet Subdivision.

(5) *Ibid.*, April 17, 1890.

(6) *Ibid.*, May 5, 1890.

(7) Arthur Mullen, *Western Democrat*, Wilfred Funk, 1940, pg.70.

(8) A. Bower Sageser, "Holt County During the 1890s" *in Nebraska History*, Vol. 40, June 1959, pg. 108.

(9) *A Piece of Emerald, O'Neill — Nebraska's Irish Capital*

(10) *The Frontier*, September 20, 1894.

IV. Frontier Justice

(1) Records of the Holt County District Court, Case No. 3023, County of Holt vs. A.J. Meals, et.al.

(2) *The Frontier*, July 20, 1893.

(3) Records of the Holt County District Court, Case Nos. 4022 and 4023, County of Holt vs. G.C. Hazelet, et.al.

(4) Harold Hutton, *Vigilante Days*, Chicago: The Swallow Press, 1978, pg. 202.

(5) *O'Neill Sun*, August 10, 1893, op.cit. *Vigilante Days*, pg. 203.

(6) *Vigilante Days*, pg. 202.

(7) *Western Democrat*, pg. 68.

(8) *Vigilante Days*, pg. 205.

(9) Records of Holt County District Court, Case No. 4093, County of Holt vs. Barrett Scott, J.S. Bartley, W.D. Matthews, W.E. McRoberts, Dell Akin, J.J. McCafferty, Hugh Allen, N.B. Bisbee, J.F. Brady, W.H. Hendrix, H.L. Putnam, Howard Miller, David L. Darr, Michael M. Sullivan, J.L. Hershiser, G.C. Hazelet, David Adams, Bennett Martin, Sanford Parker, Frank Toohill, B.A. DeYarman, and C.C. Millard.

(10) *Ibid.*

(11) *Vigilante Days*, pg. 206.

(12) *Ibid.*, pg. 209.

(13) *O'Neill Sun*, October 19, 1893. Op. cit., *Vigilante Days*, pg. 210.

(14) *Vigilante Days*, pg. 210.

(15) *Sun*, April 26, 1894. Op. Cit., *Vigilante Days*, pg. 212.

(16) *The Frontier*, July 26, 1894.

(17) *Ibid.*, September 6, 1894.

(18) *Vigilante Days*, pg. 213.

(19) *Holt County Independent*, December 30, 1897. Op. cit. *Vigilante Days*, pg. 214.

(20) *Vigilante Days*, pp. 221-231.

(21) *The Frontier*, April 28, 1892.

(22) *Ibid.*, August 2, 1894.

V. Chicory

(1) *The Frontier.*, August 24, 1893.

(2) *Ibid.*, November 28, 1889.

(3) Nellie Snyder Yost, *Before Today, A History of Holt County, Nebraska — Centennial Edition*, O'Neill: Miles Publishing Co., 1976, pg. 92.

(4) *The Frontier*, June 1, 1893.

(5) Yost, *Before Today*, pg. 92.

(6) Sageser, "Holt County During the 1890s," pg. 110.

(7) *Ibid.*, pg. 108.

(8) *The Frontier*, February 14, 1895.

(9) *Ibid.*, August 15, 1895.

(10) Sageser, pg. 110.

(11) *A Piece of Emerald*

(12) Yost, *Before Today*, pg.92.

(13) *Ibid.*

(14) John A. Hazelet, "History of the Chisna Alaska Property," Unpublished manuscript from his grandson, Richard Osborne.

VII. Stephen Birch — Eastern Opportunist

(1) L.A. Levensaler to W.E. Dunkle, June 6, 1953. Polar Collections, U.A.F., Fairbanks.

(2) *Ibid.*

(3) W.R. Abercrombie, *Copper River Exploring Expeditions, 1898* Government Printing Office, 1899. Report of Lieutenant Lowe.

(4) *Ibid.*. All subsequent quotations in this chapter are also from the report of Lieutenant Lowe.

VII. Lieutenant David Henry Jarvis — Arctic Hero

(1) Charles Brower, *Fifty Years Below Zero*, pg. 212.

(2) Lt. David H. Jarvis, *Report of the Cruise of the U.S. Cutter Bear and the Overland Expedition — Nov. 27, 1897-Sept. 13, 1898*. Govt. Printing Office, 1899, pg. 33.

(3) *Ibid.*, pg. 53

(4) *Ibid.*, pg. 46-7.

(5) *Ibid.*, pg. 64-5.

VIII. Winter on the Chistochina

(1) *The Pathfinder*, July 1920, pg. 13.

(2)   Taped accounts of early prospecting in Southcentral Alaska featuring mining engineer, W.E. Dunkle and Henry Watkins, available in the archives of the Anchorage Museum of History and Art.

After participating in the development of the Chisna gold mine, Watkins served as business manager for the Kennecott Copper Company between 1907 and 1914.

Watkins was a good friend of both Stephen Birch and George Hazelet. In later years, according to the tapes, Hazelet visited Watkins in Virginia and they commisserated about McNeer's failure to tell his partners about his findings on the Miller Gulch so that they could file claims before other prospectors beat them to it. Hazelet is said to have commented: "You know, Henry, if McNeer had played square with us, there would have been enough for us all."

(3)   John Hazelet, "History of the Chisna Alaska Property."

IX. Gold Mine at Chisna

(1)   *The Frontier*, O'Neill, Nebraska, January 25, 1900.

(2)   John Hazelet, "History of the Chisna Alaska Property."

(3)   "A True Account of the Alaskan Adventures of Henry Fleming — Gold Rush of 1900-1902," unpublished manuscript compiled by Christina Counselor, pg. 1.

(4)   *The Alaskan*, Sitka, April 7, 1900.

(5)   *Hazelet Diary*, February 2, 1900.

(6)   *The Valdez News*, April 20, 1901.

(7)   *Copper River Exploring Expedition, 1899*, "Report of Oscar Rohn," pp. 119-129.

(8)   *Hazelet Diary*, April 12, 1900.

(9)   *Ibid.*, May 28, 1900.

(10) *Ibid.*, July 4, 1900.

(11) *Ibid.*

(12) *Ibid.*, May 28, 1900.

(13) Fleming Manuscript, p. 10.

(14) *Hazelet Diary*, September 2, 1900

(15) *Ibid.*, August 24, 1900.

(16) *The Alaskan*, April 7, 1900.

(17) *Hazelet Diary*, August 24, 1900.

(18) *Ibid.*, Setember 28, 1900.

(19) *Ibid.*

(20) *Ibid.*, October 24, 1900.

(21) *Ibid.*, November 12, 1900.

X. Hydraulic Mining at Chisna

(1)   *Omaha World-Herald*, September 6, 1900.

(2)   *Hazelet Diary*, February 14, 1901.

(3)   *Ibid.*, February 5, 1901.

(4)   *Ibid.*

(5) Soldier's Additional land scrip (sometimes referred to as script) was the only land scrip applicable for obtaining public lands in Alaska. "The Story of Scrip," a brochure published by The Collins Land Co. of Helena, Montana and Washington, D.C., prior to 1910, describes land scrip as "written evidence of a right to a specified area of public land under the terms and limitations of the act of Congress creating the same." Soldier's Additional land scrip consists of the uncertified rights of soldiers of the Civil War to make homestead entry on less than 160 acres in return for 90 days or more service in the Civil War. Organizations like the Collins Land Co. bought up this scrip, certified that it was valid and offered it for sale.

(6) *The Valdez News*, March 8, 1902.

(7) *Hazelet Diary*, April 18, 1901.

(8) *The Valdez News*, May 11, 1901.

(9) Holdrege papers, Ms. 303, Box 3, Folder 41, at Nebraska State Historical Society, Lincoln, Nebraska.

(10) *Hazelet Diary*, August 21, 1901.

(11) *The Valdez News*, July 13, 1901.

(12) Fleming Manuscript, pg. 17.

(13) G.C. Hazelet to Thomas Donohoe, December 2, 1901, in Donohoe-Ostrander-Dimond Papers at Rasmuson Library, University of Alaska-Fairbanks.

(14) John A. Hazelet, "History of the Chisna Alaska Property."

(15) *Hazelet Diary*, March 4, 1902.

(16) *Ibid.*

(17) *Ibid.*

(18) *Ibid.*, May 1, 1902.

(19) Walter C. Mendenhall, *Geology of the Central Copper River Region, Alaska*, Government Printing Office, pg. 110.

(20) John A. Hazelet, "History of the Chisna Alaska Property."

(21) *The Valdez News*, March 9, 1907.

(22) *Hazelet Diary*, March 4, 1902.

XI. Bonanza Discovery

(1) W.R. Abercrombie, *Copper River Exploring Expeditions, 1899* Government Printing Office, 1900, pg. 11.

(2) Micheal Sean Sullivan, *Kennecott, Alaska*, pg. 17.

(3) James Wickersham, "Copper River Mining Co. v. McClellan et al., Nov. 23, 1903 in *Alaska Reports*, Vol. 2, pgs. 137-8.

(4) *Ibid.*, pg. 139.

(5) Stephen Birch to Governor Ernest Gruening, January 1940 in *Territorial Governor's Papers*. U.S. Government Archives, Seattle.

(6) Stephen Birch to H.O. Havemeyer, December 2, 1900. Kennecott Library, Salt Lake City, Utah.

(7) Stephen Birch to D.S. Kain, January 24, 1901. Kennecott Library.

(8) D.S. Kain to Stephen Birch, February 1, 1901. Kennecott Library.

(9) Stephen Birch to H.O. Havemeyer, March 9, 1902. Kennecott Library.

XII. Bonanza Lawsuit

(1) Stephen Birch to H.O. Havemeyer, November 9, 1903. Kennecott Library.

(2) Jeanette Paddock Nichols, *Alaska*, pg. 269.

XIII. Jarvis And Wickersham

(1) *The Alaska Prospector*, Valdez, April 17, 1902.

(2) *Daily Alaska Dispatch*, Juneau, January 20, 1902, and *The Alaska Prospector*, Valdez, April 17, 1902.

(3) *Daily Alaska Dispatch*, May 1, 1903.

(4) *James A. Wickersham Diary*, September 25, 1901, on microfilm in University of Alaska-Anchorage Archives.

(5) *Daily Alaska Dispatch*, February 8, 1902.

(6) *Wickersham Diary*, July 4, 1902.

(7) *Daily Alaska Dispatch*, April 17, 1903.

(8) *Wickersham Diary*, August 17, 1903.

(9) *Ibid.*, September 17, 1903.

(10) *Nome News*, March 22, 1904.

(11) *Daily Alaska Dispatch*, September 17, 1904.

(12) *Wickersham Diary*, July 31, 1904.

(13) *Ibid.*, November 10, 1904.

(14) *Ibid.*, November 13, 1904.

(15) *Seattle Post-Intelligencer*, March 12, 1905.

(16) *The Sea Chest*, Vol.10 (June 1977), pp. 135-6.

(17) *Alaska Daily Guide*, Skagway, March 25, 1905.

(18) *The Daily Record Miner*, Juneau, March 31, 1905.

(19) *Seattle Post-Intelligencer*, February 16, 1906.

(20) *Wickersham Diary*, March 10, 1906.

(21) *Daily Alaska Dispatch*, July 2, 1906.

(22) Jeanette Paddock Nichols, *Alaska, A History of its Administration, Exploitation and Industrial Development during the First Half Century Under the Rule of the United States*, Cleveland: Arthur H. Clark Co., 1924, pg. 269.

(23) Lone Janson, *The Copper Spike*, Anchorage: Alaska Northwest Publishing, 1975, pg. 32.

XIV. Railroad Fever in Valdez

(1) J.R. DeLamar to W.B. Holdrege, May 13, 1902. In Holdrege Collection, Nebraska State Historical Society.

(2) W.B. Holdrege to J.R. DeLamar, May 18, 1902, Holdrege Collection.

(3) *The Valdez News*, June 7, 1902.

(4) *Ibid.*, May 3, 1902.

(5) *Ibid.*, April 12, 1902.

(6) *Seattle Post-Intelligencer*, June 15, 1902.

(7) *The Alaska Prospector*, Valdez, June 26, 1902.

(8) E. Gillette to W.B. Holdrege, June 25, 1902, Holdrege Collection.

(9) E. Gillette to W.B. Holdrege, June 27, 1902, Holdrege Collection.

(10) *The Valdez News*, July 19, 1902.

(11) *The Alaska Prospector*, August 21, 1902.

(12) *The Valdez News*, August 9, 1902.

(13) *Ibid.*, September 6, 1902.

(14) G.C. Hazelet to T.J. Donohoe, September 26, 1902, Donohoe-Ostrander-Dimond Collection.

(15) *Ibid.*, August 13, 1903.

(16) G.C. Hazelet to T.J. Donohoe, January 15, 1903, Donohoe-Ostrander-Dimond Collection.
(17) Holdrege Collection.
(18) *The Valdez News*, May 9, 1903.
(19) *Ibid.*, April 11, 1903.
(20) *Ibid.*, May 16, 1903.
(21) *Ibid.*
(22) *The Alaska Prospector*, August 6, 1903.
(23) *The Valdez News*, March 5, 1904.
(24) G.C. Hazelet to T.J. Donohoe, July 10, 1904, Donohoe-Ostrander-Dimond Collection.
(25) *The Alaska Prospector*, May 12, 1904.
(26) *The Valdez News*, August 6, 1904.
(27) *The Alaska Prospector*, September 20, 1904.
(28) G.C. Hazelet to T.J. Donohoe, December 31, 1904, Donohoe-Ostrander-Dimond Collection.
(29) *The Alaska Prospector*, March 22 1905.
(30) *The Pathfinder*, July 1920, pg. 14.
(31) *The Valdez News*, March 18, 1905.
(32) *The Sea Chest*, Vol. 10 (June 1977), pg. 136.
(33) *The Valdez News*, June 10, 1905.
(34) *The Alaska Prospector*, August 10, 1905.
(35) *Ibid.*, September 21, 1905.

XV. Alaska Syndicate
(1) Stephen Birch to Judge James Wickersham, March 26, 1906. Wickersham Papers, Box 8, A.S.H.L., Juneau.
(2) Nichols, *Alaska*, pg. 269.
(3) Michael Sherin, "William Ross Rust and His Tacoma Legacy." Unpublished manuscript in Washington State Historical Society Library, Tacoma.
(4) Lone Jansen, *The Copper Spike*, pg. 26.
(5) Archibald W. Shiels, *The Kennecott Story*. Bellingham, Washington: Privately published, 1964, pgs. 5-6.
(6) *The Pathfinder*, July 1920, pg. 14.

XVI. Railroad Warfare
(1) Jansen, *The Copper Spike*, pg. 74.
(2) *The Alaska Prospector*, June 27, 1907.
(3) Jansen, *The Copper Spike*, pg. 109.
(4) *Ibid.*, pg. 112.
(5) Testimony of Stephen Birch, quoted in *The Post-Intelligencer*, March 6, 1910.
(6) *Fairbanks Weekly Times*, July 27, 1907.
(7) Jansen, *The Copper Spike*, pp. 37-8.
(8) *Ibid.*, pg. 39.
(9) *The Alaskan*, Sitka, June 6, 1891.
(10) *The Katalla Herald*, August 10, 1907.
(11) Hazelet testimony at Hasey trial, on Microfilm #84-193-1, Records of United States Department of Justice relating to Keystone Canyon Case, in Polar Collections, Rasmuson Library, University of Alaska-Fairbanks.

(12) "Renascent Valdez," in *Alaska-Yukon Magazine*, September 1907, pg. 166.

(13) *The Alaska Prospector*, August 15, 1907.

(14) Testimony of M.B. Morrisey in Wickersham Papers, Keystone Canyon file, Alaska Historical Library, Juneau.

(15) Governor Hoggatt to Secretary of Interior, October 26, 1907 on Microfilm #84-193-1.

(16) Statement of James Lathrop to Special Agent Bryan on Microfilm #84-193-3.

(17) Deposition of James O'Reilly on Microfilm #84-193-1.

(18) Hazelet to Hasey, September 2, 1907. On Microfilm #40, Keystone Canyon Transcripts, U.S. Department of Justice at Valdez Museum Archives.

(19) Hazelet testimony at Hasey trial on Microfilm #84-193-1.

(20) Hazelet to Hasey, September 6, 1907. On Microfilm #40, Valdez Museum Archives.

(21) Special Agent Bryan's discussion with Hasey, Microfilm #84-193-3.

(22) Microfilm #84-193-3.

(23) Statement of James Lathrop to Special Agent Bryan, Microfilm #84-193-3.

(24) Microfilm #84-193-3.

(25) Deputy Marshal James Lathrop to Marshal Perry, September 19, 1907, Microfilm #84-193-1.

(26) Testimony of Colonel Swanitz at John Phillips vs. Copper River and Northwestern Railway trial, Microfilm #84-193-2.

(27) Testimony at Hasey trial, Microfilm #84-193-1.

(28) An analysis of early railroad development in Valdez and the Keystone Canyon conflict written by George Hazelet himself provides essentially the same sequence of events recounted here. Hazelet's account, which is in a draft of a letter to Cordova journalist, Katherine Wilson, was provided by Hazelet's grandchildren and published in *Alaska History*, Vol. 9, No. 2, Fall, 1994.

XVII. *Trials and Tribulations*

(1) *Fairbanks Weekly Times*, September 26, 1907.

(2) *Ibid.*

(3) Testimony of Dr. Boyle at Hasey trial. Microfilm #40, Valdez Museum Archives.

(4) *Ibid.*

(5) Hazelet to Hoggatt, September 26, 1907, Microfilm #40.

(6) *Seattle Daily Times*, September 25, 1907.

(7) Hoggatt to Ostrander and Donohoe, September 26, 1907, Microfilm #40.

(8) *Fairbank Weekly Times*, October 5, 1907.

(9) Statement of James Lathrop, Microfilm #84-193-3.

(10) James A. Wickersham, "The Hasey Affair," Keystone Canyon Riot file, Box 30, Wickersham Papers, Alaska State Historical Library, Juneau.

(11) Keystone Canyon Transcripts, Microfilm #40, Valdez Museum.

(12) *The Katalla Herald*, September 14, 1907.

(13) Jansen, *The Copper Spike*, pg. 50.

(14) *The Alaska Weekly*, Seattle, January 6, 1928.

(15) *Daily Alaska Dispatch*, October 28, 1907.

(16) Governor Hoggatt to Secretary of Interior Garfield, October 26, 1907, Microfilm #84-193-1.

(17) *Daily Alaska Dispatch*, October 28, 1907.

(18) *Wickersham Diary*, March 12, 1907.

(19) Judge James Wickersham to Attorney General Charles Bonaparte, February 19, 1908, Microfilm #40, Valdez Museum.

(20) Nathan Harlan to Attorney General Bonaparte, Microfilm #84-193-1.
(21) John Y. Ostrander to Thomas J. Donohoe, March 28, 1908, Donohoe-Ostrander-Dimond Collection, Rasmuson Library, University of Alaska-Fairbanks.
(22) U.S. Department of Justice Keystone Canyon Transcripts, Microfilm #40, Valdez Museum.
(23) Special Agent McAdams to Secret Service Chief John Wilkie, March 18, 1908, Microfilm #40.
(24) John A. Carson to David H. Jarvis, April 20, 1908, Microfilm #84-193-3.
(25) *Daily Alaska Dispatch*, April 30, 1908.
(26) *Ibid.*
(27) *Fairbanks Weekly Times*, May 2, 1908.
(28) *The Katalla Herald*, February 1, 1908.
(29) Elizabeth A. Tower, *Ghosts of Kennecott*, pg. 57.
(30) Jansen, *The Copper Spike*, pg. 52.

XVIII. Frontier Politics — 1908

(1) Stephen Birch to Judge James Wickersham, April 8, 1907 in Wickersham Papers, Box 8, A.S.H.L., Juneau.
(2) Stephen Birch to Judge James Wickersham, June 3, 1907 in Wickersham Papers, Box 8, A.S.H.L., Juneau.
(3) *Cordova Daily Alaskan*, September 14, 1909.
(4) Governor W.B. Hoggatt to President Theodore Roosevelt and Governor W.B. Hoggatt to Interior Secretary James R. Gerfield, September 13, 1907, Alaska Territorial Governors' Chronological Files, Records of the Office of the Governor of Alaska, Microfilm Roll 11, A.S.H.L., Juneau.
(5) Stephen Birch to Hon. James Wickersham, November 15, 1907 in Wickersham Papers, Box 8, A.S.H.L., Juneau.
(6) D.H. Jarvis to James Wickersham, November 29, 1907, Ms. 107, Box 14, File 1026, Wickersham Papers, A.S.H.L., Juneau.
(7) James Wickersham to Stephen Birch, December 19, 1907 in Wickersham Papers, Box 14, A.S.H.L., Juneau.
(8) James Wickersham to Stephen Birch, February 1, 1908 in Wickersham Papers, Box 14, A.S.H.L., Juneau.
(9) Stephen Birch to James Wickersham, March 17, 1908 in Wickersham Papers, Box 14, A.S.H.L., Juneau.
(10) James Wickersham to Stephen Birch, Esq., April 8, 1908 in Wickersham Papers, Box 14, A.S.H.L., Juneau.
(11) Stephen Birch to James Wickersham, May 6, 1908, Ms.116, Box 14, File 1026, Wickersham Papers, A.S.H.L., Juneau.
(12) Stephen Birch to James Wickersham, May 11, 1908 in Wickersham Papers, Box 14, A.S.H.L., Juneau.
(13) D.H. Jarvis to James Wickersham, June 24, 1908, Ms. 107, Box 14, Folder 76, Wickersham Papers, A.S.H.L., Juneau.
(14) Stephen Birch to James Wickersham, July 6, 1908 in Wickersham Papers, Box 14, A.S.H.L., Juneau.
(15) Stephen Birch to James Wickersham, September 9, 1908 in Wickersham Papers, Box 14, A.S.H.L., Juneau.

XIX. Cordova

(1) Thomas J. Donohoe to George C. Hazelet, May 5, 1908, Donohoe-Ostrander-Dimond Collection, Polar Collection, Rasmuson Library, University of Alaska-Fairbanks.

(2) Hazelet to Donohoe, May 21, 1908.
(3) Hazelet to Donohoe, July 6, 1908.
(4) Hazelet to Donohoe, August 15, 1908.
(5) *Daily Alaska Dispatch*, July 29, 1908.
(6) Ostrander and Donohoe to Hazelet, August 27, 1908.
(7) *The Cordova Alaskan*, August 22, 1908.
(8) *Cordova Daily Alaskan*, November 12, 1908 and January 16, 1909.
(9) *Cordova Daily Alaskan*, December 4, 1908.
(10) John Y. Ostrander to Thomas J. Donohoe, June 10, 1908 and May 10, 1908. Hazelet to Ostrander and Donohoe, October 22, 1908.
(11) *Cordova Daily Alaskan*, March 10, 1909.
(12) *Ibid.*, March 22, 1909.
(13) Hazelet to Ostrander, April 3, 1909.
(14) Hazelet to Ostrander, May 22, 1909.
(15) *Cordova Daily Alaskan*, July 15, 1909.

XX. Muckraking

(1) Martin Harrias, "Gold Lunatics." Unpublished manuscript in Polar Collections, Rasmusson Library, U.A.F., Fairbanks.
(2) Testimony of John N. Steele at Pinchot-Ballinger hearings.

XXI. Wickersham's Scapegoat

(1) H.J. Douglas to James Wickersham, January 6, 1910, Box 31, (Muckraking 1908-15), Wickersham Collection, A.S.H.L.
(2) Stephen Birch to James Wickersham, April 8, 1907. Wickersham Collection, A.S.H.L.
(3) *Wickersham Diary*, December 17, 1909.
(4) Hazelet to Ostrander and Donohoe, December 26, 1907, Donohoe-Ostrander-Dimond Collection, UAF.
(5) Ostrander to Donohoe, June 10, 1908.
(6) Report of Special Agent Bryan, December 1, 1910, U.S. Justice Department Transcripts, Microfilm #84-193-3, UAF.
(7) *Wickersham Diary*, February 8, 1910; January 25, 1910.
(8) *Ibid.*, April 26, 1910.
(9) *Ibid.*, May 9, 1910.
(10) *Ibid.*, May 23, 1910.

Colonel Dick

(1) Richardson to Stimson, April 15, 1912 in Records of the Adjutant General's Office, 1780 to 1917, A.G.O. Doc. File, various files pertaining to Alaska.
(2) Wilds P. Richarson, "Alaska" in *Atlantic Monthly*, January, 1928, pp. 111-121.

XXII. Cordova's Coal Party

(1) *Cordova Daily Alaskan*, February 12, 1910.
(2) *Ibid.*, November 11, 1909.
(3) *Alaska Daily Dispatch*, October 7, 1909.

(4) Report of Special Agent Bryan's conversation with Hasey, November 28, 1910, Microfilm #84-193-3, UAF.

(5) Report of Special Agent Bryan's conversation with W.H. Bogle, December 1, 1910, Microfilm #84-193-3.

(6) George C. Hazelet to Thomas J. Donohoe, February 16, 1910, Donohoe-Ostrander-Dimond Collection, UAF.

(7) *Alaska Daily Dispatch*, February 9, 1909.

(8) *Cordova Daily Alaskan*, August 23, 1910.

(9) Testimony of George C. Hazelet at John Phillips vs. Copper River and Northwestern Railway, Microfilm #84-193-2.

(10) *Cordova Daily Alaskan*, April 4, 1910.

(11) *Ibid.*, September 23, 1910.

(12) *Ibid.*, June 23, 1910.

(13) Hazelet to E.C. Hawkins, February 17,1911, Donohoe-Ostrander-Dimond Collection, UAF.

(14) *Cordova Daily Alaskan*, April 26, 1911.

(15) Hazelet to Donohoe, April 28, 1911.

(16) Hazelet to Donohoe, May 9, 1911.

(17) Hazelet to B.F. Millard, May 19, 1911, Donohoe-Ostrander-Dimond Collection.

(18) Hazelet to Donohoe, June 12, 1911.

(19) Ostrander and Donohoe to Hazelet, June 14, 1911.

(20) *Cordova Daily Alaskan*, July 6, 1911.

(21) *Ibid.*, July 28, 1911.

(22) Hazelet to Donohoe, July 23, 1911.

(23) Hazelet to Donohoe, July 27, 1911.

(24) Hazelet the Donohoe, August 22, 1911.

(25) *Cordova Daily Alaskan*, March 25, 1911.

(26) *Ibid.*, April 17, 1911.

XXIII. Tired and Worn Out

(1) *Daily Alaska Dispatch*, June 21, 1911.

(2) *Wickersham Diary*, June 16, 1911.

(3) Report of Special Agent Bryan, November 5, 1910, Microfilm #84-193-3, UAF.

(4) Report of Special Agent Bryan, November 7, 1910, Microfilm #84-193-3.

(5) D.H. Jarvis to John A. Carson, March 28, 1910, Microfilm #84-193-3.

(6) Report of Special Agent Bryan, November 18, 1910, Microfilm #84-193-3.

(7) Report of Special Agent Bryan, December 1, 1910.

(8) D.H. Jarvis to W.P. Hamilton, November 25, 1910, and W.P. Hamilton to D.H. Jarvis, December 1, 1910, are letters provided by Mary Jarvis Cocke, granddaughter of D.H. Jarvis.

(9) U.S. Attorney Elmer E. Todd to Attorney General George Wickersham, April 14, 1911, Microfilm #84-193-3.

(10) *Daily Alaska Dispatch*, June 22, 1911.

(11) *Nome Daily Nugget*, June 27, 1911.

(12) *Ibid.*, July 14, 1911.

(13) *Washington Post*, June 25, 1911.

(14) *Daily Alaska Dispatch*, December 29, 1906.

(15) *Wickersham Dairy*, September 30, 1913.

(16) C.A. Jeffry, private secretary to General John C. Bond, March 5, 1915, Ms. 417, Box 31, Wickersham Collection, Alaska State Historical Library, Juneau.

(17) United States vs. Charles E. Houston and John H. Bullock, Docket 938, U.S. Federal District Criminal Court, Federal Archives and Record Center, Seattle.

(18) *Wickersham Diary*, October 29, 1910; April 10, 1911; March 10, 1916.

XXIV. Depression and Death

(1) *Cordova Daily Alaskan*, November 28, 1911.

(2) *Ibid.*, January 6, 1912.

(3) *Ibid.*, February 20, 1912.

(4) George C. Hazelet to Thomas J. Donohoe, March 20, 1912, Donohoe-Ostrander-Dimond Collection, UAF.

(5) *Cordova Daily Alaskan*, March 20, 1912.

(6) Hazelet to Donohoe, April 9, 1912.

(7) *Cordova Daily Alaskan*, September 23, 1912.

(8) Interview with Harriet Hazelet Flynn, granddaughter of George C. Hazelet, March 18, 1991.

(9) *Cordova Daily Alaskan*, August 22, 1912.

(10) *Ibid.*, September 11, 1912.

(11) *Ibid.*, October 7, 1912.

(12) *Ibid.*

(13) Hazelet to Donohoe, January 13, 1913.

XXV. High Road to Chisana

(1) *Hazelet Diary*, July 21, 1913.

(2) *Ibid.*, July 31, 1913.

(3) Stephen R. Capps, "The Chisana White River District, Alaska" in *USGS Bulletin No. 639*, GPO-1916, pg. 92.

(4) *The Daily Alaskan*, Skagway, September 18, 1913.

(5) *Hazelet Diary*, July 31, 1913.

(6) *Ibid.*, August 14, 1913. — Description corresponds to site of Chisana village on USGA survey map of Chisana district, *USGS Bulletin No.622*, Plate IX.

(7) *Fairbanks Daily News-Miner*, July 25, 1913.

(8) *Valdez Daily Prospector*, August 20, 1913.

(9) *Cordova Daily Alaskan*, August 2, 1913.

(10) *The Chitina Leader*, August 26, 1913.

(11) *Dawson Daily News*, December 9, 1913.

(12) *Cordova Daily Alaskan*, August 13, 1913.

(13) *Dawson Daily News*, August 28, 1913. There is no evidence that the plan for herding reindeer ever materialized.

(14) *Ibid.*, August 30, 1913.

(15) *Ibid.*, August 26, 1913.

(16) *Fairbanks Daily News-Miner*, September 5, 1913; September 15, 1913.

(17) *Cordova Daily Alaskan*, August 28, 1913.

(18) A detailed account is given in "Report of Oscar Rohn," *Copper River Exploring Expedition -1899*, GPO, 1900.

(19) *The Chitina Leader*, September 2, 1913.

(20) *Cordova Daily Alaskan*, September 20, 1913.

(21) *Dawson Daily News*, September 23, 1913.

(22) *Cordova Daily Alaskan*, November 5, 1913.

(23) George C. Hazelet to Anthony J. Dimond, October 14, 1913, Donohoe-Ostrander-Dimond Collection, UAF.

(24) *Cordova Daily Alaskan*, November 26, 1913.

(25) *Dawson Daily News*, December 9, 1913.

(26) *Cordova Daily Alaskan*, December 9, 1913.

(27) *The Chitina Leader*, February 24, 1914.

(28) *Ibid.*, July 7, 1914.

(29) Interviews with Hazelet grandchildren, Harriet Flynn, Charlotte Turtainen, and Calvin Hazelet, March 18, 1991.

(30) Fred H. Moffitt, "Geology of the Eastern Part of the Alaska Range and Adjacent Area" in *USGS Bulletin 989-D*, GPO, 1954, pg.200.

(31) *Fairbanks Daily Times*, August 5, 1914.

XXVI. *Terminal for a Government Railroad*

(1) *The Alaska Times*, Cordova, March 8, 1914.

(2) *Ibid.*, March 15, 1914.

(3) *Ibid.*, May 18, 1913.

(4) *Ibid.*, March 8, 1914; May 15, 1915.

(5) *Ibid.*, June 13, 1914.

(6) *Ibid.*, January 9, 1915.

(7) Thomas J. Donohoe to George C. Hazelet, October 23, 1914, Donohoe-Ostrander-Dimond Collection, UAF.

(8) *The Chitina Leader*, November 3, 1914.

(9) *The Alaska Times*, November 28, 1914.

(10) *Ibid.*, April 5, 1914.

(11) *Ibid.*, October 31, 1914.

(12) *Ibid.*, December 19, 1914.

(13) *Cordova Daily Alaskan*, January 10, 1915.

(14) *Wickersham Diary*, January 10, 1915.

(15) *The Cordova Daily Times*, January 7, 1915.

(16) *Ibid.*, January 30, 1915.

(17) *The Alaska Times*, March 13, 1915.

(18) *Cordova Daily Alaskan*, March 4, 1915; March 15, 1915; March 17, 1915; March 18, 1915; March 24, 1915; March 30, 1915.

(19) *The Cordova Daily Times*, March 16, 1915.

(20) *The Alaska Times*, May 1, 1915.

(21) *The Cordova Daily Times*, March 23, 1915.

(22) *The Alaska Times*, May 1, 1915.

(23) *The Cordova Daily Times*, May 21, 1915.

XXVII. *Kennecott Corporation*

(1) Lewis A. Levensaler, "Early Days of Kennecott, Alaska — as told to Henry S. Carlisle." Polar Collections, U.A.F., Fairbanks, pg. 4.

(2) H. DeWitt Smith, "Early Days of Kennecott Copper Corporation." Unpublished manuscript in Kennecott Library, Salt Lake City.

(3) L.A. Levensaler to Ralph McKay, July 19, 1966. Polar Collections, U.A.F., Fairbanks.

(4) Annual Reports of the Kennecott Corporation. Kennecott Library, Salt Lake City.

(5) Smith manuscript.

(6) Kennecott Corporation Annual Reports.

(7) Carpel L. Berger, "Story of Kennecott Copper" in *The Financial World*, May 30, 1921, pg. 962.

(8) Interviews with William Collins, great-nephew of Stephen Birch.

XXVIII. Katalla Oil Wells

(1) *The Alaska Times*, October 30, 1915.

(2) *The Cordova Daily Times*, July 21, 1915.

(3) *New York Times*, November 24, 1915.

(4) *Wickersham Diary*, November 1, 1915.

(5) *Ibid.*, November 17, 1915.

(6) *The Cordova Daily Times*, May 9, 1916.

(7) *Ibid.*, May 15, 1916.

(8) *Ibid.*, June 13, 1916.

(9) *Ibid.*, July 1, 1916.

(10) Falcon Joslin to his wife, November 6, 1916, Joslin Collection, Polar Collections, Rasmuson Library, University of Alaska-Fairbanks.

(11) *The Cordova Daily Times*, June 17, 1918.

(12) *Ibid.*, June 21, 1918.

(13) Falcon Joslin to his wife, May 14, 1919, Joslin Collection.

(14) *The Cordova Daily Times*, May 31, 1919.

(15) Falcon Joslin to his wife, May 14, 1919.

(16) *Anchorage Daily Times*, May 3, 1919.

(17) *The Cordova Daily Times*, November 13, 1919.

XXIX. Frontier Politics — 1920

(1) Falcon Joslin to his wife, April 26, 1919, Joslin Collection, UAF.

(2) *Wickersham Diary*, April 10, 1911; March 10, 1916; May 19, 1916.

(3) Falcon Joslin to Thomas J. Donohoe, September 13, 1918, Donohoe-Ostrander-Dimond Collection, UAF.

(4) *The Cordova Daily Times*, March 22, 1919.

(5) Evangeline Atwood, *Frontier Politics*, Portland, Oregon: Binford and Mort, 1979, pg. 331.

(6) *The Cordova Daily Times*, December 26, 1919.

(7) *Wickersham Diary*, January 29, 1920.

(8) *The Cordova Daily Times*, February 18, 1920.

(9) *Wickersham Diary*, March 16, 1920,

(10) *Ibid.*, March 26, 1920.

(11) *Ibid.*, March 25, 1920.

(12) *The Cordova Times*, April 7, 1920.

(13) *Ibid.*, March 24, 1920.

(14) *Wickersham Diary*, April 7, 1920.

(15) *The Alaska Sunday Capitol*, Juneau, April 11, 1920.

(16) *Anchorage Daily Times*, April 21, 1920.

(17) *The Alaska Daily Capitol*, April 24, 1920.

(18) *Anchorage Daily Times*, April 24, 1920.

(19) *The Cordova Daily Times*, May 4, 1920.

(20) *Ibid.*, May 17, 1920.

(21) *The Alaska Dispatch*, May 21, 1920.

(22) *The Cordova Daily Times*, June 14, 1920; July 28, 1920.

XXX. Fight for the Governorship

(1) Falcon Joslin to his wife, July 6, 1920, Joslin Collection.

(2) *The Alaska Dispatch*, Seattle, August 6, 1920.

(3) Falcon Joslin to his wife, July 6, 1920.

(4) Falcon Joslin to his wife, July 16, 1920.

(5) Falcon Joslin to his wife, August 3, 1920.

(6) *The Cordova Daily Times*, October 8, 1920.

(7) *Ibid.*, October 12, 1920.

(8) *Ibid.*, November 4, 1920.

(9) *Ibid.*, November 5, 1920.

(10) *Wickersham Diary*, November 11, 1920.

(11) *Ibid.*, November 13, 1920.

(12) *Ibid.*, November 17, 1920.

(13) *The Cordova Daily Times*, December 2, 1920.

(14) *Wickersham Diary*, December 1920.

(15) *The Cordova Daily Times*, January 6, 1921.

(16) *Wickersham Diary*, January 8, 1921.

(17) Matilda A. Snyder vs. Edward Kelter and George C. Hazelet, Trustee, Cordova Records, Third Judicial District Court, Box 3, File 38, United States Federal Archives, Anchorage.

(18) *The Cordova Daily Times*, January 22, 1921.

(19) *The Alaska Dispatch*, January 28, 1921.

(20) *Wickersham Diary*, February 13, 1921.

(21) *Ibid.*, January 29, 1921.

(22) *Juneau Daily Capitol*, February 21, 1921.

(23) *Ibid.*, February 25, 1921.

(24) *The Cordova Daily Times*, March 10, 1921.

(25) *Wickersham Diary*, April 17, 1921.

(26) *Ibid.*, May 11, 1921.

(27) *The Cordova Daily Times*, June 1, 1921.

(28) *Ibid.*, June 21, 1921.

XXXI. Chilkat Oil Company

(1) *The Cordova Daily Times*, July 7, 1921.

(2) *Ibid.*, August 8, 1921.

(3) *Ibid.*, March 11, 1921.

(4) *Ibid.*, July 7, 1921.

(5) *Ibid.*, April 3, 1922.

(6) *Ibid.*, September 5, 1922.

(7)   *Ibid.*, March 23, 1923.
(8)   *Ibid.*, February 21, 1923.
(9)   *Ibid.*, February 1, 1923.
(10) Falcon Joslin to his wife, April 15, 1923, Joslin Collection, UAF.
(11) *The Cordova Daily Times*, June 15, 1923.
(12) *Ibid.*, July 20, 1923.
(13) *Ibid.*, July 30, 1923.
(14) George C. Hazelet to Craig Hazelet, August 20, 1923. Courtesy of Hazelet grandchildren.
(15) *The Cordova Daily Times*, July 17, 1924.
(16) *The Alaska Weekly*, Seattle, April 18, 1924.
(17) *The Cordova Daily Times*, August 9, 1926.
(18) *Ibid.*, August 6, 1926.

XXXII. Ghosts

(1)   *The Alaska Weekly*, March 16, 1923.
(2)   Alaska Petroleum Chronology compiled by John R. Roderick.
(3)   *The Wall Street Journal*, December 31, 1940.
(4)   *Who Was Who In America*
(5)   Edward E.P Morgan, *God's Loaded Dice*, pgs. 256-7.
(6)   Katherine Wilson, *Copper Tints*, pgs. 43-4.
(7)   Lone Jansen, *The Copper Spike*, pg. 16.
(8)   Harrais, "Gold Lunatics."
(9)   Statement of John N. Steele before the House Committee on Territories, February 16, 1911. Copper River and Northwestern Railway in Alaska, pg. 36.
(10) Melody Webb Grauman, "The Beginnings of the Kennecott Copper Corporation."
(11) James Wickersham to Hon. Ernest Gruening, November 23, 1938. Wickersham Papers, Box 44. A.S.H.L., Juneau.
(12) Stephen Birch, "Pioneering Capital" in *Alaska-Yukon Magazine*, Vol. IX, No.5, April 1910, pg. 300.

Icebound Empire

BIBLIOGRAPHY

Abercrombie, W.R. *Copper River Exploring Expedition-1899*. U.S. Government Printing Office, 1900.

Arends, Dorothea. *The Guggenheims in Alaska: An Essay*. Masters Thesis, Columbia University, 1936.

Atwood, Evengeline. *Frontier Politics: Alaska's James Wickersham* Portland: Binford and Mort, 1979.

Birch, Stephen. "Pioneering Capital" in *Alaska Yukon Magazine*, Vol.IX, No.5, April 1910.

Breger, Carpel. "Story of Kennecott Copper" in *The Financial World*. May 23, 1921; May 30, 1921; June 6, 1921.

Brower, Charles. *Fifty Years Below Zero*.

Capps, Stephen R. "The Chisana White River District, Alaska" in *USGS Bulletin No.639*.

Douglass, William C. *A History of Kennecott Mines, Kennecott, Alaska*. Anchorage: State of Alaska Division of Parks, 1971.

Fleming, Henry. *A True Account of the Alaskan Adventures of Henry Fleming — Gold Rush of 1900-1902*. Unpublished manuscript compiled by Christina Counselor.

Grauman, Melody Webb. *Big Business in Alaska: The Kennecott Mines* Fairbanks: Coop. Park Studies Unit, University of Alaska, 1977.

Hampton, Benjamin B. "Shall Alaska Become a `Morganheim Barony'?" in *Hampton Magazine*, May 1910.

Harrison, E.S., "What Is the Alaska Syndicate Doing?" in *Alaska Yukon Magazine*, Vol.IX, No.6, May 1910.

Holeski, Carolyn Jean and Marlene Conger. *In Search of Gold*. Anchorage: The Alaska Geographic Society, 1983.

Hazelet, George Cheever. *Diary*. Provided by grandchildren, Harriet Flynn, Charlotte Turtainen and Calvin Hazelet, Jr.

Hazelet, John. "History of the Chisna Alaska Property." Unpublished manuscript provided by grandson, Richard Osborne.

Hunt, William R. *North of '53, The Wild Days of the Alaska-Yukon Mining Frontier 1870-1914*. New York: MacMillan Co., 1974.

Hunt, William R. *Golden Places, The History of Alaska-Yukon Mining*. Anchorage: National Park Service, 1990.

Hutton, Harold. *Vigilante Days*. Chicago: The Swallow Press, 1978.

Janson, Lone. *The Copper Spike*. Anchorage: Alaska Northwest Publishing, 1975.

Jarvis, Lt. David H. *Report of the Cruise of the U.S. Cutter Bear and the Overland Expedition — Nov.27,1897-Sept.13,1898*. U.S. Government Printing Office, 1899.

Joslin, Falcon. "Railroad Building in Alaska" in *Alaska Yukon Magazine*,

Lowe, Lt. P.G. "Report from Valdes Inlet to Belle Isle on the Yukon" in *Explorations in Alaska — 1898*. GPO, 1899.

McDonald, Lucile. "John Rosene's Alaska Activities" in *The Sea Chest*, Vol.10, No.4, June 1977.

Mendenhall, Walter C. "Geology of the Central Copper River Region, Alaska" in *USGS Bulletin #498*.

Moffitt, Fred P. "Geology of the Eastern Part of the Alaska Range and Adjacent Area" in *USGS Bulletin 989-D*. GPO, 1954.

Morgan, Edward E.P. *God's Loaded Dice*. Caldwell, Idaho: Caxton Printers, 1948.

Mullen, Arthur. *Western Democrat*. Wilfred Fink, 1940.

Naske, Claus-M. *Paving Alaska's Trails*. Lanhom, Md.: University Press of America, 1986.

Nichols, Jeanette Paddock. *Alaska, A History of its Administration, Exploitation and Industrial Development During the First Half Century Under the Rule of the United States*. Cleveland: Arthur H. Clark Co., 1924.

O'Conner, Harvey. *The Guggenheims*. New York: Covier-Friede, 1937.

Powell, Addison. *Trailing and Camping in Alaska*. New York: Wessels and Bissell, 1910.

Pinchot, Gifford. *Breaking New Ground*. New York: Harcourt-Brace, 1917.

Remington, C.H. *A Golden Cross (?) on Trails from the Valdez Glacier*. Los Angeles: White-Thompson, 1939.

Richardson, Wilds P. "Alaska" in *Atlantic Monthly*, January, 1918.

Sageser, A. Bower. "Holt County During the 1890s" in *Nebraska History*, Vol. 40, June 1959.

Shiels, Archie W. *The Kennecott Story*. Bellingham, 1967.

Spude, Robert I.S. and Faulkner, Sandra McDermott. *Kennecott, Alaska*. Anchorage: National Park Service, 1987.

Stearns, Robert Alden. *The Morgan-Guggenheim Syndicate and the Development of Alaska, 1906-1915*. Ann Arbor: University Microfilm International, 1968.

Sullivan, Michael Sean. *Kennecott Alaska. A Historic Preservation Plan*. Prepared for the Alaska Historical Society.

Wilson, Catherine. *Copper Tints*. Cordova: Daily Times Press, 1923.

Wold, Jo Anne. *The Way It Was*. Anchorage: Alaska Northwest Publishing Co., 1988.

Yost, Nellie Snyder. *Before Today: A History of Holt County, Nebraska, Centennial Edition*. O'Neill: Miles Publishing C., 1976.

Archival Sources

Alaska State Historical Library, Juneau, Alaska.
   Wickersham State Historical Site Collection, Boxes 8, 14, 30, 31, 44.
Kennecott Corporation Library, Salt Lake City, Utah.
   Letters from Stephen Birch to H.O. Havemeyer II and D.S. Cain.
   Corporate Reports of Kennecott Copper Corporation, 1915-1940.
   Smith, H. DeWitt, "Early Days of Kennecott Corporation."
Nebraska State Historical Society Library, Lincoln, Nebraska.
   W.B. Holdrege Papers.
   Newspapers including *The Frontier*, O'Neill, *O'Neill Sun*, *Omaha World Herald*.
Polar Collections. Rasmusson Library, Univ. of Alaska Fairbanks.
   Harrais, Martin. *Gold Lunatics*. Unpublished manuscript.
   L.A. Levensaler Papers in Verical File.
   Donohoe-Ostrander-Dimond Papers.
   Falcon Joslin letters to his wife.
   Records of United States Deptartment of Justice relating to Keystone Canyon Case, Microfilm #84-193.
Records of Holt County District Court at O'Neill, Nebraska.
Records of Alaska Third Division Court in Anchorage Federal Achives.
University of Alaska-Anchorage Archives.
   Territorial Governor's Papers on microfilm.
   Wickersham Diary on microfilm
   Alaska newspapers on microfilm.
University of Washington Library, Seattle.
   Seattle newspapers on microfilm.
   John Rosene papers.
Washington Historical Society Library, Tacoma.
   Sherin, Michael. *William Ross Rust and His Tacoma Legacy*. Unpublished manuscript.

INDEX